T0326308

The Orchestration
of
Joy and Suffering

The Orchestration
of
Joy and Suffering

—

Understanding Chronic Addiction

Dr. Corinne F. Gerwe

Algora Publishing
New York

Algora Publishing, New York
© 2001 by Algora Publishing
All rights reserved. Published 2001.
Printed in the United States of America
ISBN: 1-892941-64-3
Editors@algora.com

Library of Congress Cataloging-in-Publication Data 2001-004085

Gerwe, Corinne.
 The Orchestration of Joy and Suffering. Understanding Chronic Addic-
tion/ by Corinne Gerwe.
    p. cm.
 ISBN 1-892941-64-3 (alk. paper)
 1. Substance abuse—Etiology. 2. Psychic trauma in children. 3.
Acting out (Psychology) 4. Addicts—Rehabilitation. I. Title.
 RC564 .G384 2001
 616.86—dc21

                               2001004085

Cover illustration by Lyn Smuts
Courtesy of E. Heinze,
The Chelsea Gallery, Cape Town, South Africa

New York
www.algora.com

This book is dedicated to my beloved husband, David, who tragically was killed by a drunk driver in March 2001. His dedicated work with troubled youth coincided with my work with chronic addiction patients and offenders and gave me a parallel view into the adolescent age group that makes manifest the pressing need for positive early childhood interventions.

ODE TO THE WEST WIND

If I were a dead leaf though mightest bear;
If I were a swift cloud to flee with thee;
A wave to pant beneath thy power, and share
The impulse of thy strength, only less free
Than thou. O uncontrollable! If even
I were as in my boyhood, and could be
The comrade of thy wanderings over heaven
As then, when to outstrip thy skiey speed
Scarce seemed a vision; I would ne'er have striven
As thus with thee in prayer in my sore need
O' lift me as a wave, a leaf, a cloud!
I fall upon the thorns of life! I bleed!
A heavy weight of hours has chained and bowed
One too like thee — tameless, swift, and proud.

SHELLEY

Table of Contents

Introduction

I have thought so many times, listening to addiction relapse patients, how tragic it was that nothing was done for them at the beginning. And even though I have designed a method for addressing the complex conditions that later surface, they are very difficult to treat. I have therefore concluded many of the chapters with examples that illustrate the depth of the problem. In many respects, the only true prevention can and must be done in the early stages.

The HRIPTM (High Risk Identification and Prediction Treatment Method) brings forth crucial information that supports the need for early childhood interventions at every level of development. And the most important thing about this is that parents need to be much more aware that the seeds of later problematic conditions can be created during experiences that are characterized by the dynamics described in this text. Once created, the seeds are germinated by the behavioral response that occurs and they grow from behavioral repetition that is often overlooked by all those who surround the child.

This is *everyone's* problem. Many of the problematic behavioral patterns that lead to obsession do not necessarily lead to addiction, but do lead to life-sabotaging actions that overpower the individual. Addiction is just one of the most likely outcomes for many of these people.

In today's approach to addiction treatment, shortcut methods addressing here-and-now solution-focused outcomes don't even put a dent in the chronic potential of these people. This is a society problem and the current youth population is exposed to an increasing amount of insecurity and dangerous stimuli that produce the right conditions for these types of experiences. Intervention programs designed to help troubled and/or delinquent children are expanding, but their waiting lists are very long, and getting longer. The mental health issues of the young people they accept are getting more complex. The increase in reliance on prescribed medications is astounding, and the abuse and neglect issues reported are appalling. And these boys and girls are not just from poor families; the private-pay clients come from some of the wealthiest. It is an across-the board-problem. If society continues to depend on later treatment, instead of early prevention, the cost will continue to grow — unnecessarily.

What is the HRIPTM?

The High Risk Identification and Prediction Treatment Model (HRIPTM) was developed to increase patient and clinician ability to identify, assess and treat chronic behavioral and addiction risk symptoms more effectively. The HRIPTM was developed over many years of work with chronic patients and criminal offenders within a wide range of addiction treatment and rehabilitation settings, including military, corrections and hospital-based facilities.

The primary focus of this method is to unearth information that otherwise would not be revealed, and therefore could not be addressed by whatever treatment approach the individual finds. When core issues remain buried and the individual cannot personally identify, or even understand, what events are important to share or reveal, the most crucial information is often lost in superficial disclosure and mimicking of other patients or clients involved in the treatment process. Therefore, the following chapters focus more on the unearthing process, and what comes forth, than on the treatment approach that is prescribed based on these revelations.

The cases chosen as examples for this book represent people who have been in treatment multiple times and who, in most cases, never previously revealed what came forth until they participated in the *Orchestration Group Process*. When you realize that, then you can see why, for years, I worked on developing a way to identify and expose underlying developmental issues. I knew, from my experience listening to the most chronic patients and offenders, that such issues were creating havoc in their lives and disrupting their recovery processes.

The HRIPTM was developed with a consistent and dedicated approach to addressing the chronic nature of addiction and its underlying problems. This method has recently been incorporated into a pilot project in Atlanta for the Georgia State Department of Corrections, Pardons and Parole.

From the beginning of my professional career as a counselor assigned to develop relapse prevention programming, to my work today, I have consistently accumulated data that support the link between the developmental period and chronic behavioral and addiction conditions. The HRIPTM methods were designed to investigate the developmental process of each individual, to determine the origin and nature of life-sabotaging patterns of behavior characterized by obsessive/compulsive repetition.

In practice, HRIPTM is a highly-structured approach built around the *Orchestration Group Process* (OGP), in which I used the musical concept as a model to facilitate investigation of the individual within a dynamic, organized and collective process.

The Orchestration Group Process (OGP) is a structured format in which one member of the treatment group, in the role of "group focus," shares (describes out loud) one pivotal experience. The session is structured to represent what occurs during an experience. The group facilitator is the conductor, and leads the person who is sharing through the process of identifying what is being recalled in the vivid center of detail that arises in memory. The other group members sit in a semi-circle of rows, set up like an orchestra around the person who is disclosing his or her experience. The first row represents the feeling/physical symptom response; group participants share how each of them might have felt and physically responded if the experience being shared had happened to them. The second row represents the behavioral response; each participant shares how he or she might have behaved in such a situation. The person who is sharing as "focus" listens to each disclosure from the others and gains increased insight into his or her own experience, as the others respond by identifying their most powerful feeling, physical symptoms and behavioral responses. The facilitator (conductor) gains vital information about each member of the group during this highly structured process. The case studies that conclude each of the following chapters represent the information that comes to light during the Orchestration Group Process — crucial information for the patient and his counselors, crucial information that previous treatment processes failed to reveal.

Assessment questionnaires and other materials were developed from the OGP to enhance its effectiveness. The HRIPTM Manual, for patients in the program, includes written exercises, charts and other materials designed to educate the patient about the nature and condition of chronic behavioral and addiction relapse and to pinpoint the sabotaging elements that are individual to each case. This collaborative approach to individualized treatment enables the clinician and patient to address together the psychological and physiological dynamics stemming from pre-addiction factors, while recognizing the importance of all other aspects of treatment that address the onset and process of addiction and post-addiction factors. A study conducted to determine the effectiveness of the HRIPTM was published in 2001 in the February issue *Journal of Substance Abuse Treatment*.

The Orchestration of Joy and Suffering was written to help parents, teachers, friends and neighbors to understand problematic conditions that can arise from certain childhood experiences. More importantly, it was from the voices and revelations of those who suffer these conditions to the most chronic degree that this evidence emerged.

Corinne F. Gerwe
PhD (Biological Psychology), CCAS (Certified Clinical Addiction Specialist),
CAS (National Certification) American Academy of Health Care Providers in the
Addictive Disorders (AAHCPAD)

[Sherlock Holmes speaking to Dr. Watson]

Do you remember what Darwin says about music? He claims that the power of producing and appreciating it existed among the human race long before the power of speech was arrived at. Perhaps that is why we are so subtly influenced by it. There are vague memories in our souls of those misty centuries when the world was in its childhood.

A Study in Scarlet
— Sir Arthur Conan Doyle

The orchestra that soothes me to sleep with the sounds of imagined harps and violins, only to infiltrate my dreams in the midnight hours of moonless nights, the soft sweet slumber of predawn dreams and the restless sleep of an over-excited mind, is the orchestra of my childhood memory. A memory of an experience that occurred in the sixth year of my life. A memory that is as alive in my mind today as the day it happened, so many years ago.

On this day, I was chosen from the others in my first grade class. I was instructed to lead a single-file procession down the hall to the auditorium. There was to be a surprise presentation. I had listened carefully to Sister Mary Claver's instructions. Upon reaching the side entrance of the auditorium, I was to halt my class and wait at the open doorway. From this position, I would see the class that had entered the room fifteen minutes before we were to enter. When this class moved on, I was to lead my class into their vacated position in the center of the auditorium. A mark on the floor would indicate where to stop. There, we were to remain for exactly fifteen minutes. When our time was up, I was to exit by leading my class to the opposite doorway so that the next waiting class could follow.

I took this assignment very seriously and was pleased that I had been trusted with this responsibility. I adored Sister Mary Claver. She was soft-spoken and kind. I thought she was like an angel. I loved St. Clement School and wanted to do my best there. This was sometimes difficult, because I was often distracted and preoccupied during class-time, despite my efforts to concentrate and pay attention. As a result, I would sometimes miss important information. When this occurred, Sister was never harsh or critical. I would have been devastated if she had been. I tried to stay as quiet as possible so that these episodes would not be noticed, because I could not seem to stop them from happening. I was therefore astonished when she called my name and then gave me what I considered a very special role. Desiring to do my task well, I led my group down the long corridor with concentrated determination. And everything was going just fine — that is, until I heard the music.

We were approaching the door to the auditorium when I first heard the sweet strains of an unfamiliar melodic combination of instrumental sounds. Through the doorway, in my direct line of vision, I could see the class ahead of us. They were standing side-by-side in a horizontal line. They were facing a stage that was not visible from my position. When we reached the entrance and stopped to wait, I began to feel increased excitement as I listened to the strange and wonderful music coming from the unseen source beyond my view. So as not to be distracted from my task, I focused my attention on the rows of folded chairs that lined the walls of the large auditorium. I wondered why we were not permitted to sit on them in arranged rows, like a real audience, instead of always standing in single-file lines.

But the melody was so beautiful and different from music that was familiar to me, that I began to compare it with the music that had once filled our home. My attention became re-directed to thoughts of how things had been before everything changed. I could hear the Irish songs of my grandfather and his comical and theatrical way of singing operettas like "The Lord of the Rings," and his "Hi ho, Hi ho, Hi ho!," which created gales of laughter as he outrageously recreated the forest solo. There were the strains of my father's ukulele, purchased somewhere in the Pacific during World War II, as he played and sang his favorite song, *Celito Lindo*. And the many voices surrounding the old piano in the living room upstairs — the poor, hard-beaten, yet bravely upright instrument that had been subjected to years of family gatherings and anyone who could pound a melody into submission with undisciplined

8

abandon. This old friend that now stood silent, except for the lonely sounds of my solitary daily practice.

The piano lessons that began in my first year at St. Clement would soon end. In a few weeks, I would be joining my parents and younger brother on the farm my father had purchased earlier that year. I would be leaving St. Bernard and St. Clement School to live in a farmhouse that was located some distance from the city. The farmhouse would be a place with few neighbors. What worried me more was that there would be no piano. I wondered if anyone had thought of this as a problem. "Probably not," I thought. I began to feel the very familiar feelings of dread and uncertainty.

My father had said this move would be good for us. I was not so sure. I knew his condition was worsening. He was drinking more and was increasingly unable to control his temper. I knew this had something to do with the severe injuries he had suffered during the war. But I did not then understand that he, like many other veterans of his era, was treating his own post-traumatic stress symptoms with alcohol, and that his alcoholism was creating a deteriorating condition that would eventually take his life. The only thing I did know for certain was that there would be no music on the farm and that, for me, this would be a great problem.

As my thoughts continued to stray, the feeling of dread became overwhelming. I wondered what was happening there, and what it would be like to live in such an isolated place. Suddenly, I felt a slight nudge from behind and saw the class ahead begin to move toward the exit. The music had stopped. Quickly trying to regain focus on my job, I led my class to the vacated area in the middle of the auditorium, looking straight ahead to make sure I reached the correct spot. Once there, and only then, did I give myself permission to turn toward the stage.

There is something insidious about the feeling of dread. It can work inside of you like a sponge, absorbing other feelings, like anticipation, into it as it expands. Had my anticipation and excitement not been interrupted by my worried thoughts, I might not have had such a reaction when I turned toward the stage. Or maybe the light was just right, that day. . . streaming in from the high windows to transform shining brass into a brilliant glow. Maybe it was the contrast of this illumination against the otherwise dark, cavernous space that surrounded the diminutive audience standing at attention. Or the momentary silence that followed our systematic march, when our small shuf-fling feet stopped and a quiet stillness fell over the room. Whatever it was, the combination of light, movement and sound created an atmos-phere that set the stage for what happened next.

There, before us, dramatically elevated and framed by soft velvet drapes on an otherwise spartan platform, was a sight that to me seemed magnificent. Gleaming instruments accentuated the elegant appearance of the musicians, who were dressed in black suits and white ties. Sit-ting erect and semi-circled, they were staring attentively at the tall and imposing man who stood before them. Slowly, he turned away from them and looked down upon us with a fierce hawk-like expression. His piercing eyes glinted under a mass of thick wiry eyebrows and grayish black hair. Although I suspected he was just pretending to be fierce, like my grandfather did when telling one of his stories, I was transfixed by his stern gaze and looming presence.

Then, after what seemed several minutes, he bowed gracefully and turned away from us once more to face the orchestra, and raised his ba-ton high above his head where he again dramatically paused. I felt sus-pended by this action and pulled toward him. It was as if the space be-tween us disappeared until I was held there in his pose. When he fi-nally moved, I felt light, breathless and swept along with the baton. It was like entering a world of musical enchantment. Somehow, in what seemed to be only a few moments of intense and exquisite joy, em-braced by the loveliest melody I had ever heard, the worry, dread and everything around me ceased to exist. Captivated by the music, held within the music, the stage and all it encompassed, I was aware of every detail of sound and position. The clarity of each tone, coming from each instrument, combined to make a luxurious sound that lifted me into a place of happiness, calm and weightlessness. A place that I wanted to stay forever.

"Corinne!" "Corinne!" The voice came from some distant place — then closer — followed by sounds of laughter. I felt a hand on each shoulder. . . gentle movement, and then the face above me, slowly be-coming clearer and the voice repeating, but this time more softly, "Corinne." It was Sister Mary Claver. Beyond her, far away now, I could see the faces of the musicians as their expressions began to change. No longer serious, several began to smile. They had stopped playing their instruments and some started laughing quietly. They were looking in my direction. And then I became more aware of laughter coming from each side of the auditorium. I suddenly realized that except for Sister, I was standing alone. The classmates I had led into the auditorium, who should have been standing to my left, were gathered in the doorway at the exit to the right. They were laughing uproariously. At the left door entrance, another class was waiting and laughing with equal ferocity. They were all laughing. . . laughing at me.

It dawned on me that our time had been up for some minutes and that my class must have moved past me without my knowledge. I wondered how long I had stood there like that. How could this have happened, and worst of all, how could I have failed in my task and let Sister Mary Claver down? I desperately wanted to disappear, to go back, to hide or somehow make everyone go away. I could only stand there, shrouded in misery, staring down at the marked spot where I had earlier so conscientiously positioned myself. Sister gently began to move me along with her toward the back door of the auditorium. As she led me from the room, her sweet protective voice and the folds of her black habit were my only shields against the terrible gales of laughter.

From this point on, I remember nothing more of this day. However, there were significant changes in my behavior from that day forward. Whenever I became overwhelmed with worry, without even trying, the problem formulated in my mind into an orchestrated concept that compartmentalized the problem and reduced my irrational state so that I could once again think rationally and attempt to solve the problem. I continued to experience periodic episodes of distraction and detachment when I would lose space and time and become unaware of my surroundings. I gradually became driven obsessively to solve problems and, later, to find solutions to problems related to my childhood — particularly the time when the orchestration experience happened. Music became an essential ingredient in my life.

Is it possible that an extraordinary experience can change the course of a child's life? Can such "singular episodes," or a series of episodic experiences, have as much significance in childhood development as heredity and environmental influences? Can actions that are constructed during a highly intense emotional and physiological state create a framework for repetition? Are these behavioral actions driven by a need or desire to repeat that can be more powerful than a child's intentions or fear of consequences? Are these patterns of behavior different from learned behavior that develops during the stages of childhood? Does the level of emotional and physical intensity that is felt during these experiences generate neuronal activity in areas of the brain that are not accessed in less intense states? Can this intensified activity result in an encoding process that is more entrenched and complex than in lesser states? Can behavior that is constructed during extreme conditions, and which is repeated in association with repetition of these conditions, evolve in scope and dimension to such a degree that self-esteem, personality, relationships, career choices, life course and mental and physical health are dramatically affected?

In my own personal experience, I believe the answer to these questions is yes, and the theory has been borne out in the course of my life and my work in the field of substance abuse treatment. My professional experience provided a forum in which the full implication of these questions could be explored. This investigation led to research that developed into a High Risk Identification and Prediction Treatment Method (HRIPTM). The HRIPTM was formulated based on an orchestration framework that provides a structured investigative process focused on identifying present-day emotional/physiological symptoms and behavior patterns and pinpointing their earliest indication of origin. The HRIPTM explores the link between conditions arising from childhood experiences that persist and the development of chronic addiction and other disorder conditions.

The case examples presented below represent years of study that reached beyond clinical research. While these individuals may initially seem to have little in common, they reveal, through contrast and comparison, the common bond of behavior that affects us all. The case summaries chosen for this text exemplify the unlimited diversity of behavior that stems from a certain phenomenon of experience. The examples demonstrate how this behavior can be camouflaged, disguised, hidden, misunderstood, ineffectively punished or very effectively praised, and often tragically unaddressed until it is so firmly entrenched neurologically that it becomes powerfully resistant to treatment and rehabilitation efforts.

The case histories of notable figures were gathered from literary diaries and letters, literature and poetic texts, autobiographies biographies and media interviews. The clinical case summaries concluding each chapter are taken from the HRIPTM research. Collectively, they provide a fascinating account of how an intricate and far-reaching web of problematic behavior can originate and evolve. This orchestration of interwoven experiences will, hopefully, play before you as powerfully while you read as the orchestra that played before me, so many years ago.

CHAPTER I

A BEGINNING OVERTURE: PIVOTAL CHILDHOOD EXPERIENCE

There is a comfort in the strength of love;
'Twill make a thing endurable, which else
Would overset the brain, or break the heart.
Michael[1]
— William Wordsworth, 1800

In recent years, scientific breakthroughs in mind/brain research have revolutionized theories on childhood development. Although the Nature vs. Nurture debate continues, it is now recognized that each child is born with a unique biology that greatly influences, but does not predetermine, life course. The expression or influence of the genes depends on interactions with those in the cell, the body, and in the social and physical world of the child.[2]

Early childhood is the most crucial and the most vulnerable time in how a child develops, emotionally and intellectually. During the first two years of life, a child learns to regulate feelings and behavior through reciprocal interactions with the parents or caregiver. This vitally important relationship provides the nurturing and protection that is essential to a child's level of security. Within the boundaries of this relationship, a child learns to perceive and respond to emotional cues, develop empathy and form a sense of self. As the child develops the ability to regulate emotions within the framework of a secure environment (one that provides consistent care and guidance), difficult experiences that present challenges can be negotiated with increasing success and autonomy.

A child's neuronal development is not only shaped by experiences, but by how a child responds to his or her experiences. Early experiences affect children's later ability to learn and reason.[3] When a child does not learn to regulate emotions, or if an experience occurs that propels a child into an emotional realm that is beyond his or her ability to regulate, a behavioral dynamic can be spontaneously constructed to help the child compensate during and after the de-regulating experience. Pivotal experiences are those that result in a distinct change in behavior that alters the child's development and life course to some degree.

This work is an effort to shed light on the origin and development of problematic behavior that arises from a unique level of childhood experience. Although childhood trauma and abuse are, of course, highly represented here in relation to this pivotal phenomenon, a much wider range of childhood experience is brought into view to demonstrate the individual nature of a pivotal experience. The conditions and common factors that link certain experiences to behavior that is characterized by repetition, obsessive/compulsive thought and action, and behavior pattern development that insidiously evolves from childhood into adulthood, are presented with clear theoretical explanation and interesting clinical and notable case examples. Two primary dimensions will be explored in relation to these conditions and common factors:

- experiences that generate an extreme distress state of *Suffering*, and
- experiences that generate an extreme arousal state of *Joy*.

For the purpose of clarity, the terms *Suffering* and *Joy* were chosen to represent the two extremes of a spectrum of emotional and physiological states generated by pivotal childhood experience. These states are comprised of a variety of feeling and physical symptom combinations that are unique to each individual.

The role of pivotal experience, experience that propels a child into a highly intense-to-extreme dimension of joy or suffering, will be explored in depth in relation to the origin of behavior that sabotages healthy childhood development and creates vulnerability to addiction and many other psychological disorders. Pivotal childhood experience is one of the most underestimated areas of concern in relation to prevention and treatment of these conditions.

Behaviors that develop into repetitive and/or obsessive patterns can be linked to a dynamic that occurs during experiences that produce in the child a highly intense-to-extreme emotional state. As feelings occur in response to an experience, the most forceful feature is the set of physical symptoms that is also generated. When feelings and physical symptoms begin to escalate to an extreme level of intensity, the child can experience an emotional state and physiological condition that become overwhelming.

Examples of *feelings* reported during this state include: anger, fear, frustration, terror, excitement, embarrassment, rage, sadness, loneliness, desperation, jealousy, and many others.

Examples of *physical symptoms* reported include:

- Visual and hearing distortion or impairment, difficulty breathing, difficulty swallowing, vocal impairment.
- Changes in body temperature. Loss of body fluids, through tears, urine, vomit, perspiration, bowel movement. Changes in heart rate. Changes in energy level. Stomach distress. Involuntary body movement (shaking, trembling, twitching).
- Changes in skin, such as rashes, flushing, red patches, hives.
- Increased mental activity. Descriptions include mental confusion, racing mind, diminished ability to think clearly, diminished ability to think rationally, pressure or pounding in various regions of the head and face.

When a child has an experience that produces a combination of feelings and physical symptoms that increase in intensity toward an extreme level, the behavioral action that effectively works to decrease or alter the distress level to some degree will be registered in the brain and in memory as an effective response for distress-symptom relief.

The peak level of an experience of this nature is recorded in such a way that, years later, certain details of the experience can be vividly recalled whenever the episode surfaces in memory. Experiences that produce in the child an extreme state of suffering are often later described as intolerable or unbearable at the point when the behavior takes place. If another experience, or a series of experiences, triggers the feeling and physical symptom combination generated during the initial experience, the associated behavior, which has now become an integral part of the combination, will be repeated.

Conversely, when a child has a pleasurable experience that produces a combination of feelings and physical symptoms that escalate to a highly intense to extreme degree, the behavior that is enacted to extend or replicate this state of arousal becomes an integral part of the over-all combination associated with the experience. The peak level of the experience is often later described in vivid memory detail as a thrilling or powerful state of excitement, happiness, ecstasy — *an extreme state of joy* — unlike anything felt before the experience. The child most susceptible to behavior repetition that becomes an obsessive effort to once again achieve this desirable state is the *suffering* child.

Arousal experiences are the most overlooked area in relation to problem behavior stemming from childhood. It is often incorrectly assumed that severe behavioral problems are a result of abuse. While abuse and trauma are often an associated factor, some of the most diabolical behavior identified during the HRIPTM research[4] originated during an arousal experience. For example:

Tommy was almost 5 years old when the experience occurred. He lived with his parents in a modest home situated in a rural suburban area. His father was verbally and physically abusive. Tommy and his mother were often threatened. She became emotionally withdrawn and unable to protect herself or Tommy from her husband's weekly tirades. Tommy tried to avoid his father and stayed outdoors as much as possible. When his father came home from work in a bad temper, Tommy was often forbidden to leave the house. He was an unhappy, frightened child, who felt increasingly impotent and alone. His perceived his father as a threatening and all-powerful figure.

One day, Tommy made the mistake of leaving his wagon in the driveway. His father ran over it with the car when he arrived home from work. This accident resulted in a harsh physical beating, and Tommy was ordered not to leave the house. He felt overwhelmed with pain. He felt alone, trapped and powerless. His body felt weak and drained of energy. He also felt the first stirrings of anger about the unfairness of his situation.

Instead of going to his room, where he knew he would feel even more confined, he went into the kitchen where there was a window with a view of the nearby field and forest where he often played. His mother was not in the kitchen. When he climbed on the stool by the window, he noticed a large box of stick matches on the stove. He had been warned never to play with matches.

His first rebellious act was to reach for the matches. He climbed down from the stool and sat on the floor in a shadowed corner of the kitchen. He awkwardly struck one of the matches along the side of the box, as he had seen his mother do. Suddenly, the head of the match burst into flame. He became instantly fascinated and a surge of exhilaration sent a sudden thrill through his body. He felt powerful and energized. He no longer felt the pain from his beating. The thrill lasted until the match burned his finger. When Tommy felt the burn, he was amazed at the power of the single little flame. And he immediately felt a desire to light another match.

Fearing he would be caught, Tommy took the box of matches to his room and hid them behind his toy box until he could find a safe place to use them again. Just thinking about being able to do it again made him feel better. His mother later missed the box of matches, but she did not suspect Tommy. She had extra boxes in the cupboard and simply thought she had misplaced them.

Tommy continued lighting matches. He soon discovered how to build small fires. He set his fires in a small gorge area between the field and woods, out of view from his house. The fires grew larger and harder to hide. He began starting fires in clearings in the forest, and became more proficient at piling sticks a certain way to make the flame higher. The first time he lost control of a fire, he ran away to the house. The smoke was reported and a portion of the woods was destroyed before the fire was put out. Although Tommy was terrified that he would be suspected, he was not. He also felt guilty for the damage caused by the fire, but not about the size of the fire. He had been able to see it from the kitchen window. He felt powerful and strong while watching the flames and smoke rise into the sky.

Tommy was so frightened by the possibility of being caught that he tried to stop the behavior. Instead, he became more preoccupied with it. He needed the fire and desired the way it made him feel. It was the only good feeling in his otherwise difficult life. He was in school now, and not doing as well as the other children. But he did have more freedom than he had previously known. He used this freedom to find locations further from home for starting fires.

Tommy is an example of a child who developed a pattern of fire-starting that led to an advanced pattern of criminal arson. A fire-starter begins with a lighted match. Age four is a particularly vulnerable time for match and flame fascination. The older child will not be as impressed with it; the younger child would have greater difficulty obtaining and/or lighting the matches. Children at this age are often warned about matches. A child who feels powerless and helpless to change a fearful situation or environment will remember a warning about something he or she *is presumed to be able to do*. A powerless child, who can do nothing to stop what is occurring and who then rebelliously obtains the matches, may be susceptible to feelings that arise during the act of lighting a match or the visual experience of seeing a flame. If the flame generates a visceral feeling of power in a powerless child, the *seed* of fire-starting behavior is germinated. The need to feel powerful continues if the child continues to feel intensely powerless and helpless. If so, the behavior will be repeated and continue to evolve.

The evolution of the pattern is determined by the innovation and skill that develops along with the child's need to replicate the desired feeling. The flame becomes less satisfactory as the child develops and the pattern continues. Innovation occurs when the child begins to accumulate and hide matches, becomes more secretive, and advances the pattern into starting small fires. At first, the bigger the fire, the more powerful the feeling. Then at some point, it takes a bigger fire to achieve the desired feeling at all. But the bigger the fire, the harder it is to hide. If the child gets caught, he will have to innovate an advanced or different way to perpetuate the pattern. For example, he (or she) might start fires in other locations. Even if the child is punished, the behavior will not be deterred if the punishment coincides with or simultaneously increases the child's need to feel powerful. Punishment, for this child, is less intolerable than life without the feeling produced by fire-starting.

The child may feel tremendous guilt after being caught and punished, and may desperately want to stop. He may try to stop, only to become more compulsively preoccupied and obsessed with the behavior — without understanding why. This frustrating dynamic adds to the child's feelings of powerlessness.

Innovation in relation to these patterns requires skill and determination. A child who cannot stop, but who desperately wants to behave appropriately, may find a socially acceptable avenue for the behavior — a place and position where the pattern is accepted. Criminal arson investigators are aware of this propensity and it is not unusual for them to include local and volunteer fire departments in their arson investigations.

Tommy's pattern of fire-starting is one example of how problematic behavior can originate and develop from a pivotal experience that takes place within a dysfunctional and insecure environment. During the *seed* phase of the pattern, the behavior can go unnoticed; it can be hidden, kept secret or camouflaged. Self-harm patterns, harm to others, destruction of objects, withdrawal, fantasizing, plotting, planning, manipulating, hiding, hoarding, stealing, lying, risk-taking, food refusal, object ingestion, binging, poisoning, retaliation, running, avoiding, pretending or acting can all begin in early childhood as a result of pivotal experience. The one thing these behaviors have in common, in relation to this dynamic, is that they are obsessively repeated and continue to evolve. Another identifiable trait is their resistance to punishment. The child will continue the needed/desired behavior, one way or another, despite the consequences.

The American Psychiatric Association classifies all known mental disorders in its *Diagnostic and Statistical Manual.*[5] Obsessive-compulsive disorder is characterized by recurrent, time-consuming obsession or compulsions (trying to ignore or resist the action) that are severe enough to cause marked distress or significant impairment. Recent studies indicate that people with obsessive-compulsive disorder (OCD) have distinctive neurological differences from those without the disorder. These differences are most pronounced in the limbic lobe, the caudate nucleus and the orbital frontal cortex. Brain scans show intense brain activity and prolonged firing of neurons when patients with OCD are presented with a potentially distressing scenario. Photo-imaging has given us a window into brain activity that previously could not be analyzed; it is producing growing evidence that physiological crisis occurs when extreme neurological activity is generated. It is this same type of crisis that occurs in a child when an experience propels feelings and physical symptoms toward an extreme dimension of neurological activity. The difference is that the child's brain is still developing during this period.

Neuronal activity during early childhood is at peak level. Neuroscientists have now confirmed that the brain's greatest growth spurt draws to a close around the age of 10, when the balance between synapse creation and atrophy abruptly shifts. Over the next several years, the brain will ruthlessly destroy its weakest synapses, preserving only those that have relevance to the child's survival to that age. This can explain why certain behaviors are so hard to change. They have become a significant part of the brain's architecture and relevant to the child's developed means of maintaining some level of emotional and physiological balance.

Much attention is focused today on the role of early trauma in re-lation to addiction, eating disorders, violent aggression, sexual offenses, self-abuse and other psychological disorders. Abuse and trauma are, certainly, often precipitators or associated factors in these conditions. Less attention has been paid to the equally important role of arousal states that originate in early childhood. The suffering child who experi-ences an arousal state that is replicated by a certain behavior that also brings about undesirable consequences will repeat the behavior despite the consequences, if the state is the child's only relief from suffering. When childhood suffering is a factor, behaviors that become associated with extreme arousal episodes can be dangerous, secretive, dishonest, destructive, self-harming, high risk and develop into obsessive patterns that seem unexplainable, particularly when they are resistant to pun-ishment. But these behavior patterns are based as much on physiologi-cal logic as are those linked to trauma.

In biology it is understood that "the physical takes care of itself." For example, when a person with an allergy to bee stings is stung by a bee and then dies, the cause of death is not the poison injected into the system, but the system's effort to rid the body of the poison. The physi-cal taking care of itself can produce unbearable discomfort and even death when extreme conditions are present. Similarly, behavior that works to reduce an extreme state of emotional and physiological suffer-ing or that generates an arousal state that temporarily relieves ongoing suffering, is behavior that may help the child survive one extreme con-dition while placing him or her in jeopardy due to another.

Physical symptoms that are generated, and then escalate during a highly intense to extreme experience, are uniquely individual in their expression. They also affect the system as powerfully in children as they do in adults. If the symptoms are repeated as a result of similar and ongoing experiences, this repetition can put stress on the areas of the body that are most affected. If these physical areas of the body are also subject to predisposed genetic factors, this repeated aggravation in-creases risk for conditions that are already a potentially-inherited risk. It is also likely that genetic factors influence the individual nature of the physical symptoms that are generated during these experiences.

Derry (1999)[6] presents the added perspective that: "Physiology and psychology both play important, independent, interacting roles in the development of disease in what we call 'the person.' In the development and treatment of psychiatric problems, the importance of both physical structure and psychosocial factors is inescapable. . . . Human brains are not genetically specified; they develop over time and as a result of people's experiences. For example, the literature suggests that trauma and childhood depression alter the development and functioning of the brain. Even in the case of serious mental illness, heritability ratios do not completely explain the development of disease. For instance, identical twins are usually described as having concordance for schizophrenia of about 50%. Even identical twins do not share the same psychology, behavior patterns, or functional brain chemistry."

An experience that propels a child into an extreme realm of emotional and physiological distress can alter his or her view of the external world, perception of self and others, and behavior, in ways that cannot be predicted. Pivotal experiences are the factor that cannot be calculated by those who believe that success or failure in life is determined by either/or heredity and environment. It is the 00 on the roulette wheel.

The theory underlying these assumptions proposes that the root of vulnerability to addiction and many other behavioral disorders may begin during early development. While taking into consideration factors that include head injury, brain disease, genetic predisposition and environmental influences, the research underlying this theory studied the effectiveness of a High Risk Identification and Prediction Treatment Method (HRIPTM) which was designed to investigate the role of pivotal childhood experience in relation to chronic addiction conditions. The HRIPTM was developed to pinpoint the origin of patterns of behavior stemming from identified pivotal experiences. These behaviors were also identified as a contributing factor in chronic addiction relapse.[7]

The study concluded that when a child experiences a high degree of distress, he or she will take action to relieve the suffering. If a suffering child experiences a highly intense pleasurable state, he or she will take action to extend and/or replicate that state. These important adaptive mechanisms can lead to problems later in life if the action is repeated and continues to evolve to an obsessive and/or problematic degree. The high level of intensity of that early experience seems to result in both the experience and the coping mechanism being stored in the still-developing brain. The brain's organization reflects its experience. Experiences that are emotionally and physiologically overwhelming can produce neuronal activity and chemical changes that access cell areas (subsets) of the brain not engaged in less-intensified states, and can even change the structure of the developing brain if the activity is repeated again and again.

In severe cases, such as children who experience ongoing verbal, physical and/or sexual abuse, their ability to maintain equilibrium is so precarious that they come to rely entirely on the behavior enacted to relieve the distress of each episode (whether it is an internal mental behavioral action or an external behavioral action), not just to survive the abuse, but to survive the emotional and physiological distress that is created by the experience. The physiological component that is generated during high levels of emotional distress is the key factor in why the brain responds to this dynamic as a physiological attack on the system. For example, if a child experiences increased inability to breath during a fearful episode, a physical crisis occurs that exacerbates the emotional crisis, which then further increases the physical distress. Unfortunately, when a behavioral action is effective in helping a child survive experiences of this nature, the child unintentionally may begin to rely on it, despite additional problems that may result. A child's self-esteem, for example, is one of the many areas that can be negatively affected as this reliance develops.

Self-perception is dramatically affected by the patterns of behavior that evolve in relation to this dynamic. If a child repeats behavior that generates feelings of guilt and shame, or results in negative consequences, self-esteem will diminish as the pattern evolves. A child who does not feel good about his behavior is not likely to feel very good about himself.

The following is an example of how even a minor incident in a less-complicated situation can result in an extreme response and the construction of a "seed" behavior that quickly grows into a pattern.

> Johnny, who is age four, accidentally breaks a lamp. His mother discovers the lamp and becomes very angry. Johnny perceives this to be a terrible accident and begins to feel intense fear. The fear escalates when he sees his mother's angry expression. Johnny begins to experience physical symptoms (raised body temperature, trembling, sweaty palms, pressure to urinate). His mother shifts her focus from

the lamp, toward him. He tries but cannot stop the trembling in his legs and his lower lip. He finds it increasingly difficult to swallow. Johnny has never before seen his mother so upset. She begins to question him in a harsh tone, "Johnny, did you do this? Did you break my beautiful lamp?"

Impulsively, Johnny blurts out a lie, "I didn't do it. The cat did it." The lie worked. The cat was blamed. Johnny felt enormous relief. He also felt guilty and not so good about himself. He promised himself that he would not lie to his mother again. The next time Johnny got into trouble and was confronted, the fear, pressure, trembling and difficulty swallowing came back. He lied again, and someone else was blamed. Johnny's negative feelings about himself continued as the pattern evolved.

Once a pattern such as this becomes well-developed, self-perception will continue to be adversely affected if the child knows the behavior is wrong and continues to repeat it. Many patterns of behavior are not recognized by others and go unnoticed until they are firmly entrenched in the individual's personality.

The key to understanding these patterns lies in how they originate. When behavior is formulated under extreme circumstances, a child does not take time to clearly think out an effective behavioral response, nor does intention (as is so often assumed) play a major role in the action that is taken. The child is propelled into a realm of existence that often produces mental chaos and diminished ability to think rationally and function normally. Nothing learned or planned prepares a child for an extreme episode or repeated experiences of this nature. The initial momentarily-constructed response action is determined by a combination of influences. Genetic factors, such as hereditary traits, influence inclination and natural ability. Environmental factors influence what has been observed and learned up to that age period. Present factors are equally important e.g., what is happening in the situation, what is unique to the situation, and what is available to the child that can be included in the behavioral response. These crucial influences converge at the most extreme point of the experience — the point at which an action is constructed and enacted until the high level of distress is alleviated (to some degree).

Certain vivid details of images and sensory stimuli occurring at the extreme point of the experience, along with the feelings and physical symptoms that led to it, and the behavior that effectively led from it, are captured in the brain in memory, as if on photo-file. This recorded set of components has become vital information in relation to a specific crisis state and its regulation. This entire dynamic is important in understanding repetitive patterns. When a memory is stimulated by triggers that are associated with the initial experience, the feelings and physical symptoms that are generated can, in turn, trigger the associated behavior — without the memory always completely surfacing in the consciousness! In some individuals, the memory of the experience emerges regularly in the mind; in others, the painful memory or memories can be suppressed for years, only to surface later, unexpectedly. But, the feelings, symptoms and behavioral responses surrounding the experience/s can be active and evolving continually, whether the memory is at a conscious or pre-conscious level. At some point in time, the pre-conscious memories will emerge because they remain accessible due to the unresolved nature of conditions stemming from these experiences.

Negative emotional state is the condition that is most frequently reported as precipitating relapse, in the most well-documented and respected studies on substance abuse relapse (SSAOD, 1996).[8] HRIPTM research examining the relationship between negative emotional state and early childhood experiences found that the feeling/physical symptom combinations, described as present during childhood experiences that could be vividly recalled, were remarkably similar and often identical to the present day feeling/physical symptom combinations that made up the most predominant negative emotional states of these individuals. The patients involved in the study, who reported daily, weekly, monthly or occasional thoughts of memories associated with early events, also reported ongoing problems dealing with negative emotional state. In simple language, these people feel bad a lot and feel strongly compelled to self-medicate with behavior or substances or both.

A study focused on women and early abuse conducted at Emory University[9] reports that child abuse and other traumatic early experiences forever alter a woman's brain chemistry, setting the stage for future psychological problems. The study offers the first evidence in humans that early trauma can change the brain's response to stress and raise the risk of mood and anxiety disorders later in life, according to lead author Charles Nemeroff. The findings take on added meaning, Nemeroff says, in light of the more than 3 million reported cases of child abuse each year, which create a population of children at much higher risk of psychopathology later in life.[8]

A child who is reliant on behavior that works to reduce emotional and physiological stress, while also having a negative effect on self-perception and self-worth, often has difficulty making social and physical adjustments. Pre-adolescence and adolescence can bring about additional anxiety and stress. A child with low self-esteem and patterns linked to this dynamic, who is entering adolescence and experiencing puberty, is vulnerable to any situation or substance that reduces or alters this additional discomfort to a manageable degree. This child is particularly vulnerable to the effects of mood-altering substances if experimentation results in distress reduction, enhanced or altered self-perception and/or improved social integration. The mood-altering substance, in effect, can become an additional component incorporated into the problematic pattern/s to aid in self-regulation. Reliance on this additional factor can quickly lead to substance abuse and addiction.

Problematic patterns of behavior that are well-developed prior to the onset of addiction often persist rather than diminish during abstinence and addiction recovery. Pre-addiction patterns can become post-addiction nightmares. A return to reliance on behavior that competes with a positive healing and recovery process promotes internal conflict in the person who is trying to behave in accordance with recovery principles. The HRIPTM study concluded that pre-addiction problematic behavior patterns play a significant role in sabotaging recovery processes and are an identifiable factor in chronic addiction and other behavioral disorder conditions. The study also recognized a need for early identification and increased effective interventions with children to address problematic behavioral conditions at the earliest stages of development.

Child psychiatrist and Harvard professor Robert Coles has written over 50 books on child development. Coles emphasizes the importance of communicating with children, recognizing problematic conditions, and implementing effective and positive interventions when it is most crucial to do so. Referring to his 1974 tape-recorded conversation with Anna Freud, he writes, "Again we addressed the question of character, how the events in the lives of young children persist in their shaping (even at times defining) impact." Referring to infancy, he writes, "Here, as elsewhere in life, experience shapes character."[10]

One of the most consistent factors documented in the HRIPTM study, in relation to identified pivotal experiences that resulted in problematic patterns, was the lack of intervention (or effective intervention) during and after the experience occurred. There are several reasons why this can happen. A child may have a traumatic experience but not talk about it. The episode may not be witnessed by others. In some situations, parents might not be involved at all. Many of the reported episodes occurred with playmates, siblings, teachers, strangers or while the child was alone. Some occurred while parents were present but not aware of the impact of the episode on the child. Many reported incidents occurred at school, with teachers or classmates, or were isolated incidents involving accidents or other various types of calamity.

The following case is an example of one such experience and how it dramatically changed a child's behavior and self-perception. It is the first in a series of clinical case examples that will conclude each chapter. The case is a synopsis of information and revelations that came about as a result of the patient's participation in a psychiatric hospital-based addiction treatment program incorporating the High Risk Identification and Treatment Method (HRIPTM). The HRIPTM provides a systematic structured process for identifying the origins of behavior that contribute to chronic relapse conditions.

Case Summary: John

John, a 29-year-old, single white male, was admitted to addiction treatment with a history of cocaine use beginning at age 19. He reported moderate use of alcohol and marijuana since age 16. Despite one previous completion of outpatient treatment at age 22, he had very little understanding of the symptoms of addiction, particularly alcoholism. In the previous year, he had begun smoking crack, and used $8,000 worth over a five-month period. He also regularly consumed a small amount of beer and used marijuana, which he did not consider a problem.

John had never been married and had no children. He graduated from high school and completed two college semesters. He worked in a printing company for nine years. He quit, partly because of health concerns; he had developed allergies to dust and was having a lot of trouble breathing. He started his own landscaping company, which he described as still in the growth phase. He was not involved in a relationship. He stated that he was heterosexual. He was living with his grandmother at the time of admission. He had no history of legal problems. Other than allergy to aspirin and house dust, he was not aware of any medical problems and was on no medications.

His mental status evaluation reported that he was alert, oriented, pleasant and cooperative. He emphasized that he wanted to regain control of his life and knew just what he needed to do. He was under the impression that he was in treatment to learn better self-control. His short- and long-term memory were intact. Cognitive functioning was intact. There was no evidence of hallucinations, delusions or thought disorder. He denied suicidal ideation or homicidal ideation. His intelligence was estimated to be average.

John was admitted to the intensive outpatient program for a period of eight weeks. His initial attitude and behavior during the orientation phase of the program was positive and motivated. He stated that he had been out of control for months and wanted to regain control of his life. He said he would follow all orders and do what was necessary to obtain this goal. He approached treatment as if he were entering the military. He said he had analyzed his condition, knew he had fallen under the control of cocaine, and was ready to battle this control to a winning outcome. He agreed to begin attending Narcotics Anonymous and to obtain a sponsor. He followed all treatment stipulations and directives. But from the onset, it was evident that his interactions with treatment peers were less than positive. The apparent reason was his openly expressed views on recovery and a clear misunderstanding of basic recovery philosophy.

John was short in stature, with a strong physical frame. His features were even, his coloring fair and his complexion clear and healthy. He was neat, well-groomed, organized, self-disciplined, energetic, attentive and eager. He appeared to be in excellent physical condition. His posture was erect and his physical actions, quick and efficient. His body language was unusual. He sat at almost perfect attention, stiff and controlled. He stared straight ahead as if preventing any distraction and appeared to be trying to stay focused and attentive. During breaks, he eagerly approached staff to share his self-analysis. He explained that he was a complex case and that it might be helpful if he could describe his symptoms in detail. He seemed to have more interest in talking to staff than interacting with peers. When he did interact with other patients, his behavior created a gap that set him apart from the others and provoked antagonism.

During his first week of treatment, John shared his current efforts to gain the self-control and discipline necessary to remain abstinent. His body language in a group setting exemplified self-restraint. His approach to the daily meditation group session was more militaristic than holistic. He seemed to gain little insight from educational and spiritual readings or the personal disclosures of others in the group. His own disclosure infuriated some group members, who viewed his remarks as a challenge to 12-Step recovery principles. Advised to focus on listening and learning, he responded with increased zealous resistance. As a result, he met with increased hostility from members of his treatment group and his NA (Narcotics Anonymous) recovery support group. Despite this adversity, he appeared determined to continue and maintained perfect attendance. He adhered to the belief that he could over-. come his addiction with willpower and self-control.

John's efforts became more productive when he began to focus on identifying consistent feeling and physical symptom responses to a variety of presented situations. Imagining himself at various age periods in his childhood, he described himself prior to age 6 as a happy, good-natured child who was helpful to others and who had good feelings about himself. Toward the end of this age period, his parents divorced. John's written assignments also cited this event, but he reported no negative response to the divorce, noting only that his grandfather took over as a father figure.

During the second week of treatment, John focused on identifying consistent behavioral responses to a variety of situations. Around age 6, he described his behavior as increasingly introverted, withdrawn and isolated. He described fantasizing, attempts to "steel himself" against emotions, retaliation thinking and planning, and secretive actions in response to increased peer abuse. He described becoming increasingly fascinated with his "dark side of self." He said he became obsessed with gaining physical power, discipline and strength. He described a pattern of fascination and fantasy with a super-hero who could transform himself into a creature of superhuman strength and size.

John's effort to honestly address behaviors revealed in group were obstructed by his reluctance to accept the problematic nature of these patterns. He appeared to be self-satisfied with the evolution of his behavior, particularly in relation to his ability to analyze and mentally challenge himself. His disclosure appeared to be an effort to achieve some level of recognition from staff and peers. He seemed to be letting everyone know that he was mentally and physically superior. While this counterproductive disclosure gave a negative impression, it also provided a window into his thinking and behavior.

John stated that he could easily pinpoint the most significant experience of his life. He described the memory of his experience as "repressed." He explained that he could only remember certain things about what occurred. He said that information beyond the details he could recall remained confused and blurred.

John learned that the purpose of the HRIPTM process is to focus on that which is recalled, rather than that which is not. He later revealed that he had tried for years to fill in the "blanks" of that memory, only to become more confused by his attempts to analyze the impact of the experience. Continuing to prefer his own self-assessment and recovery approach over presented concepts, he progressed slowly toward the group disclosure that would better explain his behavior. It was therefore revealing when, as the focus of the Orchestration Group Process, he shared the following pivotal experience.

The episode occurred when John was 6 years old. He said he thought of it often and regularly since the day it happened, despite efforts to "purge" it from his memory. He began his disclosure by providing a brief background of his family situation at the time of the experience.

John described his home environment as stable until he was approximately age five. He was an only child. Although both parents worked and were away from home much of the time, he was cared for by his loving maternal grandparents. When his parents divorced, during his fifth year, he said that his grandparents, who had assumed the primary parental role, shielded him from disruption and parental discord. He described his grandfather as a father figure, and his father as having little influence in his life. He described his grandparents as having a more predominant role than his parents in his recollections of early childhood. He said he felt secure, happy and shielded from harm until he entered elementary school. He described his experience in first grade as the end of his happy childhood.

The episode took place within the first few months of John's first-grade year. He had not attended kindergarten. As a result, he said he was somewhat overwhelmed with the classroom size and all the activity. He described the room as large and bright. There were approximately 30 classmates. He described himself as quiet, unobtrusive and good-natured. His seat was situated in the middle to back area of the classroom. He recalled his teacher as strict and intimidating. On the day of the episode, the class was involved in a reading exercise. The teacher called on him to read aloud from his book. He said he had difficulty reading and felt he was not as advanced as the others. He became fearful when he could not make out all the words as he tried to read, and instead, stared hopelessly at the page before him. He said the teacher became impatient and reacted harshly. She began to approach him from the front of the classroom, moving down the row toward him. He described her face as harsh and her expression as angry and threatening. When she reached his desk, she grabbed him tightly on his right shoulder and stated, "Are you stupid?" She continued, "What's wrong with you?" His shoulder seared with pain. He described it as a "clenching pinch that hurt so bad it brought me out of my seat."

[The following exemplifies how details surrounding a pivotal experience can be recalled while the event is being described. The person describing his/her vivid recollections may not remember what happened hours or days before or after the event, but will usually recall the feelings, physical symptoms and behavioral response surrounding the episode when questioned about these components of the experience.] For example:

John's described feeling response: "I felt that my self worth was attacked. I felt degraded, hurt, powerless and scared. I felt fear, confusion, loathing, fascination with her face and expression. I felt alone, singled out, isolated, helpless and like something was wrong with me. I felt self doubt, challenged, embarrassed, upset and angry."

John's described physical symptom response: "I felt hot, raised blood pressure, flushed, like heat rushed up and out of my head, which was blood red. My mental activity increased while my emotions became so strong they destroyed coherent thought. My chest felt like a dark pit and I experienced vertigo. Then I felt drained by the adrenaline rush which gen-erated involuntary body movement. My gut/stomach felt tied up in knots."

John's described behavior response: "Once I regained control of my mental activity, I withdrew into myself mentally. I sat down and began to observe the response of the others kids. I started to plan a strategy for prevention of another attack and came to the conclusion that I would prevent it from happening again by working harder and focusing attention toward the teacher. I would watch her at all times and be ob-servant in order to pinpoint anything that might anger her. Before the other kids could laugh at me after class, I would say something first to make them think it didn't bother me. I would try to make it sound hu-morous. I turned my humor inward and continued planning what I would say at the first opportunity. I did this while also trying to pay attention and appearing to be paying attention. I protected myself by regaining control of my body. I could not relax after this. My body re-mained on alert. I pushed my physical endurance to the limit for the remainder of the day. I planned to defend myself from then on. I pre-tended to ignore the pain in my shoulder, which continued long after she grabbed me."

Prior to the described episode, John described himself as "a happy and good-natured child." His written assignments recount this experi-ence on three separate lifespan charts. His recognition of this event as a defining experience was supported by what he revealed. From that day forward, he was changed. His relationships with others changed. His interactions with his teacher and his peers changed. The behavior con-structed during this experience changed his demeanor and body lan-guage.

The behavior that John enacted, in his effort to prevent what he perceived as intrusion and attack, appeared odd to others. These defen-sive actions produced a need for more defense because his body lan-guage set him apart from the other children, particularly when he was in a hyper-vigilant state. In written assignments, he wrote, "I intro-verted my feelings, i.e., withdrawing into self with an attempt at total negation of emotion. But, I felt loneliness, anger and inadequacy. The other kids continued giving me a hard time throughout my childhood."

John became more confused as his behavior became increasingly problematic, defensive, reactionary, and both mentally and physically retaliatory. He described these actions as an "involuntary lashing out." He recounted that on one occasion, he felt like the entire student body was against him. He said he felt an increased feeling of detachment during adolescence. John's ability to detach appeared to be present prior to the first-grade episode. His lack of bonding with his parents, and his detached response to their divorce, seemed more relevant as he revealed the defensive motives of this behavior. His tendency to self-protect by detaching was obviously present prior to the classroom episode, but was propelled to a greater and more self-protective degree as a result of that experience. His ability to detach from his problematic interactions with others and concentrate his focus on a high school trade training program enabled him to graduate and enter a printing company apprenticeship at age 18.

John's case is a good example of how environment and genetic factors influenced his constructed behavioral response to the classroom experience. John was an only child who had limited interaction with other children and no kindergarten experience prior to entering first grade. His primary caretakers were aged grandparents who, by his own account, protected him from harm and discord. He had been in school only a short time, and his interactions with the other children were in the beginning stages when the episode took place. After the episode, his manner and body language changed noticeably. This odd-appearing behavior negatively affected his peer interactions. He reported no recollection of negative interaction prior to the episode.

His frame of reference for behavioral identification during this period was the super-hero, *The Incredible Hulk*. By his own account, he was fascinated by this character and had been watching him regularly on TV. The *Hulk* character influenced his efforts to control his body. His perception of the extreme physiological response he experienced during his emotionally distressed state was compared to the transformation demonstrated by the fictional character. John also linked this transformation to physical growth and superhuman power and strength. John described his physical symptoms as very similar to what happened when *The Incredible Hulk* grew bigger and stronger, only to shrink again when adrenaline reduction occurred. He stated that he could actually feel himself grow larger, then shrink in size. Size became a greater issue later when he realized that his height would not exceed 5' 6".

By late adolescence, John had developed additional defense strategies. When it became apparent that his size and strength had limitations, he compensated by turning to weapons (primarily guns) as an additional intimidating element. He would assert that it was his right to own and collect guns as a means of self-protection. He learned to repair guns as means of acquisition. He had no history of arrest related to weapons. But he was under the impression that if he let it be known that he was armed or had access to guns, his defensive position was strengthened. In dialogue with others, John alluded to weapons, extremist groups and dangerous associations. In conversations, his attempts to interject humorous asides related to these interests (as a means of relaying this information to others) was often misunderstood and considered disturbing. His dialogue was particularly unsettling because he also alluded to belief in extreme reactionary ideals and philosophies, and knowledge of covert planned retaliations. The ideas and behavior deemed acceptable in the extremist literature he read, and the radical groups he admired, negatively influenced his interactions with co-workers and friends. In reality, it is highly questionable that he was actually involved, or even accepted, within those circles. And, that his use of guns went any further than ownership.

John worked as a printer for several years after completing his apprenticeship. While content with his profession, he could not get along with co-workers. He described being in a constant state of emotional and physical irritation throughout this period. In his written assignments, he wrote that he did not deserve the unfair treatment he experienced, that he felt angry and resentful, planned retaliations, tried to intimidate others to protect himself and held grudges. At age 19 he began using cocaine. He said it made him feel powerful, invincible and less reactionary. He blamed the negative workplace atmosphere for his inability to remain abstinent after his first addiction treatment experience. Although his perception was that cocaine helped him endure his coworkers and interact more effectively, his relationship with them continued to deteriorate. He eventually left the printing profession and started his own landscaping business with the goal of achieving independence.

While John's pattern of physically pushing himself to the limit helped him start a new business, his excessive approach to the physical labor required, and his reluctance to rely on others, contributed to his accelerated use of cocaine. He said cocaine initially enhanced his energy, strength and ability to work longer hours, and that he planned to reduce cocaine use once the business was firmly established. He said he enjoyed being his own boss, having control of his destiny and being outdoors where he felt freedom and less tension. He described his growing dependence on cocaine as an obstacle to his overall goal of being in control of his life.

John had maintained a close relationship with his grandparents since childhood. When his grandfather died, four years prior to this current treatment, he moved in with his grandmother to help her with expenses and household maintenance. His behavior toward his grandmother was respectful and loyal. He spoke of her with high regard. John also exhibited this type of behavior whenever someone gave him positive attention. He could be polite, attentive, mannerly, helpful and enthusiastic, exhibiting generous, kind and thoughtful behavior in response to approval and praise. Unfortunately, his overwhelming and obsessive response to positive attention often resulted in rejection after an initial period of acceptance. This was the case in his relationships with friends and with members of the opposite sex. His grandmother remained his one consistent source of unconditional positive regard.

In the last weeks of treatment, in a written assignment, he identified a memory of an eye surgery that occurred when he was age 2. He described the memory as vague, and said that he had no understanding of what was occurring at the time, but could recall feeling fear and using his body defensively. He identified this experience as relevant to his extreme response to the physical intrusion enacted later by his teacher.

During the last week of treatment, John stated that he adhered to his belief that he could achieve successful recovery with discipline and self-control. He argued that he had remained abstinent for a period of eight weeks and would continue to do so. He stated that his gained self-understanding helped him to recognize his behavior as an obstacle to recovery. He stated that he would continue NA attendance despite his controversial views, while working on his behavior in private therapy. He also made an appointment with the treatment facility administrator to submit a bid for a landscaping contract!

John identified several behaviors that developed into patterns, prior to the onset of addiction to alcohol. They included:

- Self protection by withdrawing into self, detachment from others and isolating. Later additional compensation elements;

weapons, associations and resources to create the illusion of power. Hyper-vigilant, alert, watchful, obsessively observant behavior.

- Physical self-containment. Determined physical control, which evolved into excessive effort to dominate and/or control the physical self by restraining or unleashing.
- Obsessive mental strategy as a means of self-protection, prevention, planning retaliation and fantasizing about strength, size, power, dual self, dark self.
- Retaliatory action, often subversive and secretive. Determined emotional detachment as a means of retaliation.
- Defensive intimidation through insinuating dialogue, often guised in darkly humorous allusion. Physical aggression when experiencing loss of control. Destruction of objects, often fixed objects that require excessive strength to remove or destroy.
- Fantasy and fascination with power, super-hero identification and dual personality.
- Self-abuse enacted through derogatory self-dialogue, humor at own expense, excessive testing of physical endurance and risk associated with destructive actions.
- Obsessive self-analysis, self-questioning, self-recrimination and unrealistic self-expectation.

These behaviors, originally constructed to relieve John's extreme negative emotional state, evolved into established patterns that he came to reluctantly identify as sabotaging factors to his addiction recovery, relationships, health, occupation and lifestyle, and as factors in his previous addiction relapses. During treatment, John recognized his limited ability to cope with stressors that trigger these behaviors. Although he made significant progress in this area by working with staff to develop positive alternative behavioral strategies to compete with these patterns, John maintained certain ideas and beliefs that could influence a regression in this area. While he accepted that the process of behavioral change as a life-long commitment could be aided by weekly therapy for an extended period of time, with ongoing commitment to his NA support group, risk factors remain that center around (1) his limited ability to cope with the identified negative emotional states (those that are generated by specific feeling/physical symptom combinations and that trigger sabotaging patterns of behavior), (2) environmental and relationship stressors, and (3) post-addiction symptoms that may produce craving for cocaine.

John identified his experience in the first grade as significant in relation to his present condition. As a result of the HRIPTM, John increased his ability to identify, assess and address relapse risk symptoms by pinpointing specific feeling and physical symptom conditions that contribute to his behavior and desire for cocaine. At the same time, the HRIPTM program increased the clinician's, and the physician's, ability to understand John and to identify, assess, and implement a plan of therapeutic and (if needed) appropriate medication to facilitate risk reduction and to structure an individually tailored approach to his case.

Notes

1. Wordsworth, W. "Michael," *The Poetical Works of William Wordsworth, with Memoir and Notes*, pp. 85-94 (Excelsior Edition). New York: American News Company.

2. Carnegie Corporation of New York: "Report on Meeting The Needs of Young Children." (1994). Internet access website.

3. Brazelton, T.B. & Greenspan, S. (2000). *The Irreducible Needs of Children: What Every Child Must Have to Grow, Learn, and Flourish.* Perseus Publishing.

4. Gerwe, C.F. (1999). "Chronic Addiction Relapse Treatment: A Study of the Effectiveness of the High Risk Identification and Treatment Model (HRIPTM)." *DAI*, Vol.60-09 9946534. UMI Company.

5. American Psychiatric Association. (1996). *Diagnostic and Statistical Manual of Mental Disorders* (DSM-IV) (4th ed. rev.). Washington: Author.

6. Derry, P. (August 23, 1999). "Genes, Neurochemicals, and Persons." *MedGenMed.* Medscape, Inc.

7. Gerwe, C.F., *op. cit.*

8. Society for the Study of Addiction to Alcohol and Other Disorders. (1996, December). *Addiction: Perspectives on Precipitants of Relapse* (Vol. 91). USA: Carfax.

9. Nemeroff, C. et al. (Aug. 2, 2000). "Childhood Abuse May Create a Hormonal Predisposition to the Development of Mood and Anxiety Disorders in Adulthood." Emory University, 2000.

10. Coles, R. (1997). *The Moral Intelligence of Children: How to Raise a Moral Child*, pp. 89-90. New York: Penguin Books.

As I came home through the woods with my string of fish, trailing my pole, it being now quite dark, I caught a glimpse of a woodchuck stealing across my path, and felt a strange thrill of savage delight, and was strongly tempted to seize and devour him raw; not that I was hungry then, except for that wildness which he represented. Once or twice, however, while I lived at the pond, I found myself ranging the woods, like a half-starved hound, with a strange abandonment, seeking some kind of venison which I might devour, and no morsel could have been too savage for me. The wildest scenes had become unaccountably familiar. I found in myself, and still find, an instinct toward a higher, or, as it is named, spiritual life, as do most men, and another toward a primitive, rank, and savage one, and I reverence them both.[1]

— Thoreau

When a combination of factors (feelings and physical symptoms) comes together during an experience, and then in response to one another produce a series of reactions, a percolating dynamic can be generated that builds to a point where the converging components spill over (much like the overflow in a percolating coffee pot). The *level of intensity*, the point when this convergence takes place, can be considered a *point of transformation*. In relation to an experience that produces an extreme level of emotional and physical intensity, this is the point where behavioral action begins to formulate and is constructed. For example:

Sally is 3 years old. She is watching a funny cartoon and suddenly there is a ferocious monster introduced into the scene. The image frightens her. Her perception is that the monster is real. Her feeling of fear increases and her heart begins to beat faster. She feels pressure in her chest and her breath begins to catch. The monster on the screen seems bigger and appears to be looking at her. She begins to cry and feels increased anxiety and agitation. The monster seems to be coming toward her and she begins to feel terror. The terror increases into panic but she cannot move. She tries to scream for her mother and cannot make a sound. Suddenly, the monster seems to loom before her and she believes he is going to grab her. Sally screams and screams and screams until the monster disappears.

In this situation, Sally's initial perception produced feelings that generated physical symptoms. Her imagination influenced her perception, which generated increasingly distressful feelings and symptoms influencing her level of fear until the situation became unbearable, and then Sally screamed. Her behavioral action was loud verbal expression, and as a result, the imagined monster in the room disappeared. The behavior (screaming) was effective and therefore will be repeated the next time Sally feels this combination of emotional and physical symptoms.

In his classic, *The Principles of Psychology*,[2] written at the turn of the last century, William James presented Herbert Spencer's theory concerning components, compounding elements, fusion and convergence of musical notes that transform, at some point, into a tone. The theory, which focused on how the brain transforms variations in sound in response to what is heard, was generally dismissed because it could not be determined at which point the transformation occurs; but it did break new ground by recognizing that physical force was the driving condition that propelled the randomly occurring components toward transformation.

Since that time, scientists and mathematicians have recognized percolation dynamics in relation to the concept of evolutionary processes (Vandewalle & Ausloos, 1994).[3] Studies are currently being conducted that look at what occurs when a species is transformed both physically and behaviorally in response to certain conditions. The focus of this chapter is to explore the dynamics that lead to a *point of transformation* in the individual — the point at which behavioral action is constructed, behavioral action that becomes necessary to the individual and continues to evolve into patterns that cause problems for the individual.

When a child has an experience that generates an extreme response, a combination of many factors must come into play to produce a transforming dynamic. This combination is unique to the individual and to the experience that generates it. Professional gamblers are well aware of the seemingly infinite variety of combinations in 10 numbers. These combinations are referred to as logarithms. The feeling/physical symptom combinations that precipitate an extreme state are as diverse as logarithms. While some children might share some of the same feelings in response to an experience, and some of the same physical symptom responses, for two children to have the same perception of an experience, respond with the same exact combination of feelings and physical symptoms, and reach the same level of intensity, is as unlikely as replicating, by chance, the same number combinations in logarithms. Children can have difficult, frightening, exciting and dramatic experiences without ever reaching an extreme level that affects them to a transforming degree. But those who do are changed forever by the experience.

The structure that surrounds a child during the earliest stages of development is the most protective measure to prevent problematic behavior arising from these occurrences. Based on direct child observation and clinical practice with adults, there is rather convincing evidence that normal development requires certain amounts of frustration (Kohut 1971, Mayer 1968, Meissner et al. 1975, Winnecot, 1953).[4-7] Optimally, extremes of deprivation or indulgence are avoided and the child is confronted by enough tolerable disappointment that a capacity to withstand emotional distress and pain is gradually built up. To summarize how this capacity evolves, the individual gradually incorporates into a sense of the self and into the ego the parents' protective role and their function as a barrier to stimuli. Used in this sense, *stimulus barrier* refers to those aspects of ego function that operate either to keep unpleasant effects or tension at a minimal level, or to defend against such feelings through appropriate action and mechanisms of defense when they reach high or intolerable levels (Khantzian, 1999).[8]

Even the most protective environment cannot shield a child from an experience of this nature. A child might experience a sudden loss, be frightened by an unusual weather event, or witness a terrifying accident that results in an extreme reaction and an uncharacteristic behavioral response. But in a positive environment with a sound parental structure, a repetition of either the event or the behavior is less likely and effective intervention is more probable.

Problematic and obsessively driven patterns develop through repetition and the need and/or desire to enact behavior that effectively regulates emotional and physiological distress. A child who experiences ongoing distress in a less structured and less protective environment is the child most susceptible to problematic behavior repetition. It is also the child who will be susceptible to arousal experiences that can also develop to relieve a state of ongoing suffering.

For example, the following review of a child murder case in England involves two children who were susceptible to this dynamic and had individual responses to the same experience. Violence is becoming more relevant to children due to increased exposure to violent content presented on television, film and in computer-generated images. While it can be argued that not all children are negatively affected by these images and information, we must consider the case of Jon Venables and Robert Thompson.

On February 12, 1993 at 3:38 P.M., James Bulgar, a child not quite 3 years old, wandered away from his mother in a shopping precinct outside Liverpool in Lancashire. He was recorded three minutes later by a security camera, on another floor, in the company of two older children. A taxi driver and a woman shopper saw two boys drag the child across a road outside the center a little later, and a further 36 witnesses watched, but did not interfere, assuming that the three were related. The boys took James, who seemed upset, on a two-and-a-half mile walk down a well-traveled bus route, past a roundabout, into a do-it-yourself shop and a pet store, out on to the verge of a railway line. There, two hours after kidnapping him, they tortured James to death. They did so deliberately, hitting him at least 27 times with bricks and a cast-iron bar weighing 22 lbs, causing 40 visible wounds and multiple fractures of his skull. Then they took off his trousers, covered parts of his face and body with blue paint (apparently stolen en route for this purpose), and finally laid him on the railway track so that the next train cut what was left of him in two. Then the two boys, both ten years old, still dressed in their school uniforms, visited a video store as if nothing had happened.[9]

John Venables and Robert Thompson were arrested less than a week later and charged with murder. There was never any question of their guilt. The two had left a trail of damning evidence, not even troubling to remove James' blood from their shoes or the traces of blue paint from their jackets. Under questioning, they blamed each other, but neither then nor at any point in their sensational trial did either of them give a clear explanation about why they might have done such a thing.

The children who killed James Bulgar were the products of poverty, broken homes and abusive parents. They were persistent truants, allies in underachievement, at odds with their own society even before the murder; but the same holds true for hundreds of thousands of disadvantaged kids who do not hang around shopping malls looking for someone to kill. It emerged during the trial that Thompson and Venables, on the same day they succeeded in kidnapping James, tried at least once to lure another child away from his mother. They were looking for trouble and had something specific in mind.

There is a chilling coincidence in that the last video rented by Venables's father before the Bulgar tragedy was *Child's Play III*, a story about a demonic doll called Chucky who wears dungarees, has blue paint splashed on his face, abducts a boy and tries to kill him under the wheels of the ghost train in a fairground called the Devil's Lair.[9]

The child who is hurt, abused, neglected, riddled with anxiety, who is seething with anger and escalating symptoms of physical distress, is a suffering child. A child who erupts in bouts of delinquent behavior that temporarily relieves an ongoing state of misery and despair is a suffering child. When this child sees something that suddenly alters this ongoing condition, an image or scene that produces feelings of excitement, exhilaration and thrill, and then just as suddenly feels these sensations slip away, he or she will become desperate to replicate them. Once the thrilling experience has been felt, the distressful state that preceded it becomes all the more unbearable. Desire begins when the child cannot extend the feeling and physical sensation — to somehow make it last — during the initial experience. In the immediate aftermath, preoccupation leads to an effort to reproduce the desired state. The seeds of obsession germinate when repetition occurs. The behavior enacted to try to replicate the experience will be constructed from information that was recorded in the child's memory during the experience.

The information registered in memory is unique to the child's perception and holds the details that are necessary to recreate the experience. For example, if a companion was present during the experience and is part of the recalled memory details of the experience, the child will want that person there again to ensure replication. If blue paint was part of the detail, blue paint will be needed. If railroad tracks were part of the detail, railroad tracks will be important. Just as the most relevant details are registered during the peak/extreme level of the experience, so too will those details contribute to recreating the event that reproduces the now desired arousal state. And also, seeing the companion or blue paint or railroad tracks at some future time, will trigger the symptoms associated with the experience.

In this case, it was difficult for the boy most affected to replicate the experience because the parent had returned the video to the store and the boys were not old enough to rent it by themselves. Therefore, he engaged the help of his companion to innovate another episode. Together, they went to great effort to recreate the exciting scene as closely as possible in a real life setting. This case demonstrates how each component of the experience that was registered in the boy's memory became vital information to its recreation as we seek to understand the behavior that followed.

How can this be explained when two boys are involved? If the child who had the extreme experience is dominant over his companion (it was noted during the trial that Thompson was the dominant of the two boys), he will try to convince his companion to participate. If the companion fears losing the friend more than he fears executing the plan, he will become an accomplice.

It would be a mistake to assume that both boys responded in the same way to the same experience. When a child is alone in an experience of this nature, the pattern will be replicated alone. If the child is in a group during an experience of this nature, the pattern will be replicated in a group or gang. Another important factor to note is that the boy who is most likely to repeat the behavior, even if punished severely, is the boy who had the extreme arousal response and who organized the replication. It also should be added that, recently, both young men were released from prison after serving their required sentences. There has been much controversy in England over the decision to give them new identities so that they have a better chance to re-enter society without persecution.

Of course, not all extreme experiences result in destructive, antisocial or diabolical behavior. But whether the behavior is socially and morally viewed as positive or negative, there is always a degree of obsession involved once a behavior related to an extreme experience develops into a pattern. This is what makes the behavior problematic. The obsession to replicate is the identifying factor in problematic behavior and it can persist and evolve into adulthood.

In his book *Visions of Innocence*,[10] Edward Hoffman focuses on the spiritual experiences of children. He collected over 250 oral accounts of vividly recalled early spiritual experiences from men and women around the globe. He was not looking for behavioral patterns that came out of these experiences, but rather at the experience itself. However, the personal descriptions provided in each case strongly indicate that behavior associated with spiritual quest arose from these related early spiritual experiences and continued into adulthood. Hoffman's growing belief in the significance of early childhood experiences in relation to adult behavior is described in the following preface of his book:

> I have long been fascinated by the unexplored dimensions of childhood. For many years I have strongly felt that as children we feel and experience much more than most adults realize. My early milieu, a New York City neighborhood of mostly concrete streets and tenements, did not provide a very uplifting outlook on life. Far more important was the religious school I attended until nearly my teens. Its teachers aroused my sense of imagination and wonder in their vivid retelling of biblical legends. I was intrigued by Abraham, whose passionate quest for God originated in his childhood. The prophetic writings, hinting of a world beyond the everyday, especially stirred me. I can still recall pondering with friends the mysteries of space and time as we rode the afternoon bus back to our homes.
>
> Later, as a student at Cornell University in the late 1960s, I chose to major in psychology. It was an exciting time of new ideas about the mind, and I became interested in comparative religion and mysticism. Such unconventional subjects hardly penetrated my psychology classes, but that didn't matter. I pursued extensive reading and outside lectures on my own.
>
> Then, as part of my undergraduate training, I began working with children from differing backgrounds. Their energetic zeal and natural spontaneity were intense, but hardly unexpected. More surprising was my discovery that some — even as young as preschool age — seemed in their own way to be genuinely grappling with spiritual questions. Sometimes, I noticed, the "trigger" for their earnest thinking was a religious event, a vivid exposure to nature, or even an unusual dream.
>
> At the University of Michigan I completed doctoral studies in child development. Through increasing involvement with young children I saw some definitely had "higher" sensitivities for compassion, creativity, or aesthetics. Yet nowhere was this early capability recognized in

my textbooks. Complementing my observations were scattered articles I found on alternative education featured in children's poetry and vivid aphorisms. These, too, suggested a depth in childhood experience almost wholly overlooked by most educators and psychologists.

More than a decade passed as I taught college courses and did clinical work. Though I had written several books dealing with psychology and mysticism, I had devoted little attention to childhood from this vantage point, until suddenly, my interest was catalyzed in the 1980s. At the time, I was writing a biography on Abraham Maslow, a brilliant American psychologist who argued that spirituality is basic to human nature. Pertaining to this notion, Maslow coined such popular phrases as "self-actualization" and "peak experience" — the latter referring to those moments when we feel uplifted out of ordinary life into a realm of bliss.

In researching Maslow's life, I discovered that he became convinced in his final years that children undergo peak experiences, but usually lack the means to relate them. After Maslow's first grandchild was born, he planned to begin research on this unprecedented topic in psychology. Unfortunately, the great psychologist's death from heart failure prevented the realization of this project.

In 1989, after the birth of our second child, I too felt uplifted in a special way and decided to follow Maslow's unfinished quest for the highest reaches of childhood experience. During the past three years, my research has clearly demonstrated that childhood indeed harbors experiences and insights generally unrecognized in our time.

It is interesting to note that Hoffman's recollection of his early experiences attending religious school include his "stirring" response to the spiritual quest of Abraham. This experience influenced his intellectual query and research investigating spiritual questions, which led to writing an autobiography of another "Abraham," who argued that "spirituality was basic to human nature."

Hoffman's study explored recollections of childhood spiritual experiences that were described as blissful, joyous states. In reference to Hoffman's book, author and priest Andrew M. Greeley described it as "the most beautiful and most powerful collection of accounts of ecstatic experiences that it has ever been my pleasure to read."

However, it should be noted that, in 1901, a book entitled *Cosmic Consciousness: The Evolution of the Human Mind*,[11] written by Richard Maurice Burke, M.D. (who, prior to its writing, had been Medical Superintendent of the Asylum for the Insane in London, Canada), presented a similar topic. The photograph of Burke, in profile, on the inside cover, is striking; a soft light illuminates his magnificent forehead and long white beard. His sidelong gaze that looks upwards toward some unknown entity or vision represents, as one discovers in the early section of the text, his obsession with spiritual "enlightenment" as a result of his own "illuminating" pivotal childhood experience.

Burke writes the he could recall the experience vividly after fifty years. Within the core of his vivid memory, his attention centered on one key element present during his point of transformation (in his case, light, sunshine, illumination), which remained central to the behavior pattern that evolved from it. This central element of his experience, which he described in detail, influenced his way of thinking and eventually developed into a philosophy on spiritual enlightenment. While Burke recognized this element of his experience as a guiding force in his behavioral development, he did not acknowledge the core aspect of his experience as having greatly influenced the development of his theory. This is not unusual with many who do not connect their later obsessive behavior with an early childhood experience, even when they recognize the experience as having had an important influence on their life. As such, Burke ironically determined mid-life as the most likely time for pivotal cosmic consciousness experiences to occur. Unlike Hoffman's later view, he did not recognize the childhood period as significant in this regard, despite his own experience and the recorded early experiences of those he chose as examples.

This is crucial in understanding why pivotal experiences are often underestimated in their significance to later conditions. During the HRIPTM research, participants were often surprised to learn that their most vividly recalled experiences were linked to current beliefs and obsessions. Although Burke's beliefs and behavior regarding his philosophy do not fall into the disorder category, he did reveal in his introduction and throughout the text how he attempted to replicate his early experience again and again. And in this sense, he demonstrates in his following remarkable account (below), how the obsessive nature of behavior arising from a certain level of experience can originate and flourish.

In *Cosmic Consciousness*, Burke explores the concept of man's higher elevation of consciousness that results from an illuminating experience that is life-transforming. Examples include Walt Whitman, Gautama the Buddha, Jesus Christ, Mohammed, John Yepes, Behmen, Francis Bacon and others who have written on the subject or their own experience. Throughout the text, Burke describes this phenomenon repeatedly in terms of light and color, using descriptive terms such as *illumination, cosmic radiance, dazzling flashes of light, lightning, subjective light, intellectual illumination* and *enlightenment*. He begins the first chapter by providing a brief personal background, which, although somewhat tedious in its antiquated language and detail, is most revealing. In fact, his entire story is so markedly influenced by one dramatic episode in the sunshine that I chose it for this text and I have "illuminated" some of his words in italics, for effect.

The purpose of these preliminary remarks is to throw as much light as possible on the subject of this volume, so as to increase the pleasure and profit of its perusal. A personal exposition of the writer's own introduction to the main fact treated of will perhaps do as much as anything else could to further this end. He will therefore frankly set down a very brief outline of his early experience of what he calls cosmic consciousness. The reader will readily see therefrom whence came these ideas and convictions presented in the following pages.

He was born of good middle class English stock and grew up almost without education on what was then a backwoods Canadian farm. As a child he assisted in such labors as lay within his power: tended cattle, horses, sheep, pigs; brought in firewood, worked in the hay field, drove oxen and horses, ran errands. His pleasures were as simple as his labors. An occasional visit to a neighboring small town, a game of ball, bathing in the creek that ran through his father's farm, the making and sailing of mimic ships, the search for birds' eggs and flowers in the spring, and for wild fruits in the summer and fall, afforded him, with his skates and handsled in the winter, his homely, much loved recreations. While still a young boy he read with keen appreciation Marryat's novels, Scott's poems and novels, and other similar books dealing with outdoor nature and human life. He never, even as a child, accepted the doctrines of the Christian church; but, as soon as he was old enough to dwell at all on such themes, conceived that Jesus was a man — great and good no doubt, but a man. That no one would ever be condemned to everlasting pain. That if a conscious God existed he was the supreme master and meant well in the end to all; but that, this visible life here being ended, it was doubtful whether conscious identity would be preserved. The boy (even the child) dwelt on these and similar topics far more than anyone would suppose; but probably not more than many other introspective small fellow mortals. He was subject at times to a sort of ecstasy of curiosity and hope.

As on one special occasion when about ten years old he earnestly longed to die that the secrets of the beyond, if there were any beyond, might be revealed to him; also to agonies of anxiety and terror, as for instance, at about the same age he read Reynold's "Faust," and, being near its end one sunny afternoon, he laid it down utterly unable to continue its perusal, and went out into the sunshine to recover from the horror (after more than fifty years he distinctly recalls it) which had seized him.

After describing his life from the time of his "experience" until the age of 21, Burke continues:

His life for some years was one passionate note of interrogation, an unappeasable hunger for *enlightenment* on the basic problems. Leaving college, he continued his search with the same ardor. Taught himself French that he might read Auguste Comte, Hugo and Renan, and German that he might read Goethe, especially "Faust." At the age of thirty he fell in with "Leaves of Grass," and at once saw that it contained, in greater measure than any book so far found, what he had so long been looking for. He read the "Leaves" eagerly, even passionately, but for several years derived little from them. At last light broke and there was revealed to him (as far as such things can be revealed) at least some of the meanings. Then occurred that to which the foregoing is preface.

It was in the early spring, at the beginning of his thirty-sixth year. He and two friends had spent the evening reading Wordsworth, Shelley, Keats, Browning, and especially Whitman. They parted at midnight, and he had a long drive in a hansom (it was in an English city). His mind, deeply under the influence of the ideas, images and emotions called up by the reading and talk of the evening, was calm and peaceful. He was in s state of quiet, almost passive enjoyment. All at once, without warning of any kind, he found himself wrapped around as it were by a *flame-colored cloud*. For an instant he thought of *fire*, some sudden conflagration in the great city; the next, he knew that the *light* was within himself. Directly afterwards came upon him a sense of exultation, of immense joyousness accompanied or immediately followed by an *intellectual illumination* quite impossible to de-scribe. Into his brain streamed one momentary *lightening-flash* of the Brahmic Splendor which has ever since *lightened* his life; upon his heart fell one drop of Brahmic Bliss, leaving thence-forward for al-ways an aftertaste of heaven. Among other things he did not come to believe, he saw and knew that Cosmos is not dead matter but a living Presence, that the soul of man is immortal, that the universe is so built and ordered that without any peradventure all things work to-gether for the good of each and all, that the foundation principle of the world is what we call love and that the happiness of every one is in the long run absolutely certain. He claims that he learned more within the few seconds during which illumination lasted than in pre-vious months or even years of study, and that he learned much that no study could ever have taught.

The *illumination* itself continued not more than a few moments, but its effects proved ineffaceable; it was impossible for him ever to forget what he at the time saw and knew; neither did he, or could he, ever doubt the truth of what was then presented to his mind. There was no return, that night or at any other time, of the experience. He sub-sequently wrote a book in which he sought to embody the teaching of *illumination*. Some who read it thought very highly of it, but (as was to be expected for many reasons) it had little circulation.

The supreme occurrence of that night was his real and sole initia-tion to the new and higher order of ideas. But it was only an initia-tion. He saw the *light* but had no more idea whence it came and what it meant than the first creature that saw the *light of the sun*. Years after-ward he met C.P., of whom he had often heard as having extraordi-nary spiritual insight. He found that C.P. had entered the higher life of which he had had a glimpse and had had large experience of its phenomena. His conversation with C.P. threw a *flood of light* upon the true meaning of what he himself experienced.

Through the experiences of Hoffman and Burke we can see the influence of an experience that leads to a quest for spiritual enlighten-ment. But not all children who have an early pivotal spiritual experi-ence develop healthy patterns of behavior in relation to spiritual con-nection. The following clinical case example provides a window into the distorted perception of an insecure child who senses that she does not belong in her family, who believes that her mother may harm her, and that somehow, by reaching toward God, she will be saved.

Case Summary: Janie

Janie, a 36-year-old white female, was voluntarily admitted for alcohol dependence, increased depression, agoraphobia and increased anxiety. She had been on benzodiazepines the previous 6 months. About 2 or 3 months prior to admission, she began drinking mouthwash, got intoxicated and suicidal, and overdosed on her medication. It took intensive care and a respirator to bring her back. When she was discharged from the hospital, she intended to stay off all benzodiazepines and asked her physician to cancel any further medication refills. She became increasingly anxious at home (panicky) and was unable to leave the house most of the time. She began craving alcohol to give her relief. During the late evening, prior to a morning re-admission, she started to drink the remaining half-bottle of mouthwash. She called the hospital requesting help and was admitted several hours later.

Janie agreed to try taking Antabuse along with medication in order to have her severe anxiety disorder treated safely and hopefully to avoid another relapse and overdose. She was admitted into intensive outpatient treatment for a period of 8 weeks. From the beginning of treatment, Janie followed all directives. She had been in treatment many times previously and was acquainted with all standard procedure except for the HRIPTM, which was incorporated into this program. She quickly became involved with her treatment group and began attending Alcoholics Anonymous (AA) meetings with group members who offered her transport.

Janie could be described as medium in height, thin, fair in complexion, with attractive features and pale blonde hair worn long. She was well-spoken and interacted with others with an intelligent and knowledgeable manner. She phrased her words carefully, with modulated and flowing expression. She was quite dramatic when attempting to be compassionate, caring, interested and thoughtful, or when offering helpful guidance to her peers. Those who knew Janie were aware of how quickly her behavior and manner could change. But treatment peers who were newly acquainted with her were impressed with her seemingly confident air, knowledge of protocol, easily assumed leadership role and her "guardian angel" approach to their welfare.

On occasion, she "overdid it." This was particularly evident in group sessions that gave her a forum for expounding recovery wisdom gained from her vast experience. The problem with this facade of confidence was that Janie could not maintain it for an extended period of time. She had the ability to initially captivate others and win their respect and allegiance only to lose them when, momentarily and surprisingly, her instability became shockingly apparent. At times, she could convincingly appear so knowing, ethereal and spiritual that it was difficult to believe that she had been suicidal since childhood.

During the first week of treatment, Janie actively and openly participated in process and meditation group. She said her primary focus was on spiritual issues, which she described as essential to her recovery. She explained that she had recognized years ago that she was powerlessness over addiction and now realized that her only hope for survival was in the hands of the "Divine." She attributed her regained ability to leave her apartment, attend meetings and participate in treatment to "spiritual guidance." She described the months prior to her current spiritual awakening as a "vacuum of spiritual depletion."

Janie addressed current issues involving a possible change in residence. She was considering moving into a halfway house facility where she could be with others in recovery. She said she realized that living alone was "too dangerous." A recent relationship with a boyfriend, with whom she had been living, had ended prior to her entering treatment. She said the break-up contributed to her anxious state and the relapse. She expressed no regrets about the loss of the relationship and stated she was "glad it was over."

She described her relationship with her adoptive parents as persistently troublesome. She explained that she was no longer dependent on them financially, but was dependent on their love and support. She said arguments with her adoptive mother were a source of continual guilt, anger and suffering and put a strain on her relationship with her adoptive father. She expressed hope that things would change now that her plan was to live a life of "celibacy and spiritual commitment." Her plan included active 12 Step Program participation and commitment to a recovery lifestyle.

During the second week of treatment, Janie began describing consistent feeling responses to a variety of presented situations. Fear and a sense of being alone were identified as the most prevalent feelings in her life. From early childhood to the present, she could not recall a time when she did not feel alone. She described experiencing positive feelings of happiness, joy, love and peace during her early childhood that she associated with "God" and a "spiritual, heavenly place." She said she first felt compelled to communicate with God at around the age of 2 to 3.

Janie's disclosure in response to a variety of presented situations revealed behaviors beginning in early childhood that involved preoccupation with death, acting, pretending, fantasizing, planning, hypervigilance, "enclosing" into herself, wrapping or covering herself up "like in a cocoon," suicidal thoughts and attempts, wishful prayer for death, quiet rebellion and self-harm actions, most of which were hidden or disguised in appropriate behavior and self-defeating attempts to live up to her parents' expectations.

Janie's efforts to identify feelings, physical symptoms and behavioral responses to a variety of presented experiences revealed many early patterns of behavior. When Janie was 3-4 years old, she began enacting behavioral dynamic that developed into a dangerous and self-harmful pattern. She identified this period in her childhood as significant in relation to her early perception of herself, her adoptive mother and her family and home situation. She reported memories from this period as regularly present in her current daily thoughts and relevant to how she dealt with the many painful and traumatic experiences that occurred during her adolescent and adult life. Beginning with a brief background of her family and home environment, the following is her account of one in a series of nightly experiences that dominated this period of her life.

Janie was adopted at age 3½ months by parents who were both educated professionals. Her adoptive father was a scientist and professor at the time, and her mother a physicist. Three years prior to the adoption, her mother began teaching part time after the birth of their son. When Janie was adopted, her mother took a temporary hiatus to stay home with the new baby. Their home was situated in an upper-middle class suburb located near the university where both parents held teaching positions. Janie and her brother would be their only children. Janie described herself as a frightened child. She said she knew that she was adopted long before she was told, but never let her parents know this. She insisted that she had had a fear of bedtime since infancy. She said she was certain of this because of the knowledge of nightly fear that was present in her memories from her age 3-4 period.

"I was so scared of bedtime. Every night I was scared. I remember one night in particular, although it was like many others. But this night must have been worse, because it is always the one in my mind. I was in my bed. The bed was small. My brother had his own room down the hall. There was no night light, but I always asked that the door be left open. The closet doors were closed. My Barbie dolls and stuffed animals lined the shelves. There was one window with white curtains. I had lots and lots of covers, even in the summer. My mother came in to kiss me goodnight. I had this fear and believed that my mother wore a mask that made her look younger and at night she was going to take it off because she was really really old and she was going to kill me. I thought this every night."

Janie's described feeling response: "Absolute sheer terror. Fear, scared, confused, alone. Feeling like I was going to be killed."

Janie's described physical symptom response: "Panic, frozen, paralyzed, crying softly, shaking, heart beating rapidly, hot and cold, sleeplessness, nightmares and bed-wetting."

Janie's described behavior response: "Lay awake with my covers over me, except for my face, so I could watch the door. Waiting, praying about death, thinking about death, watching the door, not being able to sleep, being alert for sounds, for her to come for me, planning to die, praying for my family to die and fantasizing about heaven, about being God's special angel that he would save, asking God to help me. I would watch the door until I finally passed out with exhaustion. Sometimes I'd wake up scared and the house would be dark. I'd go into Mom and Dad's bedroom (they slept in separate beds). I'd want to wake Mom up because of a bad dream, but she would just say 'Everything's all right,' and 'Go back to bed.' So I'd lie on the cold hardwood floor next to her bed and sleep there. Sometimes I'd wake up before she did and go back to my bed so she wouldn't know. When it was morning, there was a garage (a carport) attached to the house. There was a ladder to the roof. I thought God was on the other side of the roof up the ladder and I wanted to climb it, but couldn't. I was too afraid. I remember, before going to kindergarten, learning to climb the ladder so I could wait for God to come to get me. I wore my white nightgown so he would know I was his angel. I thought I was too little for him take me but I was able to send and receive messages from him when I reached the top of the ladder."

In reviewing Janie's written lifespan chart assignments and other memory worksheets, this early episode may seem minor in comparison to her later experiences. At age 13, Janie was violently attacked, beaten and raped one evening on her way home from a school event. The assailant was identified and arrested. A lengthy court case followed in which Janie had to appear several times. Janie described this period as devastating, humiliating and frightening. When addiction, eating disorder and suicide threats and attempts followed, the rape was deemed the probable cause of Janie's problems and condition. Prior to the rape, she had presented no signs of behavioral disorder at home or in school. As a result of this assumption, Janie had addressed the rape experience repeatedly during a multitude of previous treatments and hospitalizations.

Her early preoccupation with death and thinking of death as a solution was never disclosed to her parents. She hid hear fears and preoccupations behind a facade of "angelic" behavior. However, preoccupation with death, from age 3-4, was Janie's primary means of relieving intense to extreme fear and panic symptoms. Preoccupation with dying, the death of others, and suicide began a pattern of death-related ideation that evolved and was well-developed by pre-adolescence. Her perception of her mother, the mask and the old woman behind it, however distorted, was real to her at age 3-4. The behavior patterns that emerged from this distorted reality were very real, and very deadly. Her later adversarial relationship with her mother, which emerged during a rebellious period after the rape and continued into adulthood, had its roots in this early perception. The rape that destroyed her innocence and perception of herself as "angelic" was a pivotal catalytic event that made it impossible for her to maintain her facade of perfection. To her parents and those who knew her, her behavior seemed to change so dramatically that there seemed no other conclusion than to blame her change in behavior on the rape.

The numerous self-destructive experiences that followed could fill several more pages. With each vulnerable period, she became more compelled to die; but before and sometimes during each suicide attempt, she cried for help. As a child, Janie experienced joy, happiness and love in an early spiritual connection and perception of God. She developed a pattern of preoccupation with death as way out of her nightly terror, and as a means of attaining and perpetuating the love, joy and peace she found in this spiritual connection. Janie continued to be drawn toward a connection with her perception of God, yet her belief in her own lack of "perfection" created enormous fear when she faced the prospect of death in her attempts to fully experience this connection.

Janie's case demonstrates the influence of an experience that generates extreme feelings and physical symptoms, and resulting behavior, on pivotal experiences that follow. It is interesting to note that stated in her group disclosure, and written next to this identified experience on her lifespan chart, she emphasized her early belief that she was "God's favorite angel" and could receive messages from God. Her written description of this belief, and her attempts to communicate and receive messages from God, were replicated in the behavior she exhibited during treatment. This "angelic" behavior emerged almost immediately after her admission into treatment. It followed an almost two-month period of suicidal ideation, relapse, overdose and emergency hospitalization. Her spiritual declarations and stated commitment to remain celibate would have been misleading if one supposed she had a solid spiritual foundation for recovery. Since early childhood, Janie's spiritual perceptions and beliefs had not prevented, but rather supported some of her most life-endangering patterns.

Janie identified several behaviors that, prior to the onset of alcohol addiction, were established patterns. They began with suicidal ideation and fantasizing about death within a spiritual context, developing into a complex pattern of behavioral disorder and suicide attempts. Janie threatened and repeatedly attempted suicide in a variety of ways, beginning at age 13.

The behaviors in question were originally constructed to relieve Janie's extreme negative emotional state and to replicate a state of spiritual joy, peace and exhilaration. But they subsequently evolved into patterns that she has now identified as actions that dangerously sabotage her addiction recovery, and her relationships, health and lifestyle. She also identified them as a major factor in her chronic addiction relapse.

During treatment, Janie acknowledged her limited ability to cope with stressors that trigger her identified negative emotional states and resulting behaviors. Although she made significant progress in this area (working with staff to develop positive alternative strategies to compete with self-harming patterns), Janie accepted that her behavioral and addiction recovery process requires a life-long commitment, psychiatric care and appropriate medication as needed, weekly therapy for an extended period of time that will help her restructure a context for positive spiritual growth, and active participation in her AA support group. Even with this highly structured continuing care plan, Janie remains at high risk. Information revealed during her participation in the HRIPTM produced substantial evidence to advocate for this level of continuing care treatment.

An interesting addendum to this case was the interview that took place with Janie's parents, who were then retired. Her mother described Janie as "a joy" as a child. She said the only problem they had with her was right after the adoption. She explained that a much older couple had taken care of Janie until the adoption went through. When they brought Janie home, her mother said she cried day and night for almost that whole first year. But after that, she was quiet, imaginative and well-behaved. Her mother and father both agreed that it was a shock to them when she began to have problems later.

The positive or negative evolution of a pattern depends greatly upon the child's unique perception of his or her pivotal experiences, and each contributing element involved in subsequent pivotal experiences. When behavior patterns that have evolved from pivotal experiences are framed in religious, psychiatric, criminal or other categorical contexts, even those that are socially acceptable, they may seem to have little in common with one another, and therefore are often viewed as separate or distinct conditions. The common thread that connects them is the obsessive need and/or desire to repeat the behavior to a problematic degree, despite the context in which the behavior is framed.

Notes

1. Thoreau, H. D. (1854). "Higher Laws." *Walden: Or Life In The Woods*. In *Crowned Masterpieces of Literature That Have Advanced Civilization*, p.3777 (1902). (D.J. Brewer Ed.). St. Louis: Ferd. P. Kaiser.

2. James, W. (1890). *The Principles of Psychology*, (Vol.1) pp. 151-56. New York: Henry Holt & Company.

3. Vandewalle, N. & AusLoos, M. (August, 1994). "Lacunarity, Fractal, and Magnetic Transition Behaviors in Generalized Eden Growth Process." *Physical Review, E (Statistical Physics, Plasmas, Fluids, and Related Interdisciplinary Topics)*. 50, 635-638.

4. Kohut, H. (1971). *The Analysis of the Self*. New York: International University Press.

5. Mahler, M.S. (1968). *On Human Symbiosis and Vicissitudes of Individuation*. New York: International University Press.

6. Meissner, W.W., Mack, J.E., and Semrad, E. (1975). "Classic Psychoanalysis." In *Comprehensive Textbook of Psychiatry*, ed. A. Freedman et al., pp. 482-566. Baltimore: Williams & Wilkins.

7. Winnicott, D.W. (1953). "Transitional Objects and Transitional Phenomena." *International Journal of Psycho-Analysis* 34:89-97.

8. Khantzian, E.J. (1999). *Treating Addiction as a Human Process*, pp. 33-34. Northvale, New Jersey, London: Jason Aronson Inc.

9. Watson, L. (1995). *Dark Nature: A Natural History of Evil*, pp. 205-6. New York, New York: Harper Collins.

10. Hoffman, E. (1992) *Visions of Innocence: Spiritual and Inspirational Experiences of Childhood*. pp. xiii-xiv. Boston & London: Shambhala.

11. Burke, R.M. (1931) (7th ed.) *Cosmic Consciousness: A Study in the Evolution of The Mind*. pp. 7-10. New York: Dutton & Company, Inc.

Lunch Dates

We had a rendezvous
each noon
my mother and I,
at the soda fountain
of Nate's Pharmacy
where she bought me
burgers and phosphates
soup and hot dogs
grilled cheese and fries,
where she watched me
eat apples for dessert
then kissed me goodbye
at the bus stop
before I walked
back to school and
she rode back to
her job at the paper.

Well fed, well loved,
much envied
I thought myself
until at age 10
I had lunch at my friend
Laurel's house
where in front of the TV
we ate baloney sandwiches
and chocolate chip cookies
made with margarine
while her mother drank
instant Nescafe in the kitchen
with a neighbor woman.
I heard them talking about me:
"Poor little thing. . . her mother
works."

Victual Reality, 1999[1]
— Bellamy

In the 1st century AD, the Greek philosopher Epictetus wrote, "People are disturbed not by things, but by the view which they take of them." The experience of human existence depends largely on our ability to make sense of the world and ourselves. The struggle to discover what things are and what they mean begins in infancy and depends on three closely related processes: sensation, perception, and conceptualization.

Sensation is what happens when physical stimuli are translated into neural impulses that can then be transmitted to the brain and interpreted. Thus, sensation depends on the activity of one or more of our specialized sense organs — eyes, ears, and taste buds, for example.

In its simplest sense, *perception* is the brain's interpretation of sensation. Thus, wavelengths corresponding to the color red affect our retinas in specific ways, causing impulses that are transmitted to the part of our brain that deals with vision, causing us to *perceive* the color red. That we can now *think* about the color red, compare it to other colors, or make some decision based on it, is a function of the third process, *conceptualization* (Lefrançois, 1996).[2]

When a child has an experience that produces an extreme emotional/physiological reaction that affects ability to think, function and decide, both the perception of the experience and the conceptualization of the experience can alter dramatically what would otherwise have occurred during less extreme conditions.

Einstein's Theory of Relativity showed us that our conceptual relationship to the world around us is extremely flexible — that our perception of the world is determined both by our position in and of itself, and our position in relation to others. His theory of physics has had an immense impact on our epistemological endeavors, in that it imposes limits on what and how we can know due to our location in space/time. If we add to this the factors of age, stage of brain development, level of understanding and knowledge, then the concept of individual perception becomes a fascinating and complex issue — one that has been underestimated in relation to problematic behavior construction and pattern development.

One of Einstein's better-known parables of relativity is that of the physicists and the elevator. Einstein presents us with the following thought-experiment. There are two groups of physicists, having all the necessary equipment for measurement of velocity. The physicists inside the elevator have no means of looking outside it, and indeed, they have never been outside it. Effectively and ideally, they are in a closed system. They notice that they are in a three-dimensional space, and can only walk on one side of it, that is, on the floor. They decide to try to figure out the cause of this and, using their instruments, they measure and calculate and, in the end, determine that the force of gravity is responsible. The group of physicists outside the elevator chance to observe it, and notice that it is accelerating rapidly through space. They determine that all objects inside the elevator would be held to the end opposite the direction of the acceleration, and attribute this phenomenon to the force of acceleration. Einstein's relativity says that both groups are right in light of their location relative to the elevator — from inside, the force of gravity is indeed responsible, and from outside, the force of acceleration is responsible, and neither statement has more or less truth than the other.

Einstein's theory is particularly relevant to what occurs when a child experiences an event that produces extreme emotional/ physiological response. How that child perceives what is occurring, if observed, will most likely be understood not from the child's perspective but from the perspective of the observer. The child may not be able to translate to the observer his or her perception of what occurred. Thus, the event is addressed in relation to the reality of the observer. If the child, years later, should recall this experience and perception of what occurred by describing a vivid recollection of the event to the observer, there would be a discrepancy of view about what had actually taken place. When there is no observer present during the experience, the credibility of the child is even more challenged.

Children are often not able to adequately describe what they have experienced, if they attempt to do so at all. If a child perceives the experience to be shameful or embarrassing and the event is kept secret, and then shared years later, the recollection might be dismissed as improbable by those who have a different perspective on the period in question. Truth often becomes the argument between differing perspectives in relation to memory.

The core details that are recorded in memory are the only truth that matters to the brain in relation to behavioral response. When these memories are shared in an appropriate and structured context and environment, and without provocation, the patient's revelations need not be discounted or challenged. This would be as counterproductive as the two groups of physicists arguing the theoretical validity of each others' perspective regarding the elevator problem. The Thomas Aquinas statement of compromise, *"Pulcra sunt quae visa placent,"* which allows for and respects individual vision despite seeming discrepancy, makes the point that we need not scrutinize what comes into a person's mind and is then recounted, but instead recognize that in these revelations are clues to understanding the individual. Otherwise, the individual sharing the experience is placed in a defensive position against a doubting offensive, an opposing opinion that has to be convinced.

From an Einsteinian perspective, an experience revealed from an individual's space/time position and from inside the closed system of self is a reality that is legitimate, regardless of how odd it may seem from another perspective. This is especially relevant in relation to what is recalled from early childhood because of the remarkable and some-times extraordinary ways in which a young child can perceive an ex-perience. The following is an example of one such case.

Audrey, and Buster Toad

An in-patient addiction treatment setting is like a small and di-verse community. Substance abuse occurs on every level of society, and has in recent years, become a more recognized problem within the growing senior citizen population. Many elder citizens have difficulty adjusting to the role of patient under these circumstances, and find it hard to believe that after a lifetime of hard work and accomplishment, they have developed an addiction. Older patients are often mistaken for hospital workers by newly admitted patients. Some are approached for advice and solace, and some offer their advice to staff. Others, like Aud-rey, just try to blend in and avoid notice.

Quiet, reserved, fragile in appearance, timid, childlike in manner and agreeable in disposition, Audrey graced the treatment unit like a church volunteer delivering flowers. She exhibited polite behavior and vague interest in lectures and group dynamics. She spent much of her recreation time pruning and watering the plants. She was such a benign presence that she had somehow been able to "successfully" complete treatment three times before a fourth admission. Audrey's condition was chronic and severe, and she was about to celebrate her 64th birth-day.

On this day, after three weeks of participating in group therapy and listening to the experiences of her treatment peers, something sud-denly inspired Audrey to make this bold announcement: "I don't know if this is important, but I have something I would like to share because I still think about it almost every day." She began to share the following experience.

> I had a wonderful father whom I loved very much. He loved nature, flowers and wildlife and I was always by his side. He drew pictures of birds and little animals and told me stories about them every night.

My favorite animal was Buster Toad who, through the voice of my father, would make me laugh and feel happy before going to sleep. My father told me to respect all creatures and think of them as if they were people because their lives were important to all things in nature. My father had a large garden in which he worked every day. I followed him up and down the rows with my watering can.

One day, he surprised me with a little hoe and told me I was now old enough to help with the weeds. It was my 4th birthday. I was thrilled with my gift and new responsibility. As I was weeding and chopping my way down one row, my father was in the next, almost hidden from view by the corn stalks. I looked up for a moment to see if he was watching the good job I was doing. When I looked back down, I froze in terror and disbelief. I simply could not move. It seemed as though I stood there frozen for hours but it must have just been seconds. There before me lay the severed head and body of a little toad with the blade of my hoe in-between.

Suddenly, I heard my father's voice and his approaching footsteps as he said, "How is my little helper doing?" Before I knew it I had used the hoe to dig a small hole where I hurriedly pushed the little toad body, but his little head looked up at me and all I could see was Buster Toad. I thought, "How could I have done such a thing? How could I have been so careless? It was him — it was Buster!" It was horrible! I thought, "He will never make me laugh again. I don't deserve to ever laugh again." These were my thoughts as I pushed his little head into the hole with his body. My father's shadow fell over me just as I covered the hole. He didn't see what I had done. I felt so ashamed. He would be so disappointed in me. He would have never made a mistake like this. He was always careful and so kind. I never wanted to ever make another mistake again. I never wanted to be four years old again. Today is my sixty-fourth birthday, and it still bothers me.

Audrey's father (at the time of the experience) was a widower, an older parent and a quite well-known naturalist artist. He died suddenly of a heart attack when Audrey was ten years old. During the remainder of her childhood and throughout her adolescence and adult years, Audrey had no reported history of problem behavior. She married a "wonderful man" and raised four "wonderful children." Audrey became a widow in her late fifties, and appeared to be coping well, according to her adult children. She had a lovely home and grounds, was financially secure, loved to garden and seemed content in her environment. How-

ever, she was somewhat reclusive. When she began having health problems in her early sixties, her children became concerned and began visiting more frequently. On one occasion, Audrey was found unconscious
and near death. During this first emergency room visit, they were
shocked to learn that a high level of alcohol was the cause of their
mother's condition.

The discovery of Audrey's secret habit of drinking alcohol
throughout the day occurred as a result of several more substance
abuse related emergency room admissions. Her children were confused
by Audrey's denial of alcohol abuse, the fact that they had never witnessed their mother drink alcohol, and that there had been no visible
signs of alcohol around the house. A search of the premises by her old-
est son led to the discovery of many little bottles and small containers
filled with vodka. They were hidden in the pantry, the garden shed, and
even in her hospital room, disguised as baby oil.

Audrey's children loved her very much and were bewildered. They
were also afraid that she would die. They could not understand why,
despite their support throughout several in-patient addiction treatments, she continued to drink after repeatedly promising that she
would not make "another mistake" (Audrey's preferred reference to her
relapses). With each relapse to drinking, Audrey agreed to re-enter
treatment while profusely apologizing for her behavior, stating, "I am
so sorry to be such a bother. I don't deserve such wonderful children.
They are so good and kind. They take after my father, you know."

Audrey's perception of what occurred in the garden that day was
the perception of a four-year-old child who was traumatized by what
she had done to the toad. Her response was as uniquely individual as
the situation and her imagination could inspire. Her perception of herself changed dramatically that day, and so did her behavior. From that
day forward, she covered up every mistake she made, even the most minor. Her self-esteem perished as her mistakes accumulated in her mind.

As Audrey grew older she realized, of course, that the toad was
not really Buster Toad, but that did not change her perception of herself or stop the pattern of behavior that developed in relation to this
perception. Another important element in Audrey's episode was the
loss of life that resulted from her perceived "horrible mistake." In Audrey's perception, the toad had human characteristics. She described
how, with each loss in her life, beginning with the death of her father,

she felt responsible in some way; that if maybe she had been a better child or better wife, the sudden death would not have occurred, although there was no logical basis or evidence to support this.

The weight of this internal burden was carried throughout her childhood and later became magnified during her widowhood after the unexpected death of her husband. It was during this period that she began abusing alcohol and came to rely on it to relieve what she described as "unbearable feelings of guilt and sadness."

The point should be made here that there is often a mistaken assumption in the treatment of addiction that revelations that bring about a catharsis, a realization, or a change in belief about a past experience will "cure" the problem that is standing in the way of recovery. This assumption underestimates the power of these patterns. Once repeated and entrenched in the neuronal structure of the still-developing brain, the pattern evolves in relation to the way the child continues to feel, while it gathers strength and dimension beyond the initial experience. While there are certainly many healing factors in the appropriate disclosure of a pivotal experience, an objective focus should center on the details that are revealed that contain vital information in relation to what has symptomatically and behaviorally developed from that experience. In Audrey's case, her startling revelation was just the beginning. Her longstanding pattern of hiding her mistakes and problems did not dissolve because she shared the experience. But the information she revealed completely changed the future course of her treatment.

The child's world can encompass as many chilling realities as the world of an adult. However, a child does not have the power of an adult. A child may perceive that he or she made a mistake, caused an accident, created a problem or made a terrible error in judgment. If the child is not caught, avoids responsibility, and has no exposure to another explanation that could change this perception, the perception is not likely to change. For example, if Audrey's father had seen the toad and realized what happened, he could have talked to her and helped Audrey realize that what occurred was just an unfortunate accident.

When this immediate positive source of resolution did not occur and Audrey's feelings of guilt and shame continued, her level of distress was only lessened to the degree that she could once again function. While hiding the toad effectively addressed her panic state and symptoms, the remaining distress added to her new perception of herself as "bad." This new self-image created a vulnerability that did not exist before the experience.

When another mistake occurred, the *effective and registered* action of hiding repeated. Each repetition made Audrey fearful of another mistake. Guilt and fear increased with each mistake — mistakes that would have been normal for any child, but to Audrey seemed monumental. The behavior pattern that evolved developed like a rolling snowball gathering size and mass, gaining momentum and taking onto it all that adhered along its pathway. A child has little power to stop this dynamic without help. It is difficult for a child to communicate something that he or she may be afraid to reveal. This is one of the primary reasons why experiences of this nature and the behavior arising from them escape interventions that could effectively disrupt problematic behavior pattern development.

The documented early childhood memories of adults with chronic addiction and behavioral problems compiled during the HRIPTM research are riddled with episodes of this kind. Case after case revealed that intervention and resolution did not occur. Not only is it difficult for the child to communicate what has occurred, it is often difficult to recognize when a child has an experience such as Audrey's. It is doubtful that her father noticed any difference in her at all.

One of the most important future research challenges toward more effective early childhood problem intervention is to find better ways to see what children cannot communicate. Identification and intervention at the earliest stages of pattern development is the ideal prevention strategy. While the more obvious cases of abuse and trauma are easier to identify, trauma can occur in some children from an experiences that an adult might not identify as traumatic at all. For example:

Soren Kierkegaard (1813-1855), the Danish philosopher, is a major influence in contemporary existential philosophy. In his work he dealt with three levels of existence — the aesthetic, ethical, and religious — and the first two of these were his primary concern in his first great work, *Either/Or*,[3] published shortly after he had broken his engagement — a crucial event in his life.

Although Kierkegaard wrote no autobiography, the whole story of his life, including his childhood and youth, can be told in his own words. He did not start keeping his journals[4] until he was well along in the university, and even then they did not contain a great deal of bio-graphical material. However, in his pseudonymous works (precisely because they were pseudonymous) he felt free to describe his own ex-periences, and because of his lonely life and his morbid reticence he found satisfaction in revealing himself in books and journals, knowing that the journals would not be seen until he was dead and that the per-sonal references in his books would not be understood. He felt no re-luctance whatsoever in revealing himself to a coming generation, but rather was desirous of doing so. The careful revisions of his journals, including the elision of passages which he did not wish to have read, are proof that he expected them to be published. In one place he said: "Some day, not only my writings but especially my life will be studied and studied." He was confident that his books would some day be un-derstood, and that the personal passages they contain would be under-stood as a revelation of his own life and experience. No one ever fol-lowed more seriously the Socratic injunction 'Know thyself', and surely no one ever probed more deeply for this knowledge. It was by studying himself that Kierkegaard became a psychologist.

The following is a quote from *Training in Christianity*.[4] This passage, confidently regarded as part of Kierkegaard's autobiography, recalls how his father (desiring to impress upon the child the most poignant truths of Christianity) inserted among his toys a picture of the Cruci-fixion. He introduces this reminiscence in order to suggest how we might all of us be affected by this picture and its story, if we were not familiar with it, if we might see it and hear it now for the first time. Here, Kierkegaard shares his own individual perception, interpretation and response to a pivotal experience in his life, while assuming the same reaction would hold true for other children. The lengthy quote below is preceded in the text by a lengthy description of himself as a sensitive, imaginative, studious child influenced greatly by his close relationship with his father.

> Suppose then such a child and give this child delight by showing him some of those pictures which one readily finds in the shops, which from the artistic point of view are so trivial but to the child are precious. — This one on a snorting steed, with the tossing feather, with the lordly mein, riding at the head of the thousands and thou-sands you cannot see, with hand outstretched in a gesture of com-mand: 'Forward! — forward over the crests of the mountains which

you see plainly in front of you, forward to victory — that is the Emperor, the unique figure of Napoleon. — This one here is dressed as a huntsman; he stands leaning upon his bow and gazes straight before him with a glance so piercing, so self-confident, and yet so anxious. That is William Tell. You now relate to the child something about him and about that extraordinary glance of his, explaining that with the same glance he has at once an eye for the beloved child, that he may not harm him, and for the apple on the child's head, that he may not miss it. — And thus you show the child pictures, to the child's unspeakable delight. Then you come to one which intentionally was laid among the rest. It represents a man crucified. The child will not at once, nor indeed easily, understand this picture, and will ask what it means, why he hangs on a tree like that. So you explain to the child that this is a cross, and that to hang on it means to be crucified, and that crucifixion in that land was not only the most painful death penalty but also an ignominious mode of execution employed only for the grossest malefactors. What effect will this have upon the child? The child will have a very strange feeling, he will wonder what could have prompted you to lay this ugly picture among all these other lovely ones, the picture of a gross malefactor among all these glorious heroes. For just as, to do despite to the Jews, there was written above His cross "The King of the Jews," so that the picture, as it comes forth anew regularly every year for a reproof to the human race, is a remembrance which the race never can and never shall be rid of, it shall never be represented otherwise; and it shall ever seem as if it were this present generation which crucified him. As often as this generation for the first time shows the child of the new generation this picture, for the first time explains how things actually go in this world; and the child, the first time he hears this, will become sorrowful and anxious about his parents, about the world and about himself; and the other pictures — yes, they all (as it is said in the poem [of "Agnes and the Merman"] will "turn their backs" — so different is this picture. Meanwhile — and we have not yet come at all to the decisive thing, the child has not yet learnt who that gross malefactor was — the child, with the curiosity children always show, will surely ask, Who is he? What did he do? Then tell the child that this crucified man is the Saviour of the world. However, he will not be able to form any clear idea of what that means; tell him therefore only that the Crucified One was the most loving man that ever lived. Oh, in common intercourse, where one can recite all that story by rote, in common intercourse a half-word thrown out as a hint suffices to recall it to every one — so glibly it goes; but truly he must be an extraordinary man, or rather an inhuman man, who does not instinctively cast down his eyes and stand like a poor sinner at the moment he tells to the child for the first time, to the child who has never heard a word of it before, and consequently never has surmised anything of the sort. But so the parent stands also as an accuser of himself and the whole race! — What impression do you think this will make upon the child — who naturally will ask, But why were people so bad to him then? What?

But what impression do you think this story will make upon the child? First and foremost surely this, that he forgets entirely the other pictures which you have showed him; for now he has got something entirely different to think about. And now the child will be in the deepest wonderment at the fact that God in heaven did nothing to prevent this being done; or that this was done without God — if not beforehand, at least at the last minute — raining down fire from heaven to prevent His death; that this happened without the earth opening to swallow up the ungodly. . . That was surely the first impression. But by degrees, the more the child reflected upon the story, the more his passion would be aroused, he would be able to think of nothing but weapons and war — for the child would have made the resolute decision that when he grew up he would slay all these ungodly men who had dealt thus with the Loving One; that would the child have resolved, forgetting that it was 1800 years ago they lived.

Then when the child became a youth he would not have forgotten the impression of childhood, but he would now understand it differently, he would know that it was not possible to carry out what the child, overlooking the 1800 years, had resolved to do; but nevertheless he would think with the same passionateness of combating the world in which people spat upon the Holy One, the world in which they crucify Love and beg acquittal for the robber.

Then when he became older and mature he would not have forgotten the impression of childhood, but he would understand it differently. He would no longer wish to smite; for, said he, I should thus attain to no likeness with Him, the humiliated, who did not smite, not even when he himself was smitten. No, he would only wish one thing, to suffer in some way comparable to his sufferings in the world. . . .

All of these descriptions quoted here go well beyond the period of childhood; but it is no disadvantage that they enable us to see how the religious impressions of early childhood, though Kierkegaard revolted against them, availed in the end to shape his life.

Kierkegaard's experience not only influenced him toward a life of spiritual pilgrimage, but led to a pattern of behavior that developed in response to his perception of the crucifixion, and the sacrifice he expected from himself in this regard. Whether through rebellion against a world that had allowed the crucifixion of Christ, or his later attempt to suffer in a comparable way, his obsession with self-denial led to the broken engagement that preceded his writing about the crucifixion experience in *Training in Christianity*, and a philosophy that effectively denied him other worldly attachments.

Kierkegaard's experience also exemplifies the impact that story illustrations and visual images can have on a child. When a child has an extreme response to what is seen and heard and individually perceived, the behavioral response that manifests itself can impact his or her life-course significantly. When we consider the effect of today's media exposure on children, it is important to recognize that a child responds not only to violent content, but to content that has a particular relevance to the child.

In the previous examples, both Audrey and Kierkegaard responded to their experiences with a profound sense of guilt that propelled their patterns of behavior and undermined their ability to feel worthy of happiness. The following case demonstrates how feelings of guilt arising from experience can propel a much more destructive dynamic.

Case Summary: Max

Max, a 38-year-old white male, manager of a family-owned restaurant and former motorcycle gang leader, was voluntarily admitted for relapse to cocaine dependence. He agreed to admit himself to the hospital when his mother threatened to have him committed involuntarily. He had been using $3,000 worth of cocaine and methamphetamine over a period of three days prior to admission. He had a recent history of cocaine-induced heart attacks. He reported that he would soon be receiving a quarter of a million dollars after a lawsuit settlement. He said he wanted to be clean before receiving his money. He had not been able to work regularly and was disabled due to chronic physical pain. The cocaine had also interfered with his work and his relationship with his fiancée who was reported to be very angry about his drug use. He was delusional while using cocaine and methamphetamine. He said he had been using sporadically for the past several months but had only recently lost control.

During his initial orientation into intensive outpatient treatment, Max exhibited a positive attitude and willingness to follow all treatment directives. His manner was polite and engaging. Although he reported feeling anxious, depressed and sad about his current legal and relationship problems, he was friendly and open in discussion with group peers. Within one week, he had won the respect and admiration of several group members who gathered around him when he arrived. Others kept a cautious distance and were intimidated by his presence.

Much of this caution was a result of his interactive dialogue in group sessions and during breaks. He often made reference to his recent former gang membership, and his role as state-wide president of a well-known, nationally organized and reputedly notorious motorcycle club. Max had long history of gang-related activities and arrests. While emphatically stating his intention to change his life and separate from his club, it was evident in his disclosure and manner that his identity was enmeshed in his previous leadership role and lifestyle. For example, his ingratiating diplomacy often gave way to intolerant, opinionated and racist views. He was particularly disdainful of anyone with gender issues. He appeared to expect others to agree with him and defer to his perceived superior wisdom on each issue he chose to address.

He made no objection to immediate and active involvement in the 12 Step Program. He offered to transport members of his treatment group to both AA and NA meetings. He also offered rides to and from the treatment facility. Max assumed, from the first day, that he functioned well in group situations because he took charge from the onset and did favors at every opportunity. His manner with women was both charming and patronizing. The elder women in the group were especially taken with him. He teased them with mildly flirtatious comments and mannerly attentions. He offered rides to those who had to take the bus, and brought donuts for everyone each morning. Unfortunately, this pattern of behavior was more in keeping with attaining group power and status than attaining recovery.

His assumption of responsibility for others reinforced his inclination to protect the treatment peers he befriended. Those who succumbed to his influence were indebted to him in a way that was both subtle and insidious. He exacted loyalty that demanded recognition of his authority and agreement with his opinions and actions. If he rejected certain peers from his circle of friends, he expected those within the circle to do the same. All of this was evident within the first week of treatment, and therefore had to be addressed immediately.

Max was tall, moderately overweight, thickset in body-frame, with muscular shoulders and arms. His physical build and facial features gave the impression of embattled strength and endurance, despite his disability status. His upper body and arms were tattooed with gang symbols (skulls and crossbones, chains and dripping blood). He dressed simply in denims, T-shirt and motorcycle boots. He said he never wore much gang regalia; he relied on his personality and presence rather than costume. He exhibited bravado, swagger and confidence. He would have easily dominated peer and group interactions if he had not been encouraged to do otherwise.

During the first week of treatment, he interrupted group and lecture processes with commentary, opinion, input and disclosure. It was obvious that he viewed this behavior as helpful and appropriate. He was encouraged to listen instead and to wait for the appropriate time to share feedback. His response to this "encouragement" was a bit resistant; however, he did try to restrain himself to some degree. Confrontation is not used in the HRIPTM process and would have been counterproductive with Max. The Orchestration Group Process (OGP) was helpful, in this regard, because it is structured to give everyone a turn to speak, a specific role, a specific component to address, a time limit and a responsibility to maintain order.

By the second week of treatment, Max revealed consistent feeling and physical symptom responses to a variety of presented situations. He described his most consistent feeling state as a pervasive feeling of guilt. He said he would have felt intense guilt if his response to any situation in the past was inadequate, wrong or cowardly. In response to situations that posed a potential threat or harm to others, he identified feelings of anger and frustration, and intense fear in relation to loss of home or loved ones due to disaster, death or destruction.

He consistently described physical symptom responses as intense pressure in his chest and head that affected his vision, "blinding rage — red flashes," increased energy and strength, and raised body temperature that created a sensation of explosive pressure moving from chest to head. He described mental confusion as a chaotic state that affected his ability to think clearly when the pressure reached his head (he indicated with his hand how the pressure moved from his frontal cortex area to temporal lobe region).

During the third week of treatment, Max revealed consistent behavioral responses to a variety of presented situations. Violent aggression was identified as a consistent response to situations that triggered his most distressful feeling and physical symptom states. His aggression was particularly respondent to situations in which he perceived potential harm to others, outnumbered odds, outweighed odds, outpowered odds, lack of support, lack of protection, lack of preparation and lack of "back-up." His first response to most situations involving threat of harm or a harmful occurrence was to immediately gather group support, obtain additional weaponry, develop a strategic plan of action, demand allegiance and collective agreement to follow his plan, then move into retaliatory action with intention to inflict injury or death despite potential consequences.

As treatment progressed, Max identified a consistent combination of feeling, physical symptom and behavioral actions that he assessed as dangerous and potentially sabotaging to his recovery. Through group process and written assignment, he came to recognize a pattern of destructive violence dating back to pre-adolescence. He also identified guilt as a primary component of his most negative emotional state.

Although he functioned in group on a much more equal level, with improvement each day, outside of the group structure he continued to dominate most interactive situations. When asked to evaluate his progress in this area, he described lack of authority and loss of power as frustrating. He identified several feelings associated with his need for group involvement, stating that separation from his motorcycle club produced feelings of alienation, loneliness and powerlessness. He said his recovery support group and participation in recovery-oriented activities did not alleviate these feelings.

During the fourth week of treatment, Max began to share concerns about his former gang involvement and revealed anxiety and fear about their policy that, "No one is allowed to resign from the club." He said there were death threats and a $25,000 price on his head posted on the Internet. He admitted that he often felt compelled to return and regain his club position, which he believed was possible. He then reflected that, after a previous attempt to leave the organization and find recovery, his decision to return had resulted in relapse, injury and criminal charges.

He also addressed his estranged relationship with his fiancée, describing her as a violent, verbally abusive alcoholic. When talking about her, he often became emotional and tearful; he was surprisingly sensitive to her criticism of him. He explained that she did not want him to use drugs because he became too dangerous when he did, but she did not support his involvement in recovery groups because she was jealous of other women. He said he wanted to be free of her and his former club, but felt powerfully compelled to return to both.

During this period of treatment, Max started attending a small Christian church in the area. The minister there took a special interest in him and recognized his leadership skills. He suggested that Max could be a positive influence to the youth of his congregation, once his recovery had progressed more substantially. Max responded positively to this encouragement, and as a result, began to focus enthusiastically on spiritual issues, which enhanced his understanding of 12-Step principles. This involvement coincided with a behavioral development plan that Max helped to design, accessing the identified skills and natural abilities present in his already existing patterns, to be incorporated into positive alternative actions. The church activity fit well into this plan. While he was beginning to understand the counterproductive nature of assuming a leadership role at this phase of his recovery, his ability to influence others and lead was an integral part of his identity. This minister was helping him to see a future in which leadership could be developed in a more positive way.

During the fifth week of treatment, Max volunteered to be "focus of group." The experience he chose to share occurred when he was 14 years old. He stated that an earlier experience, at age 11, was important in relation to this later episode. It was agreed that he briefly describe the earlier episode while giving introductory background information on his family and home environment.

Max described his family as very male-dominant. His father was deceased. His mother had three sons when she married for a second time to a farmer and tradesman. Max was the youngest son. His stepfather had two brothers who lived nearby, with whom he "did business." The nature of their business dealings was unclear and probably involved illegal activity under the cover of legal trade. The family home was located on the outskirts of town, in a rural, mountainous region of Tennessee.

Max respected and admired his stepfather, uncles and older brothers. The family was often involved in conflict with others, and sometimes with each other. Despite this, a strong bond of male camaraderie grew in this environment. Although Max loved and respected his mother, she had little control over the men of her household. However, she was regarded highly as "mother" and was affectionately placated whenever she expressed concern regarding their behavior. Her concerns were usually ignored or dismissed.

One day, while the rest of the family was in town, Max came home from school to find the family home empty, and on fire! At first he ran toward the fire to put it out. When he realized the fire was out of control, he ran away from it and toward town. He desperately tried to find help. His frantic efforts were unsuccessful until the volunteer fire department belatedly responded. By the time they arrived, it was too late; the home was destroyed.

Max recalled that his primary feeling during this experience was fear that developed into panic. He described his behavior as chaotic. "I had run around like a chicken with my head cut off. After it was over, I felt guilty and responsible for not saving the home. I felt that everyone thought I should have saved it, even though no one said anything like that. I thought, if my brothers had been there, we could have saved it."

Max was 14 at the time of his next identified pivotal episode. He said, "I think about this experience all the time, and sometimes every day."

Max and his older brother were standing on the front porch of the family home (then located on a side street in town) where they had moved after the fire. It was dusk, and their habit was to "hang out" on the porch in the early evening. Earlier that day, he and his brother had had a verbal altercation with two boys in town. Threats were exchanged. Max and his brother were not concerned; they did not view the boys as a threat. Therefore, it was a surprise when one of the two boys suddenly appeared at the front gate, opened it, and started coming up the walk toward them. The boy seemed to be holding something behind his back. Max angrily started down the porch steps to confront and intimidate the boy for this intrusion. He recalled, "I can still see the expression on that boy's face. He looked odd; funny; not scared. . . kind of crazy-like. I'll never forget that look." The boy's arms came forward. He was holding an automatic rifle. He raised it and began firing wildly. Max turned back toward his brother, who had fallen in a heap on the porch floor. He started to reach for his brother when he saw blood gushing from several wounds. Then Max felt a piercing pain in his shoulder blade and another in his thigh.

Max's described feeling response: "At first, I felt surprised, shocked and astounded that this boy would have the nerve to come to our house. And then, I felt angry and determined. Then, when he began shooting, everything was chaos. When I saw my brother laying in a pool of blood, I felt panic — like fear multiplied a thousand times — which exploded when I felt myself being shot. I wanted to help my brother. I thought he was dying and I felt terror."

Max's described physical symptom response: "I couldn't think straight. My heart was pounding in my chest and the pressure felt explosive. There were blotches of light and dark in front of my eyes, sweating and blood rushing to my head and red flashes. I felt tears in my eyes and on my cheeks."

Max's described behavioral response: "My body just started moving. I didn't think, 'move', I just started moving. I ran. I ran down the steps and around to the right side of the house toward the back, reached the back of the house and leaned against the back wall with my face pressed against the boards. The shots stopped. There must have been twenty or thirty shots. My head began to clear while the shots were still ringing in my ears. Then I felt overwhelming shame and guilt for running, and fear that my brother was dead and that I had abandoned him. The anger I had felt before the shots, came back like a blinding rage. I felt increased strength and energy even with my wounds. I didn't even feel them. My vision cleared, but the pressure inside my head was intense and further back to the sides of my skull it was pulsating. I could feel the blood pumping above my ears, but I could see clearly now. I ran back to the front and turned my brother over. He was still alive and was not aware of anything. He was moaning. People started coming to help. I had only been gone for seconds even though it had seemed longer. The boy was gone. I felt guilty and ashamed that I had run, and relieved that no one knew I had run except me and the boy who shot me. The ambulance came and my brother and I were taken to the hospital. He was in critical condition. My wounds were not serious."

"The doctor told me that my brother would survive, but I knew things would never be the same as before. I grew up that night. I started calling people from the hospital. Guys that we knew and hung out with. They were older than me, but I was big for my age. I knew I would make them listen. Within several hours, I had the support I needed. I sat there in the hospital and made a plan for revenge. My brother wasn't able to take over. My other older brother was away in the military. I knew what had to be done and I vowed that I would never be caught off guard again. I also decided that being alone, at any time, was dangerous. I had just learned a lesson; you are powerless when alone and outnumbered, especially when weapons are involved. Also, this boy thought he could come to our house and do this. I decided that no one would ever think they could do this again. We would retaliate. And we did, with guns and violence. I won't admit to murder in group, but that boy was 'dealt with'."

Max was not abusing alcohol or other drugs at age 14. While there was violence and illegal activity within his home environment, there was also a sense of belonging, loyalty, companionship and family. His mother cared for her husband and sons with kindness, affection and nourishment. She was rarely critical and often praised her boys for their positive attributes. She did not attempt to control them, but did make her opinions known when she was worried. Her concerns were acknowledged but generally viewed as irrelevant, "female concerns." Max respected his stepfather and older brothers. When he perceived that his behavior did not measure up to theirs, his feelings of shame intensified. When he did not live up to his own perception of "expected behavior," he felt guilty.

In both of these shared experiences, he had found himself alone in two very extreme situations. Each episode occurred suddenly, alarmingly, with no warning signs or time for preparation.

Max learned group dynamics from his family. He inherited physical strength and size. He identified with and respected the dominant male roles exemplified in his family. He witnessed episodic violence from an early age, but felt a certain sense of security because it was usually directed at others. As the youngest, he was usually protected and spared involvement. He was also not given much say in the matter.

While these factors played a significant role in his reactions, his individually constructed behavioral response to the episodes were also influenced by his perception of what occurred, what he felt emotionally and physically, what was previously experienced and what was available to him at the time. His constructed behavior in the shooting episode, after initially running as he had in the first episode, included assumption of leadership, strategic planning, gaining followers, influencing a group with verbal skill and authority, taking control and keeping it, demanding total loyalty, using weapons to support retaliation plans, self-protection and protection of others, exacting revenge, physical intimidation, violent aggression, and sophisticated group dynamics.

Max identified several behaviors that were well-established patterns, prior to the onset of addiction to cocaine, including:

- Running away when in extreme emotional distress
- Returning to scene of danger and life threat
- Strategic planning of revenge and retaliation
- Gathering followers, assuming leadership
- Manipulating and intimidating followers
- Using group to create power base and power edge
- Using threat, violence, weapons and numbers to intimidate, outmaneuver and overpower
- Self-abuse through repeated life-endangerment
- Hyper-vigilant, on-guard behavior and acute observation
- Self-protection through group involvement, avoiding aloneness, protection of others

Max came to realize that the behaviors constructed to relieve his most extreme negative emotional state evolved into patterns that threaten to sabotage his addiction recovery process, positive relationships and goals, and his health and new lifestyle. He also recognized their role in his previous addiction relapses. These patterns contributed to his return to a lifestyle that involved drugs, illegal activity, violence and aggression. Max stated that abstinence and recovery were impossible for him in that environment. He judged the behaviors associated with his role as club president to be unacceptable in "recovery" circles, and he admitted that his return to the motorcycle group would be a self-destructive attempt to alleviate intense feelings of separation, alienation and loneliness that he continued to experience as a suffering condition.

Max continued to feel strongly compelled to return to the bikers' club despite his stated desire to do otherwise. He described his current recovery progress, spiritual growth and church involvement as positive, but not as rewarding in some ways as his previous associations and involvements. He recognized that the behaviors that earned respect and leadership in the club did not work in his present situations.

Toward the end of treatment, Max was undergoing a difficult identity transition, and his life was in danger. He said he could easily remedy this by returning to the club. He referred to the one-year "leave time" that privileged members are given in these circumstances. He explained that less privileged members who leave as he did remain under a death threat, without reprieve, for as long as they live. Max was also under federal indictment that, he said, could easily be avoided if he were to go "underground"; but that would prevent him from collecting the insurance money he planned to use to fight his legal charges.

He also felt compelled to return to a violent relationship. His fiancée provoked him with criticism that he was not able to tolerate. She was not supportive of his recovery involvement and derided him when he shared with her his attempts to follow through with his treatment plan. He explained that he felt the same sense of loyalty to her that he did toward his former group.

Despite these dilemmas, Max strengthened his commitment to change and continued trying to improve his interactions with others. Although he continued to act as a leader and use favors, persuasion and an intimidating persona to influence people, he made a consistent effort to participate as an equal. In 12 Step meetings and his church, he openly shared his persistent feelings of guilt concerning previous actions and activities in the motorcycle gang as his motivation for moving forward in the ministry and in recovery.

Although Max progresses at high risk, he has many positives from his early life upon which to build. He had an already-developed positive sense of self before his first traumatic episode. He was surrounded by love and support throughout his early childhood. He suffers tremendous guilt for actions he considers to be wrong, while justifying other actions that were acceptable behavior in his family and cultural environment. These contradictions will be a challenge he must meet with a lifelong commitment. His inclination to be part of a social group is another positive factor that will help him maintain his recovery network and will compete with his desire to return to the motorcycle club.

Note: Max currently has been cocaine abstinent for two years and is actively involved in youth ministry. He has had some minor drug relapse setbacks due to overuse of prescribed medication for his chronic pain. He resumed his relationship with his fiancée and reports improvement in this relationship. His legal problems continue, but there have been no reported attempts to end his life.

Notes

1. Bellamy, G. (2000). *Victual Reality*. Pudding House Publications Chapbook Series.
2. Lefrancois, G.R. (1996). *The Lifespan*, 5th Ed. p.135. U.S.A.: Wadsworth Publishing Company.
3. Kierkegaard, S. (1944). *Either/Or* (Vols.1-2). Garden City, New York: Princeton. University Press.
4. Lowrie, (1989). *Kierkegaard, I: Childhood, 1813-1830, II: Youth: 1830-1838, III: Early manhood, 1838-1844*, pp. 39-41 (Vol.1). New York: Harper & Brothers.
5. "Training in Christianity by Anti-Climacus". Edited by S. Kierkegaard. Sept. 27, 1850. *Procul, O procul est profani!* Preface d by the Editor, S. K. Invocation.

> Superior musical neurology may manifest itself as an excruciating
> sensitivity to sound. It often appears early. The infant Mozart was
> made sick by loud sounds; Mendelssohn simply cried whenever he
> heard music. As a child, Tchaikovsky was supposedly found weeping
> in bed wailing, "This music! It is here in my head. Save me from it."
> This passion for sound, even for individual tones, is common enough
> that German has a word for it: *Horlust* (roughly, "hearing passion").
> But where there is pleasure there is also pain. Ugly sounds become
> torture. And also Handel would not enter a concert hall until after
> the instruments had been tuned, and Bach would fly into a rage upon
> hearing wrong notes.[1]
>
> — Jourdain, 1997

During the most important time of neuronal development, children are individually sensitive to discord, whether it arises in music, a tone of voice, or in the ugly sounds of arguing and conflict. Conflict experiences are a major factor in some of the most problematic behavior documented in the HRIPTM research. Childhood memories of conflict between parents or family members, conflict within the neighborhood, the classroom or playground, espoused ethnic and racial hatreds and community divisions are all vividly represented in these recollections. A child can be negatively affected by surrounding conflicts even when not directly targeted. Children witness and observe, listen and overhear, and too often, silently contain the disturbing impact of what they see, hear and perceive to be happening.

Children who *are* directly targeted or who are at the *center* of a dispute are sometimes put in an impossible situation. When observed, the child may appear to have minimal reaction, even when being pressured into adopting views or taking sides. But the child's emotional and physical well-being and behavior *will* be affected, although it may not be recognized at the time.

The recent case of Elian Gonzalez is an extraordinary example of a child caught at the center of a custody dispute. It is a also good example of the "out of control" nature of this type of conflict, and how its impact on the child can be disregarded despite the "good intentions" of those involved.

The dispute involved Elian's father, his extended family, the surrounding community and two governments. On Thanksgiving Day, 1999, Elian was found lashed and clinging to an inner tube off the coast of Fort Lauderdale. Rescued by fishermen, he was one of three survivors from a boat that capsized during a harrowing attempt to flee Cuba. Over a period of several hours, Elian witnessed the drowning death of his mother, Elizabet Brotons Rodriguez, and ten others.

Elian's father, Juan Miguel Gonzalez, and the Cuban government demanded his return. His Miami relatives went to court to block an INS ruling that ordered his return to Cuba. His case stirred heated debate, international controversy and media coverage on a global scale.

Besides suffering the loss of his mother and separation from his father, Elian was encouraged to decide whether he wanted to remain in Miami with relatives or return to his father in Cuba. Family members gave many interviews and allowed him to be photographed and filmed in a variety of settings. They took him to Universal Studios where he was photographed with the popular dinosaur character, Barney. They threw a bash for his sixth birthday, where he was showered with presents including a new bike, a Labrador puppy, and two cell phones. In outings with relatives, at baseball games and even when he was playing in the backyard, the camera crews, reporters and supporters were visible in the background of daily scenes depicting the "Americanization of Elian."

In the midst of this media blitz, a myth was created. Elian became the "Angel Child," who was miraculously saved from the depths of the sea by dolphins that guided him to the fishermen. Mythical legend grew into a public display of homage. Gifts were brought to the modest home in Miami's Little Havana where he stayed with relatives. Visitors tried daily to get a glimpse of him. When he was taken out in public, believers reached out to touch him. Many older, deeply religious Cubans considered him a "miracle." Some believed his life was saved as a sign that Castro will be defeated. He became an anti-Castro symbol; his rescue on Thanksgiving Day was deemed a prophetic sign.

When the federal judge overseeing his case fell victim to a stroke, speculation arose that anyone supporting Elian's return to Cuba might be struck down. Further rumors supporting this curse spread when Elian's great-uncle, Manuel Gonzalez, who openly expressed his opinion that the boy should be sent back to Cuba, was rushed to the hospital complaining of heart palpitations and numbness in his left arm.

Throughout this entire public spectacle, there seemed to be little concern about the effect these ongoing events were having on Elian. He was not shielded from the press, nor was he protected from the inappropriate display of adulation and attention. The media focused predominately on the controversy surrounding Elian, while he remained at the center of the actual conflict. Psychologist Robin Goodwin was one of the first mental health professionals to publicly express concern about the constant media attention, the conflict between relatives and the daily community demonstrations. She warned that it was far too confusing for a six-year-old.[2] Shortly thereafter, a video was released by the Miami relatives showing the child pleading that he not be returned to Cuba. Many believed that Elian appeared strained and was coached in his statements.

When Janet Reno and the Federal Courts decided the case, and it was arranged for Elian to be reunited with his father, political debate escalated. The Cuban exile community threatened violence, and the boy was forcibly removed from the Miami home. There was public outrage, but the boy appeared happy to be with his father once again. Prior to this reunion, the renowned pediatrician Dr. T. Berry Brazelton appeared on *"Larry King, Live"* to share his opinion on the Elian Gonzalez case. He expressed anger and outrage, stating, "Our nation is behaving improperly. The child is being used and battered. We are acting as immaturely and destructively as Cuba. We have two powerful countries acting like babies ignoring what they are doing to this child." From the beginning, he continued, we should have investigated his situation in depth before allowing Elian to be put into a situation that might exacerbate post-traumatic stress disorder stemming from the boating accident and loss of his mother. He said that those events alone will have an everlasting impact. He warned that Elian may be overwhelmed and developmentally stressed on one level, while shutting down on another, and that without a transition that provides help for both father and son, Elian could enter a period of regression that later manifests in severe problems.

Brazelton has written extensively on the physiological impact of stress on children. In one of his many books on child rearing, he wrote, "each child is likely to have an 'Achilles heel.' Every stress or impending illness will express itself in this organ. In this organ, there is a lower threshold for resisting stress, and as a result, it reflects the struggles of the child's coping system."[3] When King asked how early it was possible to detect problems that could affect a child's future success, Brazelton replied, "I can tell as early as 8 months old."

But rather than speculate on how Elian, who has now returned with his father to Cuba, might be affected in the future by this series of extraordinary events, the following example demonstrates how one child's life *was* affected by a pivotal series of conflict and loss experiences.

In 1971, John Lennon wrote these lyrics: "You can live a lie, until you die. One thing you can't hide, is when you're crippled inside."[4]

In Goldman's[5] extensive biography on John Lennon, he wrote that, for most of the time during the last few years of Lennon's life, he had confined himself to his bedroom. Except for summer holidays in Japan, and brief periods of creative productivity, he rarely left his queen-sized bed, sleeping in two-to-four-hour spells and spending the balance of the day sitting in a lotus position, his head enveloped in a cloud of tobacco or marijuana smoke, reading, meditating or listening to tapes (including self-hypnosis cassettes with titles like *I Love My Body* or *There's No Need To Be Angry*). Though he was surrounded by his family, John was as removed from them as if he were spending his life out on the road. With a history of eating disorder dating back to 1965 (when someone had referred to him as "the fat Beatle"), he could deny his flesh anything but coffee and cigarettes. His addiction to these legal substances bothered him far more than his use of virtually every drug listed in Schedule I.

His ravaged appearance was largely due to doing too much cocaine. He had burned a hole through his septum, which he was scheduled to have repaired (by grafting tissue from the roof of his mouth to the damaged divider) the week following his death. Extremely thin, devoid of muscle, his pale skin exhibiting an unnatural sheen from obsessive washing, he would shrink from contact with either flesh or fabric.

He claimed to resemble Prince Myshkin in *The Idiot*, the Christlike epileptic hero who screams so violently when he throws a fit that his would-be assassin drops the knife and flees in terror. In truth, he looked less like a prince than an old beachcomber. The lights were never extinguished in the bedroom because he had a horror of waking up in the dark. Darkness to him represented death. Obsessed with terrible crimes, assassinations and conspiracy theories, he was fascinated by the sight of a man taking a bullet and how it feels to be on the receiving end of a slug. Obsessed by death and dying, even crucifixion, for most of his life, he had found a solution to his fear of human mortality by embracing the doctrine of reincarnation. John wanted to die standing there like a saint, like Jesus, confronting his assassin with a soul sublimely at peace. He was assassinated by Mark David Chapman, in front of his apartment building, The Dakota, on Pearl Harbor Day, December 8, 1980.

The books that had been strewn across his bed were a testament to how hard he had been working to break the shackles of his childhood. The book that had come to mean the most to him since Arthur Janov's *The Primal Scream* was *The Continuum Concept*, which argues that the solution to the problems of neurotic dependency lies in adopting the child-rearing techniques of primitive peoples, whose women strap their children to their bodies and go about their work with the children sustained at every moment in their experience of their lives by continuous contact with their mothers. This idea had enormous appeal to John, who had always felt that his mother had abandoned him. That was the theme of his most haunting and harrowing record, "Mother," a psychodrama that exposed the anguish at his core. No matter how hard he tried, he could not get his past out of his system.[5]

John Lennon was born in Liverpool in 1940, during the Battle of Britain. The Luftwaffe was bombing Liverpool night after night. Surrounded by a family that doted on the baby John, his mother Julia, feeling deserted by his father Freddie (who was serving at the forefront of the war), found a new independence when she moved into a cottage owned by her sister's husband.

Night after night she went out dancing in the village with uniformed men. She fell into the habit of slipping out after John had fallen asleep, leaving him alone. A pampered child accustomed to being closely watched, he would awake in the dark and discover himself unattended and alone. He would imagine a ghost or a goblin by his bed and, crying out in terror, would raise such a racket that sometimes the neighbors would have to investigate.

In 1944, his father returned from the war to find Julia pregnant with another man's baby. Sent to live with his uncle during this complicated period, John returned to his mother's home after some time to find a new man named Dynkins. He was extremely upset, and manifested his anger and resentment in hostile behavior, particularly attacks on weaker children. He was expelled from Mosspits Infants School for misbehavior in April, 1946 at the age of five and a half. His expulsion was closely connected with yet another series of highly disturbing incidents at home. His father Freddie, coming straight home from his ship (the *Dominion Monarch*), confronted his usurper and a quarrel erupted. Dynkins was thrown from the house. While the quarrel was raging, John crept down from upstairs. He witnessed his father punching it out with his mother's lover — a scene he never forgot.

Things became so bad between John and Dynkins that he began to run away from home, making his way to his Aunt Mimi's house on a tram that he recognized by its black leather seats. (To the end of his life, he could remember the smell of those leather seats.) Assuming responsibility for John's care, Mimi consented to allow John a six-week vacation with his father. Alone at last with his sorely missed dad, the experience for John was highly pleasurable as he and his father formed a bond. Impulsively, Freddie decided to emigrate to New Zealand and planned to take John with him. This was wonderful news for John, who had always dreamed of going off to sea on a great white ship with his Dad. Then Julia and Dynkins turned up unexpectedly.

In the midst of a fight over who should have John, Freddie said the boy should make his own decision. "I shouted to John," recollected ·Freddie. "He runs out and jumps on my knee, asking if she's coming back. That's obviously what he wanted. I said, no, he had to decide whether to stay with me or go with her. He said me. Julia asked again, but John still said me. Julia went out the door and was about to go up the street when John ran after her. That was the last time I saw or heard from him till I was told he'd become a Beatle."[6]

Little John chose his mother, but what he got was his aunt. No sooner did Julia return with her son than she put him into the hands of Mimi, who became his foster mother. This final betrayal convinced him that his mother did not love him. In fact, he believed that nobody loved him because nobody wanted him and he felt that, at one stroke, he had lost both his mother and father.

Lennon recalled, "I soon forgot my father. But I did see my mother now and again. I often thought about her, though I never realized for a long time that she was living no more than five or ten miles away."[7]

Julia did appear at Mimi's occasionally, but her calls were not inspired by concern for her son, but the perils of her own turbulent life. John recalled one such incident vividly, "My mother came to see us in a black coat with her face bleeding. She'd had some sort of accident. I couldn't face it. I thought, 'That's my mother in there bleeding.' I went out in the garden. I loved her but I didn't want to get involved. I suppose I was a moral coward. I wanted to hide all my feelings." John's older cousin was present that day. She remembered her embarrassment as she watched Mimi denounce and turn Julia out, for what had apparently been a beating by Dynkins; "She thundered in a voice like a Jehovan judge, 'You are not fit to be this boy's mother.'"[8]

Lennon recalls, "It was scary as a child, because there was no one to relate to. Neither my auntie nor my friends nor anybody could ever see what I did. It was very, very scary and the only contact I had was reading about an Oscar Wilde or a Dylan Thomas or a van Gogh — all those books that my auntie had talked about their suffering because of their visions. Because of what they saw, they were tortured by society for trying to express what they were. I *saw* loneliness."[9]

Domineering, smothering, and more a matron than mother, Mimi raised John, maintaining strict control over him until (during a rebellious adolescence) he reunited with his mother, who had moved nearby and with whom he began to visit daily. This reunion was to be short-lived. July 15, 1958 John's mother, Julia, was knocked down and killed while waiting at a bus stop. Even years later, John recalled his mother's death with bitterness and rage.

> She got killed after visiting my auntie's house where I lived by an off-duty cop who was drunk. I wasn't there at the time. She was just at a bus stop. The copper came to the door to tell us about the accident. It was just like it's supposed to be, the way it is in the films. Asking if I was her son an' all that. Then he told us, and we both went white. It was the worst thing that ever happened to me. I thought, I've no responsibility to anyone now. I was sixteen. That was another big trauma for me. I lost her twice. When I was four and a half and I moved in with my auntie, and then when she physically died. That made me more bitter; the chip I had on my shoulder I had as a youth

really got big then. I was just re-establishing a relationship with her and she was killed.[10]

After leaving the hospital, John returned to Mimi's. Mrs. Bushnell, the next door neighbor, was shocked to hear him out on the front porch playing his guitar. She couldn't comprehend that it was John's only consolation.[11] After his mother's death, he says,

> I was sort of in a blind rage for two years. I was either drunk or fighting. It had been the same with other girl friends I'd had. There was something the matter with me. Because of my attitude, all the other boys' parents, including Paul's father, would say, 'Keep away from him.' The parents instinctively recognized that I was a trouble-maker, meaning I did not conform and I would influence their kids, which I did. I did my best to disrupt every friend's home I had. Partly, maybe, it was out of envy that I did not have this so-called home. . . . Paul's parents were terrified of me and my influence, simply because I was free from the parents' stranglehold. That was the gift I got for not having parents. I cried a lot about not having them and it was torture, but it also gave me an awareness early.[12]

During his life, John tried abstinence from alcohol and other drugs many times. He did experience some temporary periods of abstinence when he was involved with Transcendental Meditation and with Primal Scream Therapy. Throughout his career, his rage would erupt into episodes of violent and abusive behavior. Much of this was covered up by those around him, who feared for his reputation. His behavior was reported to improve when he was under the influence of heavy drugs, particularly hallucinogens. It was during those periods of heavy drug use, including heroin, that he presented the peace-loving, passive image that inspired so many to enter the Peace Movement. The only time he felt "peaceful" was when he had drugged his rage into submission. His final, almost total dependence on Yoko Ono, after an unsuccessful rebellious period, resulted in a regressive state from which he was, in his last days, trying to emerge. In 1979, one year before his death, Lennon stated, "Without Yoko I couldn't cope with life. I really need her and could not survive without her. She is the answer to everything. Being with her makes me whole."

On December 8, 1980, John Lennon was gunned down outside his New York home. "What worries me is that one day a loony will come up and God knows what will happen then" (1965). In 1980: "You know, I used to worry about death when I was a kid; now the fear of it means less and less to me. . . . It took me a while to get things sorted out in my head, mate, but now I have a new — and *bigger* — direction to go in. It's a big, wide, wonderful world out there and Yoko and I are going to explore it until we die. I just have one hope: that I die before she does because we have become so much an equation together that I don't think I would have the strength to go on without her. Oh, I don't mean I would commit suicide; I just mean life would be so empty. . . . I hope I die before Yoko, because if Yoko died I wouldn't know how to survive. I couldn't carry on."[13]

While it might be correctly assumed that substance abuse is a catalyst for "addictive behavior," it is a mistake to associate all problematic behavior observed in the addicted individual as stemming from addiction. In the HRIPTM research that focuses on the lifespan experiences of chronic substance abusers, the identified experiences and behaviors that evolved from these experiences that substantially influenced negative self-concept and vulnerability to mood-altering substance dependence, occurred most frequently in the early developmental period of these individuals. These pre-addiction behaviors were characterized by obsessive repetition that was traced to vividly recalled experiences reported by these patients.[14]

To demonstrate the impact of an experience of this nature, the following case summary presents an example of a child caught in the middle of one "singular" episode of family conflict. When this case is considered in comparison to children who suffer repeated episodes of conflict, it helps to explain how severe conditions develop when a child is exposed to this repeatedly.

Case Summary: Richard

Richard, a 34-year-old white, married male, was admitted for treatment of cocaine dependence. He had been binging on cocaine, using one gram approximately every three weeks on average. His binges occurred weekly, although there were periods of time when he went for months without using drugs. His use of cocaine had been intermittent over the previous 10 years, during which time he reported one 10-month period of abstinence following completion of a 21-day inpatient treatment program. His use went on increasing until it became an issue in the family. His reason for admission was that he could no longer control his use of cocaine. Richard had also recently been diagnosed with attention deficit disorder. He reported that his symptoms began during his elementary school days and included being easily distracted, having difficulty maintaining focus, difficulty with school despite his apparently above-average intelligence, and enjoyment of high levels of stimulation.

Richard was admitted to the intensive outpatient program for a period of 8 weeks. He reported a positive family support system, ownership and management of a successful business, varied interests and accomplishments. Although diagnosed with ADD, he reported that he had been able to compensate in positive ways unrelated to his addiction, and had experienced some improvement with medication.

During Richard's initial participation in treatment, he followed directives, exhibited cooperative behavior and agreed to begin active Narcotics Anonymous attendance and obtain a sponsor. During the first few days of treatment, he appeared anxious, cooperative, engaging, enthusiastic and motivated. His high energy was apparent in his restless body language and impulsive verbal dialogue. His repeated questions and interruptions were distracting to group peers, but they liked and accepted him. His engaging affect and expression, obvious desire for recovery, and humorous, charming manner facilitated friendships. Short to medium in stature, physically agile with the appearance of unusual strength for his size, he gave the impression of being comfortable with himself and his appearance.

Richard's initial disclosure was focused on his cocaine addiction and the enormous monetary losses he had incurred. Although he had attended NA for several months after his previous treatment, he said he could not identify with this support group and felt that he was better suited to more action/health-oriented activities. He explained that he had difficulty sitting through the meetings and found them depressing. Although he agreed to actively resume attendance, he expressed doubt that his NA experience would be different from before. In terms of spiritual gain, he insisted that his spiritual beliefs were deep and abiding. He professed belief in God, love for his family and children and extended family. He remarked that he found it very easy to love others. He said his capacity for love was the reason for his problem with worry, and that if he could stop feeling anxious and worried, he might be able to remain abstinent.

Richard's insight concerning the feelings and physical symptoms of worry and anxiety were interesting in that he had his own idea about the origin of these symptoms. During the first week of participation in the Orchestration Group Process (OGP), he volunteered to disclose as focus of group. He wanted to share a series of episodes that had occurred within a 24-hour period of one day when he was eight years old. He said the events of that day changed his life and behavior drastically. He reported his childhood as otherwise positive. He had not addressed this experience previously in treatment because, he explained, "It wasn't a case of child abuse or anything like that."

Richard was encouraged to wait until he progressed further in treatment before becoming the central focus of group. He agreed to wait, but admitted having difficulty containing what he wanted to reveal. He was instructed to begin his lifespan charting and other written exercises. In this way, his experiences could be addressed in written form, in preparation for his later focus of group sharing.

Disclosure concerning early events is not advisable in the HRIPTM Orchestration Group Process until the participant has gained an appropriate level of objectivity through systematic participation in group roles and group positions that represent the feeling, physical symptoms and behavioral response components surrounding an experience. Emotional factors can be overwhelming when premature disclosure precludes gained objectivity. When the time is right, disclosure takes place within the structured group environment in which the person chosen for focus of group has become familiar. Thus, gained understanding of the nature of a pivotal experience enables the person to share what occurred in such a way that appropriate investigation of each component surrounding the experience can be identified.

It was remarkable to note that upon review of Richard's lifespan chart and other written preparation assignments, that he identified that one solitary day as the most significant experience of his entire childhood.

Richard's behavior during group process was impulsive, attentive, eager, and initially disruptive, due to questions and comments he interjected out-of-turn which were often not applicable to his assigned role. By the second week, his participation was appropriate and revealing.

He consistently responded to the shared experiences of others with intense empathy and feelings he described as confusion, worry, concern, guilt; and he often used the word "mad." By the third week, he added anger, dread, sadness and fear to his identified feeling responses. His accompanying physical symptom responses were described as adrenaline rush, chest expansion, "feeling like I could burst," increased body temperature, "hot," trouble breathing, fidgety hands and feet, and increased strength.

Richard was anxious to focus on behavior, once he had identified his most predominant feelings and physical symptoms. Although he expressed desire to understand more about his behavior, he said he recognized that his feelings and physical symptoms would not have been adequately explored if focus on his behavior had been premature. His behavioral responses were consistently described in terms of action and achievement. He identified strategy, organization and planning as important components of his goal-oriented behaviors. Verbal expression and dishonesty were used to manipulate, control, explain, intervene, disrupt, convince, comfort, persuade, rationalize, placate, commiserate, engage and to "nag" others. It became increasingly apparent through his disclosure that he could not tolerate being ignored and was willing to go to great lengths to prevent this from happening.

Richard's ultimate goal was to achieve positive regard, love, closeness and harmony. Complex and dishonest strategies coincided with positive and productive strategies. The obsessive nature of these conflicting patterns also presented self-harm features such as sleep and nutrition deprivation, excessive work, and relentless drive to achieve his goals. Richard's efforts to identify his most predominant feelings, physical symptoms and behaviors had a positive impact on his progress. He was scheduled to be focus-of-group.

Richard described his memory of the day in question as present in his thoughts on a weekly to monthly basis.

It was a Saturday morning. Richard's cousin Joey, who was age seven, came over to his house to ride motorized bikes. They rode the bikes to their grandmother's farm to ride through her fields. After a while, Joey realized that his clothes were covered with mud. He was afraid that his mother would be upset. Richard described Joey's mother as "a hard nose." Both boys were sure Joey would be punished. Joey became very upset and Richard wanted to help him. Richard's mother owned a beauty shop where she was working that day. Knowing that no one would be at home, he took Joey home with him, and proceeded to wash his muddy clothes in the washing machine. They both felt greatly relieved that the problem was solved. Joey went home. Richard said he felt good about having saved Joey from an ordeal with his mother. He felt grateful that his own mother was more understanding.

At this point in his disclosure, Richard gave a brief background of his family. He was an only child who lived with his parents and grandmother. He described his family as loving and close-knit. He said his family had a long history of dancing and that by age 8 he, too, was a great dancer. He was on a local dance team and an important dance competition was being held that very evening at 8:00. The competition was to take place in a town that was a one-hour driving distance from their home.

Around 6:00 that evening, Richard's mother came home from work and hastily put Richard's competition clothes, which included a white shirt, into the washing machine. When the cycle finished, she hurriedly put the clothes in the dryer. As it was nearing time to leave, she got Richard's shirt out of the dryer and noticed that it was not white. It was dirty. She became very angry and started scolding Richard. She held the clothes before him. He tried to explain what happened with Joey. He said his mother didn't listen and "went on and on." His father came into the room and began to defend Richard, explaining to her that Richard was only trying to help his cousin stay out of trouble with his mother. Richard's mother started criticizing her sister-in-law (Joey's mother), and made it clear that she didn't like her "ways."

Richard's (maternal) grandmother appeared in the doorway of the kitchen to see what was happening in the living room. Richard's father responded to the criticism of his sister with anger and argument. The argument quickly escalated. Richard's mother threw the soiled clothes at his father. His father responded by slapping her. The grandmother came from the kitchen with a frying pan and hit Richard's father over the head. Richard was in the middle of all this activity and had never before witnessed such behavior from his mother, father, or grandmother.

Richard's described feeling response: "Disbelief that my good action had caused this problem, scared that my parents might divorce, mad at everyone for behaving this way, glad that my father defended me, guilty because I had caused the problem, confused . . . everything was moving too fast; sheer panic over being in trouble, embarrassed and very worried."

Richard's described physical symptoms: "Nervous energy, adrenaline rush, increased strength, increased blood pressure, tears."

Richard's behavior response: Richard described how he tried to intervene while crying, frantically explaining, and physically coming between them. When the frying pan ended the argument, his parents quickly decided to go on with the plan to attend the competition. Richard was so upset that he declared, "I'm not going." He said he was forced to go anyway.

"But," he continued, "the worst part was not over. . . . During the one hour ride to the dance, no one would speak to each other. The silence in the car was unbearable. The hour seemed like a lifetime. This day which had started with a good deed had turned into a nightmare without end. I decided in the car that I must do something to make things better and to make up for what I had caused."

He then described a concentrated effort to "focus within," with all the energy he could muster. He performed at the competition like never before. He won the competition and received a large trophy as an award. When he presented the trophy to his parents and grandmother, he did see "some happiness." Although there was still an "uncomfortable silence" on the way home, he knew that winning the award had made things better.

Richard's group disclosure helped him to identify several behavior patterns that evolved from this experience. He also identified symptoms associated with his ADD as beginning around that time; "I could either concentrate totally or not concentrate at all." He began having difficulty at school and his reading, writing and grades suffered as a result. He worried constantly about causing another episode of family conflict. He said he could not endure the thought of his family breaking up. He became more observant in order to recognize any potential problem. He became more organized and planned ahead to prevent any last-minute disaster. All of his energy went into these behaviors. Most of his concentration went toward dancing and winning awards. In school he was often tired and could not concentrate. His grades continued to decline. He tried to appease his teachers with charm and personality. He was popular with his peers.

By early adolescence, he was behind his peers scholastically and it became more difficult to manipulate his teachers. He received a failing report card and in response to his father's disappointment, secretly broke into an office at school, obtained blank report cards, learned to forge grades and replace the teacher's cards with his forgeries. He made sure his grades did not exceed C level because he feared that higher grades might cause suspicion. He was never caught, and continued this behavior for every period that followed throughout high school. He enlisted the help of trusted friends, who maintained their secrecy because they depended on him for passing grades. He felt tremendous guilt for this behavior but deemed it necessary to keep his family from getting upset. The guilt bothered him to such an extent that he decided to begin an honest approach to study when he entered college. As a result of his own endeavor, and without deceit, he made top grades.

His deceptive strategies would continue to evolve, however, in relation to any threat of family disruption. Manipulation, control, excessive work, self-induced pressure, accumulation of awards, dishonesty, and goal-oriented achievement continued to an obsessive degree. Richard states that his role with his wife and children became much like his role with his parents, except for the fact that he was now "in charge." As such, the pressure increased. When he discovered cocaine, he said it was the "magic elixir" that kept him going.

Richard concluded by stating that he has not touched a washing machine since that day. And, that silence for him is still "intolerable." He cannot endure it if his wife ignores him and will "nag" her relentlessly until he gets her attention. Impatience is a major problem: he feels intense pressure to be "on time," dress quickly, and move fast, and he gets impatient with those who don't. When the pressure increases, he erupts with verbal aggression. Family conflict and the thought of divorce are his "worst nightmare." His wife has threatened divorce if he resumes the use of cocaine.

Richard identified the following pre-addiction behaviors that developed into patterns:

- Total concentration or no ability to concentrate at all; increased efforts to concentrate and control. Primary negative emotional state triggered when loss of concentration occurs.
- Obsessive preoccupation with worry about family conflict, the family breaking up; vigilant observance in order to recognize any potential problem.

- Attempts to control outcomes with ritualistic organizing and planning ahead to prevent any last-minute disaster.
- Preoccupation with time, planning, preparing, rushing, impatience, irritability and attempts to control time.
- Verbal control, advanced verbal skills used to manipulate, pressure, intervene, "break the silence," rationalize, explain, convince, mediate, and/or take charge.
- Excessive competition to achieve an outcome that will improve or make situation better. Difficulty arises when outcome doesn't meet expectations.

These behaviors, which initially helped to relieve his extreme anxiety, have since evolved into patterns that now sabotage Richard in many key areas of life. He also recognizes their contributing role in his previous addiction relapses. Richard has accepted that his desired behavioral change requires a life-long commitment, therapeutic and psychiatric interventions and active participation in his recovery support group. Environmental and relationship stressors and craving symptoms related to his cocaine addiction, as well as his limited ability to cope with negative emotional states generated by specific feeling/physical symptom combinations, add to his high-risk status. Richard revealed information that provides a basis for a high-level approach to his continuing-care treatment. However, he is likely to fluctuate in his commitment to this plan. Any disruption in his life will generate extreme levels of anxiety that provoke his most vulnerable state. While his intentions are sincere, his priorities will most likely be determined by surrounding conditions that he cannot control. Therefore, he progresses at very high risk.

Notes

1. Jourdain, R. (1997). *Music, the Brain, and Ecstasy: How Music Captures Our Imagination* p.188. New York: William Morrow and Company, Inc.

2. *ABC Evening News* with Peter Jennings. March 30, 2000/February 21, 2000. Interview with Dr. Robin Goodwin.

3. Brazelton, T.B.(1984). *To Listen To a Child: Understanding the Normal Problems of Growing Up*, pp. 132-33. USA: Addison-Wesley Publishing Company.

4. Lennon, J. (1971). "When You're Crippled Inside." *Imagine*. Album produced by John & Yoko and Phil Spector: Capital Records.

5. Goldman, A. (1988). *The Lives of John Lennon*. New York: William Morrow and Company, Inc.

6. *Ibid.*

7. Heatley, M. (1994). *John Lennon: In His Own Words*. London/New York/Sydney: Omnibus Press.

8. Goldman, *op. cit.*

9. Heatley, *op. cit.*

10. *Ibid.*

11. Goldman, *op. cit.*

12. Heatley, *op. cit.*

13. *Ibid.*

14. Gerwe, C.F. (November, 1999). "Chronic Addiction Relapse Treatment: A Study of the Effectiveness of the High Risk Identification and Treatment Model (HRIPTM)." *DAI*, Vol. 60-09) No. 9946534 UMI Company.

See also the latest sources for this information:

Gerwe, C.F. (Feb. 2001). "Chronic Addiction Relapse Treatment: The Study of the Effectiveness of The High Risk Identification and Prediction Treatment Method, Part I." *The Journal of Substance Abuse Treatment 19* (2000) 415-427. Elsevier Science.

Gerwe, C.F. (March, 2001). "Chronic Addiction Relapse Treatment: The Study of the Effectiveness of The High Risk Identification and Prediction Treatment Method, Part II." *The Journal of Substance Abuse Treatment 19* (2000) 429-438. Elsevier Science.

Gerwe, C.F. (May, 2001). "Chronic Addiction Relapse Treatment: The Study of the Effectiveness of The High Risk Identification and Prediction Treatment Method, Part III." *The Journal of Substance Abuse Treatment 19* (2000) 439-444. Elsevier Science.

CHAPTER V

> When I started to study how Synapses work and how messages come in from the outside world, it became very clear that the diversity of the brain is even staggeringly larger than its anatomical complexity. It is the most diverse object that I could think of, except for an evolutionary jungle. Then I was naturally prompted to look at perceptual phenomena as the perhaps most simple organizing, early function of the higher brain. And when I looked at that, it became very clear that your brain *constructs*. There is no avoiding that, in some deep cases, it constructs. It doesn't mirror. Oh boy. Big problem, right? Even before language, your brain constructs and makes perceptual slices of the world, and then you have to embed this all in evolution.[1]
>
> — Gerald Edelman, 1995

When a child has an experience that is *novel* — beyond the norm — the physiological response that is activated works much like a system on alert. When the physiological symptoms that are produced continue to escalate to a point where the system is overwhelmed by the situation, increased neuronal activity can produce a state of mental chaos. Whether described as acutely intense excitement or acutely intense distress, physical symptoms appear to dominate at the transforming point where behavioral action occurs, while the brain records the action that brings order to this state of chaos. Behavior that develops under normal conditions differs from behavior formulated during extreme conditions. In these moments, a child is not always able to consider rationally the positive or negative consequences before acting. The biological impact on behavior that is constructed during a state of mental chaos helps to explain why these behaviors are characteristically problematic. They do not fit in with the normal scheme of things, and yet, they have proven effective in relation to emotional and biological regulation.

Charles Darwin, upon completion of his *Origin of Species*,[2] reasoned that if we could locate the point of origin, a place where the tree of life is growing new branches right now, we would see something less distinct and more chaotic. We would see a blur of variations shading from the individual up to the level of the species, "an inextricable chaos of varying and intermediate links."

Gerald Edelman's research strongly identifies with Darwinian theory in relation to neuronal development and behavioral manifestation. His theory of how the brain constructs responses, and the evolutionary development arising from these constructs, moves beyond Darwin's theory into the evolutionary world of the brain. Edelman has already won the 1972 Nobel Prize for his work in immunology, and has been considered for a second one for his molecular biological research based on Darwinian principles. Conducting his most revolutionary work as chairman of the Neurobiology Department at the Scripps Research Institute in La Jolla, California, his ideas on how the brain gives rise to the mind helps to explain how behavior is constructed under the most extreme circumstances. As he puts it, his ideas would not only have great importance in the world of biology, but would profoundly affect the way human beings view themselves.

Edelman maintains that the brain is not a computer but something more akin to a complex ecology, like that of a jungle. The dense interconnected tapestry of neurons is not a preordained construction but something that has evolved to cope effectively with novel circumstances. Edelman[3,4] refers to subsets of the brain that are not normally accessed in less intense states. He asserts that constructed responses that extend or alleviate a state that affects more expanded brain regions are encoded in these accessed regions. When these regions are once again accessed, the stored information is also accessed.

In other words, memories associated with experiences that result in accessing these cell regions are stored in such a way as to be accessed when stimuli associated with the experience generates activity in these regions, and triggers the effective behavioral resolution. "Behavioral development outcomes are decided not so much in the genes as in the developmental process that carries out those genes. Thus, who we are is due as much to private history as to genetic destiny. Chance events totally unanticipated by the instructions in our genes — a glance, a flash of daylight, a hurried conversation — will change the strength of certain connections between maps, cause us to categorize things in a slightly different way, and remake our minds."[5]

The role of novel experience and the individual variation of constructed response that stems from novel experience is now being explored with great success by evolutionary scientists all over the world. Evolutionary biologist teams such as the one led by Peter and Mary Grant, who are restudying Darwin's finches on the Galapagos islands, are observing evolution at a level that was totally inaccessible to Darwin: the molecular level, as the DNA in the blood samples taken from the birds reveals evolutionary change, particularly in response to radical change in climate. Not only are they recording climatic events that have resulted in evolutionary "happenings," they are recording the individual physiological and behavioral variations of these birds as they survive or perish in the midst of the extraordinary circumstances that arise from the extreme climatic conditions.[6]

Darwin studied the variation problem most deeply not in birds but in barnacles. In October 1846 he began trying to classify a single curious barnacle specimen that he found on the southern coast of Chile. It was the very last of his *Beagle* specimens, an "ill-formed little monster," the smallest barnacle in the world. To classify that barnacle, he had to compare it with others. Soon the working surfaces of his study were littered with barnacles from all the shores of the planet. The classic barnacle is an animal with the body plan of a volcano: a cone, with a crater at the top. It colonizes rocks, docks, and ships' hulls. Every day when the tide rolls in, each barnacle pokes out of its crater a long foot like feather duster and gathers food. When the tide goes out, each barnacle pulls in the feather duster and clamps its crater closed with an operculum — a shelly lid. To mate, a barnacle sticks a long penis out of its crater and thrusts it down the crater of a neighbor. Since every barnacle in the colony is both male and female, this is not as chancy as it sounds.

What could be more of a sameness than a colony of barnacles? But Darwin, staring through a simple microscope, found himself descending into a world of finely turned and infinitely variable details. He wrote to Captain FitsRoy: "For the last half-month daily hard at work in dissecting a little animal about the size of a pin's head. . . and I could spend another month, and daily see more beautiful structure." In every barnacle genus, he found astonishing variations. In one genus, "the opercular valves (usually very constant) differ wonderfully in the different species." Elsewhere he found variations in the form of "curious ear-like appendages," "horn-like projections," and, in one strange species, "the most beautiful, curved, prehensile teeth."[7]

Everywhere he looked, individual differences graded into subspecies, subspecies into varieties, varieties slid into species. Which specimens were the true species? Where should he draw the line? "After describing a set of forms as distinct species, tearing up my MS., and making them one species, tearing that up and making them separate, and then making them one again, I have gnashed my teeth, cursed species, and asked what sin I had committed to be so punished."

Darwin's friends knew just how he felt. The botanist Joseph Hooker wrote Darwin across the top of one letter, "I quite understand and sympathize with your Barnacles, they must be just like Ferns!" This profusion and confusion of barnacles helped confirm for Darwin that one species can shade into another: that there is no species barrier. In many cases Darwin discovered one barnacle subspecies, variety, or race (he did not know which to call them) on rocks at the southern edge of a species' range, and another subspecies, variety, or race at the northern edge of its range. In *Natural Selection*,[8] his sprawling first draft of the *Origin of Species*, he notes that in many of these cases, "natural selection probably has come into play & according to my views is in the act of making two species."

Of course, Darwin assumed that the split, the act of creation, would be much too slow to observe any motion in his lifetime — because evolution proceeds at a barnacle's pace. Darwin proceeded at a like pace through his barnacles. "I am at work at the second volume of the Cirripedia, of which creatures I am wonderfully tired," he wrote in 1852, when he had been plowing through barnacles for six years, and still had one more year to go. "I hate a Barnacle as no man ever did before, not even a sailor in a slow-sailing ship."[9]

In the initial stages of the HRIPTM research that is the basis for these chapters, the same dynamic occurred. In gathering data from the recalled experiences of chronic patients and habitual offenders, it became apparent that no two recalled experiences resulted in exactly the same perception, feelings, physical symptoms and behavioral response. In each case variations were formulated into combinations unique to the individual and the recalled experience. While similarities were found in relation to certain types of experiences and certain combinations of responses, it became evident that the individual nature of response to experiences related to extreme conditions created an ongoing evolution of behavior. It became clear that behavior constructed during extreme conditions could not only influence a child's developmental process, but could potentially influence change in others and change in societal norms.

For example, the child who enacted the first school shooting targeting random victims was the focus of much media attention. Other children and adolescents fueled by extreme emotional/physiological conditions were then provided with a new behavioral option that could be integrated into their own individually constructed behavioral response. The next incident was influenced to some degree by its predecessor, but was acted out in a new and very individual way and for very individual reasons.

In many respects, Charles Darwin is a perfect example of this evolutionary dynamic. A childhood experience resulted in young Charles challenging a theory that he had been taught as a truth. This set a behavioral precedent for what was to come later. His early natural curiosity about his environment led to his most obsessive pattern of behavior; specimen collecting. This obsession and a remarkably unplanned turn of events led to an extraordinary voyage that relied on his specimen collecting. The voyage had a disastrous affect on his heath but did not deter his collecting. His collected finds, sent back to England, and his perception of what he discovered, led to the development of a theory that created enormous controversy. Darwin was ill-suited for this role. His health suffered tremendously as a result of his theory, but he continued, because he could not resist or tolerate doing otherwise despite pleas from his beloved wife and vilification from the society in which he lived.

Charles Robert Darwin was born on February 12, 1809 in Shrewsbury, England on the same day that Abraham Lincoln was born, and in the same year as Chopin, Gladstone, Mendelssohn, Poe, Tennyson, Oliver Wendell Homes and Elizabeth Barrett Browning.[10] As a child, Darwin was gentle, meditative and acutely observant of his surroundings. Even when he was confronted with danger, he was able to pursue his observations in the midst of his fear. One day, absorbed in his thoughts, he was walking through the fortifications of Shrewsbury and absent-mindedly stepped over a parapet. Suddenly he found himself falling through the air — to his death, as he believed. . . . "The number of thoughts which passed through my head during this very short but sudden and wholly unexpected fall was astonishing. . . . all of which seemed hardly compatible with what physiologists have stated about each thought requiring an appreciable amount of time."[11]

This first questioning of an existing theory led to his ability to change his view in the midst of discovery. From the earliest years of his childhood, he formed the habit of noticing things for himself. He loved to collect and to study all sorts of pebbles, shells, coins, birds' eggs, flowers and insects. He rarely captured insects alive, preferring to pick them up when he found them dead, for he didn't think it right to kill them with his own hands. Yet with the naive logic of childhood, he felt no compunction about killing birds with a gun — at a distance. He enjoyed hunting for a number of years, until one day he saw the struggles of a wounded bird and made up his mind not ever again to bring suffering or death to any living creature for the mere sake of sport.[12] He would later have a similar life-altering experience that led to a decision to leave medical school.

Darwin inherited his gentle nature from his mother, who died when he was eight years old. His father, Doctor Robert Waring Darwin, had difficulty understanding his son's character. Although Darwin loved and respected his father and thought him to be "one of the wisest of men," his father considered Charles a loafer, whose mission in life was to "mess up the house with his everlasting rubbish." In order to guide him in a worthier direction, Dr. Darwin sent Charles to a classical school. But the youngster paid no attention to his Latin and Greek. Instead he fixed up a secret laboratory in his father's garden and began to dabble in chemistry and physics. This, in the opinion of both his schoolmates and of his teachers, was, "the activity of a deranged mind." His father, disgusted with his experimenting and his "rat-catching," removed him from classical school and sent him to the University of Edinburgh to study medicine.[13]

At first, Darwin was not disinclined to follow his father's footsteps — but the lectures on anatomy soon began to bore him. Moreover, his sympathetic temperament couldn't bear the sight of the surgical demonstrations. One day, as an operation was being performed on a child, he rushed out of the amphitheater. At that period they were still operating without anesthesia, and the screams of the agonized child kept haunting him for years.[14]

Charles Darwin was completed stunned when he was invited to

join the H.M.S. Beagle voyage. He had recently convinced his father, after two years of study in medicine, that he did not have the dedication nor the inclination to follow him and his grandfather, the celebrated Dr. Erasmus Darwin, in their profession. Surprisingly, he announced his preference to study at Christ College in preparation to enter the clergy. After some consideration, his father became receptive to the idea of having a clergyman in the Darwin family.

However, when the voyage invitation letters came from Professor Henslow at Cambridge and George Peacock, a fellow at Trinity College, Charles revealed to his sisters that since childhood he had felt a strong desire for a different vocation. "By the time I went to the Rev. Mr. Case's day school, at nine, my taste for natural history was well-developed. I tried to make out the names of plants, and collected all sorts of things, shells, coins, minerals . . ." He went on to describe how throughout his education he had spent most of his free time in the obsessive pursuit of this interest, with no idea that it might lead to a profession. Following this conversation, and with a great deal of apprehension, he presented the news to Dr. Darwin.

"Father, I've had the most extraordinary offer."

"Oh, what is that?"

"To travel around the world for two years as a naturalist."

"A naturalist? Since when have you become a naturalist?"
Responding to his father's concerns and objections, he tried to reassure him about the future.

"I am committed to becoming a clergyman. I have no plans other than to enter the priesthood. You yourself said it would be at least two years before I could find a parish."[15]

Until his father's eventual approval and his final appointment as ship naturalist, Charles suffered a series of setbacks and disappointments. His fluctuating excitement and reservations continued until the day of his acceptance; Charles stepped out into the streets of London, his head spinning after his two interviews, walked along the Whitehall as far as the Treasury, then cut down to the riverbank, strolled along the Thames past the majestic House of Parliament, doubled back to the Westminster Bridge and stood watching the green river water swirl beneath him on its way to the English Channel. His hands had *broken out in a rash*. This had happened before when he had been under *nervous pressure*, a condition his easygoing nature deplored. "Shakespeare was right," he thought, "There is indeed 'a tide in the affairs of men,' and I have experienced it."[7] But did he ever imagine that this tide would become a tidal wave of change in man's understanding of religion and nature?

For five years (1831-1836) the *Beagle* sailed over the seas and Darwin was privileged to behold with his own eyes "the rondure of the world and mysteries teeming with life." However, he suffered greatly during the voyage. Darwin had inherited his father's stature, but not his constitution. Besides being plagued with protracted seasickness and ill health — to the end of his days Darwin suffered from repeated attacks of vomiting — there were many other discomforts. The food was insufficient and indigestible, there were frequent spells of unendurable cold and unendurable heat. Again and again, in the swampy regions that he visited in search for scientific data, he suffered from the bites of venomous insects. On some of his explorations into the jungle he was obliged to go for days without water. After the voyage, his heath never recovered and he never set foot on a boat again. But during it and despite the tortures he endured — just as he had as a child when he fell crossing the parapet — his mind remained alert to every detail. His curiosity stimulated his racked and weakened body. He wrote in his notebook each day to catch up on ideas already formulated; and to ask himself questions such as:

"Why is life so short? Why does an individual die? We *know* [the] world [is] subject to change of cycle, temperature and all circumstances which influence human beings. We see the young of living beings become permanently changed or subject to variety, according to circumstances."

With the precision of a scientist and the imagination of a poet, he collected, observed and classified fragments of the Chinese puzzle of existence and tried to piece them together into a comprehensive and comprehensible design.[16] His transposed journal, the *Voyage of the Beagle* (a scientific treatise that reads like a romantic tale of adventure), began his reputation as an outstanding naturalist. It was to take him twenty years of laborious research before he could determine that his vast accumulation of facts, when examined impartially, pointed to a single theory — the theory of evolution.

The life of Darwin was perhaps the best proof of his own theory. His capacity for love seemed to grow from year to year. He was drawn to people, and people in turn were drawn to him. In his bluish-gray eyes there was a perpetual twinkle of sympathetic understanding. Such was the kindly serenity of his face that strangers would come away from their first visit with tears of joy in their eyes. As for his intimate friends — and he had many of them — they found in his gentle person- ality a "perpetual benediction." He never assumed a superior attitude either toward his antagonists or toward his collaborators. He looked down upon no creature, however lowly. His servants, like members of his family, were in his eyes invested with the selfsame dignity. Darwin had something of Buddha's fellow feeling toward all mankind — indeed toward all nature. He talked about trees and grass as if they were living things. He would scold a plant-leaf for its "ingenuity" in screwing itself out of a basin of water in which he had tried to immerse it. Vexed with the behavior of certain seedlings with which he was experimenting, he said: "The little beggars are doing just what I don't want them to do." He looked upon every plant as upon a living personality. He enjoyed the beauty of flowers, and he was thankful to them for the "graciousness" of all their beauty. He would touch their petals gently, with the infinite love of a sage and the simple admiration of a child. . . . . His character was Christ-like, yet he refused to call himself a Christian. He was not, however, an atheist, but regarded himself rather as an agnostic.[17] He was tenderly devoted to his wife Emma (who bore him ten children), and she to him.

During his life, his health suffered continually from the demands required by his intense and extensive research, voluminous correspon- dence, and the writing and publishing of articles and manuscripts. He could have led the life of a country squire on his substantial inheritance and sound investments. He knew from the beginning the implications of his theory and thought to have it published only after his death, but his honesty directed him otherwise as his research progressed. He was driven to seek understanding and the anxiety provoked by his discover- ies was further aggravated by the growing firestorm that surrounded his theory. His genius had enable him to come upon a great discovery and he felt it his duty to kill an old dogma in order to re-establish what he regarded as a still older truth. But although he suffered physically from the impact of his work that brought about critical wrath and con- troversy, he had said, "I would rather be the wretched, contemptible invalid which I am than live the life of an idle squire."

Herein lay the truth, as Charles Darwin acknowledged it! Why, then, was his work making him ill? In the dark of a troubled night he was properly anxious and frightened about what his theories, as written in the notebooks between 1837 and 1839 and his essays of 1842 and 1844, would unleash in a Christian nation such as Great Britain, whose history had frequently been plagued with religious upheavals. He had grown up as a friendly, uncontroversial, easygoing chap, popular at the Shrewsbury School, at Christ College, on the HMS *Beagle.* He had been born without any appetite for conflict. He had not even participated in competitive sports, preferring to walk along the river Severn, go horseback riding, catch toads in the Cambridgeshire Fens. Though he had become convinced, with Agassiz, that nature never lied, it had made a ghastly mistake in choosing him for the role of the anti-Christ! Not that he was; but the world would think him so, which amounted to the same thing![18]

The dizziness, the palpitations, the flatulence, the retching, was the price he paid in order to turn the world around. . . . To most of England's scientists, and some of his friends, this would label him an incurable hypochondriac. So be it. He knew that he would pursue the origin of life as long as he lived. His brain was searching for ultimate truths about nature; his body profoundly resented that occupation. There was no cure for it.[19] The suffering he endured throughout his life could not deter the obsessively driven behavior that was constructed during his early development and shaped the course of his life irreversibly.

The following case summary exemplifies how a pattern of behavior that leads toward a dangerous occupation can be as powerful as one that leads toward controversy.

Case Summary: Doyle

Doyle, a 40-year-old single white male and a professional electrician, was voluntarily admitted for treatment of alcoholism. He reported compulsive alcohol use and daily drinking in increasing amounts. Upon admission, he stated, "It's time to get some help."

Doyle's occupation regularly took him out of town. He was on a temporary layoff, which, he said, contributed to his increased drinking. Prior to the layoff, he said he had been drinking at work and taking poor care of himself. He said he often passed out and could not sleep when not drinking. He reported a recent increase in anxiety attacks. Prior to admission, he was drinking up to a case of beer a day, plus hard liquor. His drinking had been escalating steadily over the previous 7 years after a relapse following completion of a 28-day addiction treatment program.

Doyle's initial participation in treatment was positive. He exhibited cooperative behavior and expressed willingness to follow all treatment directives including active AA attendance and sponsorship. He exhibited polite, self-contained, mannerly, reserved behavior. Although he appeared hesitant to interact with peers, he did respond to attention from others in a friendly manner. Doyle spoke in a quiet, clear and well-modulated voice with a regional mountain accent. His manner of speaking was slow and methodical. He seemed to think before speaking, weighing each word carefully. He did not volunteer input or disclosure during group processes.

Doyle appeared self-disciplined and well-groomed, despite his admission of poor self-care upon intake. He dressed neatly every day in plaid flannel shirts and jeans with well-cared-for work boots. His posture was erect and almost stiff, his facial expressions and reactions minimal. His eyes were his most remarkable and expressive feature and they often sparked with a glimmer of amusement. He held his body firm and still while observing his surroundings. Despite his reserve, he was accepted by his peers. He exhibited good listening skills and interest in others. He was attentive in group and lecture. He was a positive and agreeable presence in his group. His questions during educational lectures reflected a natural curiosity and desire to understand the content of each presentation.

During the first week of treatment, Doyle began to reveal consistent feelings and physical symptom combinations that he identified as present prior to alcohol dependence. In response to a variety of presented situations, Doyle consistently stated that he would have felt curious about what was occurring despite danger and/or potential harm. He described the feeling of curiosity as powerful and associated with intense excitement. He associated fear with intense anxiety. In situations where he imagined himself at a variety of ages, he repeatedly identified curiosity as predominating over other consistent feeling responses. He recalled intense feelings of fear, anxiety and loneliness as a child. He identified physical symptoms described as anxiety, raised blood pressure, sweating, shaking, upset stomach ("butterflies in stomach") in association with fear.

During the second week, Doyle began to reveal consistent behavioral responses to a variety of presented situations. Imagining how he would have responded at various age periods in his life, Doyle consistently described behavior responses driven by curiosity. He repeatedly stated that he would have been curious to know more about something, even when gaining this knowledge would put him at risk for danger or punishment. He described the desire or impulse to act on curiosity as "impossible to resist." He identified a repeated pattern of solitary action in relation to this behavior. For example, whenever he would enact behavior driven by curiosity, he did so alone, and then escaped the situation alone, without revealing to anyone where he had been. Solitary action developed into a pattern of isolation and withdrawal that contributed to feelings of loneliness and being set apart from others.

Doyle revealed a pattern of dangerous, high risk behavior that was well developed prior to adolescence and alcohol abuse. He described his self-contained behavior as a means of self-protection and avoidance of the consequences of high-risk behavior. His avoidance patterns contributed to the development of secretive and deceptive actions that reduced his level of self-regard. His high risk behavior patterns became a source of approval when dangerous actions benefited others. These patterns eventually converged with his sense of identity and self-value.

As Doyle progressed in treatment, his disclosure produced evidence of behavior that had put his life in jeopardy since childhood. He became more aware of how this behavior related to later alcohol dependence and repeated relapse. Although he was progressing well in the 12 Step Program, he admitted that his behavior presented a clear and present obstacle to recovery. His occupation entailed working with high voltage wiring that involved life-endangerment. Doyle revealed that he had a reputation for taking jobs that no one else would attempt. As a result, he often continued to work when others were laid off. When he tried to resist a request to do a dangerous job, he admitted having difficulty saying "no." He also admitted having intense fear and anxiety in relation to this behavior, and identified panic attacks as a persistent factor before and after dangerous activity. He identified sleep deprivation as related to ongoing fear of death and dreams of death.

During the fourth week of treatment, Doyle stated that he wanted to share an episode as focus of group. He said he had been thinking about something that occurred when he was age 6, and had only thought of this memory periodically, until recently. He said it was now in his thoughts almost daily.

Doyle had progressed from initially reserved and hesitant to active in group participation. His increased understanding of himself was reflected in questions and statements such as, "Why do I keep doing things that I know will kill me eventually? I know my luck will run out one day. Lately I've had to drink to numb the fear of what I know I will do. The risk is greater because I cannot be careful doing dangerous activity when I'm drinking. It's just plain crazy, and yet I get excited and feel good when I'm doing something others are afraid of, even though I'm afraid."

The following is a transcription of Doyle's account of his experience at age 6.

"I was in the kitchen. My little sister was about five years old and she was sitting in a chair by the table. She had long hair which hung down her back. Her hair was hanging over the back of the chair. I had found an old lighter outside earlier that day. I had been flicking it on and off before entering the kitchen. My mother was in the bathroom. I started looking my sister's hair and wondered if hair would catch on fire if it was lit. I knew I shouldn't try this, but I couldn't stop wondering about it and moved toward her quietly. I lit the lighter and put it to her hair. It started burning and she started screaming. My mother came running from the bathroom and grabbed a towel and started putting out the fire on her hair. The smell was awful and I realized that I had done something really bad. While my mother was calming my sister, my sister told my mother that I had been behind her."

Doyle's described feeling response: "I knew I was in trouble and I felt awful for doing this. When it was happening, I had felt excited while watching it burn. But when she started screaming, I felt fearful of my mother, and guilty for doing something I knew was bad. I felt afraid of what my mother would do to me. I thought she would punish me. Then I felt extremely afraid."

Doyle's described physical symptom response: "I felt anxious in my stomach, like butterflies. I felt really hot and started sweating. I felt nervous, like trembling, then shaking all over. It was like total panic. My whole body was in trouble."

Doyle's described behavior response: "I ran out the kitchen door and ran for the field. I ran toward the area where the bees were kept. We had this beekeeping area way past the cow field, fenced in with lots of bee-boxes for collecting honey. The bees were everywhere, but I knew if I was very still and stayed quiet, they might not attack me. I had seen my father wear special clothing to go in there and collect the honey. I went in there behind him one day and the bees didn't bite me because I was very still. Even my father didn't know I was behind him, but when he finally saw me, he told me to never do that again. I figured that I could go in there and that my mother would not come after me in there. I figured that no one would, except my father who would not be home until dinner. So I stayed in there with the bees all day, being quiet and still. I was afraid the whole time but more afraid to go home. I kept thinking about what I had done and felt bad that I had hurt my sister. I wondered what made me do it. I also felt good about being able to stay in the bee pen, even though I was afraid. Finally, I was so tired, and I went home. When I got there, my mother and father were waiting. They had been looking for me and my father asked why I had done this. I told him that I didn't mean to do it and that it was an accident. But I knew it had not been an accident and that I did it on purpose. My mother took my lighter away from me. I watched her put it into a drawer. I felt bad about what I had done, but worse about her taking the lighter. I don't remember any more punishment. Later, after I thought she had forgotten about it, I got the lighter out of the drawer and hid it."

As a result of Doyle's disclosure, he began to reveal other episodes of similar behavior that continued to evolve after this episode. In one incident, he ran into a bull pen to hide, knowing that no one would follow him there. He was almost killed by the bull before he could escape. His curiosity continued to result in behavior that created problematic situations that in turn generated escape into dangerous areas for self-protection. He admitted to feeling a powerful compelling impulse to act when curious about something, and a "thrill" sensation while attempting a dangerous and even harmful action to satisfy his curiosity. Despite the knowledge of potential harm and consequences, he was more compelled to act than to resist the impulse. He said that he knew the difference between right and wrong and felt bad afterwards, but continued this behavior. Fire was often involved. He began collecting lighters.

The collection of lighters is a good example of how an object can become significant after it has been involved in the episode that is registered as memory in relation to an extreme experience. Doyle continued to collect lighters and today has an extensive collection.

Obsession with the object that is significant in an extreme event, and is included in the vivid recollection of the event, is not unusual. For example, the weapon of choice used in criminal activity usually evolves from an initial experience with the weapon. "Good luck" objects associated with arousal experiences, such as winning or success, and objects associated with security (such as blankets, dolls, money, and a multitude of others) stem from experiences of this nature. Obsessive collecting or hoarding of the "seed" object used during the experience is a common practice in relation to this dynamic. If the object is a central component involved in the experience, it will become a necessary factor in the development of the behavior pattern. In some cases, the person becomes obsessed with the object itself and develops a preoccupation with acquisition of similar objects.

In Doyle's case, collecting lighters became a hobby, while he advanced his skill with electrical tools in working with potentially explosive energies. As his pattern developed, he became increasingly fascinated with light, fire, electricity, voltage, and electric shock. As he learned more about electricity, he became more curious about working with it in its most dangerous capacity. At first, he hid this behavior as much as possible and lied to cover up when he did something wrong or had an accident. Then, one day at school, he volunteered to fix an electrical problem for his teacher, did so, and was praised for helping her. This pivotal episode opened a new and socially-accepted avenue for him to enact his behavior. He continued to be praised for his ability to help with electrical problems at school and at home. He was quiet and well-behaved and generally accepted by his peers and teachers. His dangerous experimentation with electricity continued in secret, but became less necessary when dangerous jobs began to become available in an accepted context, and with the added benefit of praise and reward. His identity began to intrinsically develop in relation to his abilities in this area.

By adolescence, his pattern of high risk behavior was beginning to affect his level of security. He began to fear his own behavior and the risks he continued to take. Despite his growing anxiety, danger produced excitement, thrill, praise, identity, and what he later described as a feeling of power and superiority. In his mid-teens, he discovered that alcohol gave him a sense of peace and well-being that initially reduced his need to act on his impulses. He said, "right from the start, I felt less alone and more content when inebriated." His skill and ability incorporated into his chosen trade developed rapidly during this period as he concentrated on the fundamentals of his profession. Dangerous risk continued to be hidden and enacted sporadically.

By young adulthood, he was a skilled electrician and began working for independent contractors, and then a company that contracted State projects. He was valued not only for his expertise but for his willingness to take on dangerous assignments. His ability to work on outdoor electrical problems in the worst weather conditions resulted in continual travel, to a variety of locations, for weeks at a time. He was paid well by his company and hired on a permanent basis.

When Doyle described himself as a "troubleshooter," valued by his company for "heroic actions," it was evident that he took pride in this role. He appeared more animated and even excited when describing situations that depended on his seemingly fearless behavior. His reputation among fellow workers was built on willingness to do jobs they would refuse. He was also known for not using a live-voltage detector. He admitted feeling pressure to "perform" in relation to his reputation, and increased fear that accumulated risk would eventually result in disaster or death. Despite fears, he continued to experience "thrill and excitement" during the actual danger period of the job. He stated that it was only afterward that he would get "shaky" and "need something to relax."

Doyle was alcohol dependent by his mid-twenties, but he said his drinking did not interfere with his work at that time. It would be several more years before he began drinking "before a job" or "to do the job" rather than afterwards. By then, alcohol was no longer producing a feeling of well-being, but was necessary for anxiety reduction. Anxiety manifested itself in physical symptoms that were generated during the increased life-risk demands of his job. But, he said, he could not stop working. His quiet, self-contained behavior limited social interaction and activity beyond his changing work environment. His growing dependence on alcohol and the transient nature of his life limited relationship opportunities.

When Doyle was "pursued" by the opposite sex, the pleasant and likeable aspects of his personality came forth enough to result in a series of temporary relationships. The constant traveling and long periods of solitary activity made it difficult for him be consistent in a relationship. His reserved and introverted manner did not help. He did manage to have one long-term girlfriend, but admitted feeling uncomfortable in this relationship. He said he felt confined, despite his desire to be intimate with her and to have a companion. He described work as a "temporary escape" from this confinement, but said he felt lonely when away from her, which contributed to his drinking. His girlfriend became frustrated with his lack of investment, lack of communication and lack of commitment. When she ended the relationship, his drinking escalated. His first entry into addiction treatment was an effort to win her back.

After treatment, Doyle had difficulty achieving successful recovery despite his desire to live a "normal" life. He described feeling so anxious and frustrated during his first attempt to remain sober that he "gave up." He said he felt "alone" in group situations because he had "nothing to do," except to be social, which he described as frustrating. He spent most of his time at meetings trying to "be still" and not call attention to himself. He said his impulse to drink became overwhelming. His employer had given him paid-leave time to enter treatment and begin the process of recovery, but he said, "I had to get back to work." And as soon as he did, he quit attending meetings and was "relieved to be out of those situations." When he resumed work, he resumed drinking.

During the HRIPTM process, Doyle identified behaviors that had become well-established patterns prior to the onset of addiction to alcohol. These included: life endangerment involving electricity, voltage, fire, lightening, shock and other similar dynamics, escape for self-protection, avoidance of punishment and avoidance of disapproval, escape into a dangerous situation or location where no one might follow, and extended-time periods in those places and situations (for example, many hours, for a child, is a long time! During the initial pivotal episode, Doyle stayed in the beekeeping area all day).

Beginning with the initial experience, during the extended period spent in the bee "danger zone," Doyle developed the ability to discipline his body. He had to be quiet and still to remain safe in the dangerous situation. The time-extension factor (how long he could stay in a dangerous situation) continued, and was later evident in his life-risk and withdrawal patterns. Non-verbal self-recrimination and self-reproach diminished his self-regard. Self-contained, solitary, introverted behaviors inhibited intimacy and connection with others and reduced his ability to relax in social situations without alcohol. He collected the object related to the initial episode, despite guilt feelings associated with the experience. Rebellion, deception, secretive behavior developed to support his identified patterns. Life risk patterns also developed in relation to identity and approval.

These patterns of behavior began before his addiction to alcohol and were originally constructed to relieve Doyle's extreme negative emotional state, and to satisfy his desire for excitement and exhilaration; but they became major factors in his initial reliance on alcohol, a major contributor to his addiction relapses, and pose a high risk threat to his current recovery process.

With full acceptance of this knowledge, Doyle collaborated with clinical staff to develop positive alternative behavioral strategies to compete with these patterns. He re-evaluated his occupation in recognition of the risk factors associated with his profession; he was referred to Vocational Rehabilitation Services where he was aided in re-planning his professional direction. After a period of evaluation and assessment, he entered training for a position as an instructor in an electrical training program where he would be teaching others about his trade and the dangers associated with electrical work. Doyle's identity was so connected with his abilities that it was an advantage to re-direct him into a position where his skill and knowledge could benefit others, while increasing his social interaction and self-esteem. This path was also chosen to bring about more consistency in his life and relationships.

Doyle increased his recovery potential with the help of Vocational Rehabilitation Services while continuing to address his addiction in AA.

When a person reveals information that helps the therapist/clinician to grasp the web of behaviors that can weave so insidiously from childhood to adulthood, compassion for that person is stirred and increased effort toward the case is inspired. When one considers Doyle, who was such a bright, inquisitive and courageous child, who also developed patterns of behavior that robbed him of his health, relationships, positive self-regard and almost of his life, it is easy to see the myriad of potential pitfalls that he faces in his sincere attempt to achieve successful recovery. When relapse risk is viewed from this perspective, it can be seen clearly and then addressed in its full complexity.

Notes

1. Levy, S. (May 2, 1994) "Annals of Science: Dr. Edelman's Brain." *The New Yorker*.
2. Darwin, C. (1964)(1859). *On the Origin of Species*. Ed. Ernst Mayr. Facsimile of 1st ed. Cambridge, Mass: Harvard University Press.
3. Edelman, G.M., Tononi, G., & Sporns, O. (1996, April 16). "A Complexity Measure for Selective Matching of Signals by the Brain." *National Academy of Science 93* (8), 3422-7. Medline: San Diego, CA: The Neuroscience Institute.
4. Edelman, G.M., Friston, K.S., Tonini, G., Reek, G.N. Jr., Sporns, O. (1994, March). "Value Dependent Selection in the Brain: Simulation in the Synthetic Neural Model." *Neuroscience 59* (2), 229-243.
5. Levy, *op. cit.*
6. Weiner, J. (1994). *The Beak of the Finch: A Story of Evolution in Our Time*, pp. 38-40. New York: Alfred A. Knopf.
7. *Ibid.*
8. Darwin, C. (1975). *Charles Darwin's Natural Selection*. Ed. R.C. Stauffer. Cambridge, U.K.: Cambridge University Press.
9. Weiner, *op. cit.*
10. Thomas, H. & Thomas, D.L. (1946). *Living Biographies of Great Scientists*, pp. 134, 136, 145. Garden City, New York: Blue Ribbon Books.
11. *Ibid.*
12. *Ibid.*
13. Stone, I. (1980). *The Origin: A Biographical Novel of Charles Darwin*, pp. 58, 91, 612-613. Garden City, New York: Doubleday & Company, Inc.
14. Thomas & Thomas, *op. cit.*
15. Stone, *op. cit.*
16. Thomas & Thomas, *op. cit.*
17. *Ibid.*
18. Stone, *op. cit.*
19. *Ibid.*

In the resignation and disciplined subservience that she had inherited from a century of forbears a change had come about: she was sure now that injustice could not last much longer, and that if God was no more, some other Force would assuredly spring up and avenge the downtrodden.[1]

The Germinal
— Emile Zola, 1932

When a child has an experience that produces an extreme emotional/physiological state, behavioral action works to reduce the intensity of the state. But in the aftermath, problems stemming from the experience may not be resolved. Behavior is the temporary solution to a condition that is produced by the experience. Behavior is repeated when dynamics surrounding the initial experience continue to occur. Problematic behavior develops by repetition in an evolutionary manner that is related more to emotional and physiological regulation than to decisive action. The child, in a sense, enacts the behavior to address an ongoing condition. This is not necessarily a conscious or intentional process. Repetition can also be influenced by the unresolved nature of the experience. In some cases, the child develops an intention and determination to change the outcome of something related to the experience that remains unresolved.

In cases involving experiences characterized by injustice, abuse, deprivation, loss, abandonment, humiliation, unfairness, confinement, powerlessness, or deception, the child may develop a pattern that is a determined effort to change the outcome by seeking vindication, safety, acquisition, security, revenge, freedom, power, deliverance, truth and/ or justice. The behavior pattern that evolves, whether positive or calamitous, is driven by an all-consuming and often fearless determination. Behavior that stems from this determination can begin directly after the experience and may go on for years, or it may emerge years later in relation to an event that is similar. For example, consider the life of the French novelist, Emile Zola (1840-1902), who took on the French military establishment single-handedly to defend a Jewish officer accused of espionage. It occurred to Henry James, who met the young Zola twice (first through his mentor Flaubert, and then years later in London when he was a guest of the Lord Mayor), that it was as if "nothing had happened to him in life but to write 'Les Rougon-Macquart.[2]'" The later championing of Dreyfus, James felt, was "the act of a man with arrears of personal history to make up. . . treating itself at last to a luxury of experience."

Zola did not simply wake up, late in life, to fight one of the great cases of injustice, personally leading a campaign on behalf of Dreyfus at the risk of criminal proceedings for defamation of the army and exile. There was one experience in his past history that would have fueled just such a battle for the vindication of someone he believed to be innocent. When Emile Zola was 7 years old, his father died. A Venetian engineer, he had made possible a reliable source of water for the city of Aix-en-Provence, where his family lived. Upon his death, a fraudulently contrived bankruptcy deprived his widow and son of their inheritance. The father's name was ruined.

The power of a pivotal experience to change or alter the course of one's life can spill over onto others'. In Zola's case, he saved the life of an innocent man. Whether fighting injustice or seeking revenge, behaviors stemming from pivotal experiences can change a child's destiny and influence the destiny of others in remarkable and sometimes extraordinary ways.

In his autobiography, *The Journal of John Woolman and a Plea for the Poor,* John Woolman described his effective work with the Indians and his active opposition of slavery. A great 18th century colonial Quaker and writer, his gentle conduct, courage and fortitude in the face of opposition (at a time when many Quakers were slave owners), are a testament to his legacy. His influence within his own group eventually extended to other groups and influenced a change in views about slavery. Through his own example, he helped his fellow Quakers look within for the truth in this matter. Their example of coming to terms with the cruelty and injustice of slavery set in motion a method of reevaluating rationalized beliefs in light of awakened insights.

Woolman recognized early on that hasty words of judgment, criticism and blame produce nothing but fierce resistance. An entry in his journal, in which he describes "a remarkable circumstance that occurred in my childhood," may explain how he developed his ability to rethink previous beliefs and actions into newly formed resolutions:

> On going to a neighbor's house, I saw on the way a robin sitting on her nest, and as I came near she went off; but having young ones, she flew about, and with many cries expressed her concern for them. I stood and threw stones at her, and one striking her she fell down dead. At first I was pleased with the exploit, but after a few minutes was seized with horror, at having, in a sportive way, killed an innocent creature while she was careful for her young. I beheld her lying dead, and thought those young ones, for which she was so careful, must now perish for want of their dam to nourish them. After some painful considerations on the subject, I climbed up the tree, took all the young birds, and killed them, supposing that better than to leave them to pine away and die miserably. In this case I believed that Scripture proverb was fulfilled, "The tender mercies of the wicked are cruel." I then went on my errand, and for some hours could think of little else but the cruelties I had committed, and was much troubled. Thus He whose tender mercies are all over his good works hath placed a principle in the human mind, which incites to exercise goodness towards every living creature; and this being singly attended to, people become tender-hearted and sympathizing; but when frequently and totally rejected, the mind becomes shut up in a contrary disposition.[3]

John Woolman's experience changed his way of thinking. The behavior that developed from his childhood experience was driven by a determination to be merciful and just, and to influence others to rethink rationalized laws that were unjust and cruel. Just as Woolman's experience led to a life-long effort to influence change through his own powerfully quiet example, the following is an example of a tragic childhood experience that led to a life-long obsession to solve a mystery.

Critically acclaimed novelist James Ellroy began talking about his experience in a series of interviews that he began to give in 1995. In a televised chat with Diane Sawyer, Ellroy described his troubled life and how he came to be one of publishing's most successful authors of crime/mystery novels. (His credits include *L.A. Confidential* and *American Tabloid*, named 1995s best novel by *Time*.) In the course of the interview, he related two incidents that occurred during his childhood which he credited as the driving force in his writing, and in his current obsession with investigating the death of his mother.

> It was my tenth birthday, June 22nd, 1958. I can still recall even the smell of my mother, the cigarettes and bourbon, her sitting in the chair — calling me to her — telling me I had to make a choice between her or my father. When, disgusted by her, her drinking, her behavior, I stated that I chose my father, she slapped me. I made up my mind, at that moment, I would never allow her to slap me again. I remember the feelings of hate and disgust I felt towards and for her. Three weeks later she was murdered!
>
> I recall standing in front of the house. The detectives showing me the snapshots, then telling me that my mother had been murdered. She had been last seen alive in a low-life nightclub/bar, in the company of a blonde woman and a swarthy man. I remember feeling tremendous guilt for the hate-filled feelings I had for her at her death. But most of all I recall feeling fear — a terror that I would end up just like her; end up an alcoholic. . . she died in such a pathetic fashion.
>
> I went to live with my father, but began stealing, shoplifting, breaking into houses, eventually taking dope, using drugs, until living a crummy, slummy, promiscuous, alcoholic, low-rent life existence. I was arrested forty times and still felt terrified, but somehow, deep down, I never blamed anyone.
>
> Somehow, I managed to get sober and with pen and paper began to transfer the life I had lived and my knowledge of this lifestyle onto paper. I sold my first manuscript for $30,000. For sixteen years, I've been writing crime novels.[4]

Ellroy's books are set in his mother's L.A., 1950's world. His mother, Jean Ellroy, was strangled in 1958. His wife commented during the interview that she felt the presence of a "very real mother-in-law," so powerful was her presence in Ellroy's mind. For 36 years, until recently, he had not visited his mother's grave because of "fear." Then, after writing one hundred crime stories, he returned to his mother's crime scene. With the help of the Los Angeles Police Department, he re-opened her "unsolved" case. Ellroy said he felt pain as he tried to recount the strangulation of his mother. He is in the process of trying to find the blonde woman and swarthy man that were last seen with her. He said he always tried to paint over his mother's murder in his fiction. He believes that the facts of her murder may finally set him free, and states that even though he is sober, until this is resolved, he will not find peace. His wife concluded, "Maybe then he'll start writing 'feel good' books instead of 'feel bad' books."

Since that interview, Ellroy's success and reputation have grown. The film adaptation of *L.A. Confidential* won two Oscars, and his compelling autobiography, *My Dark Places: An L.A. Crime Memoir*, won critical acclaim. The *Sunday Times* reviewer wrote: "Ellroy writes as if driven by demons. His brutal, staccato graffiti tips over into art." In *My Dark Places*, Ellroy looks back to his own youth to investigate the central mystery behind his mother's death. His unrelenting self-examination addresses his obsession with violence against women, homicide, and crime. The *New York Times* called it a "strenuously involving book. . . . Early on, Mr. Ellroy makes a promise to his dead mother that seems maudlin at first, 'I want to give you breath.' He describes how the murder turned an already angry boy into an angrier, violent adolescent. 'I was a terrified as a kid. I broke into houses, spent time in jail. . . . I was always frightened, I was never a tough guy. Every wild thing I did was tinged with alcohol and drug-addicted self-loathing and a large degree of fear.' He later turned his obsessions into increasingly brilliant novels about crime and then became equally obsessed with reopening the investigation of his mother's death."

When asked in a later interview about the cathartic value of the investigation (despite its still open status), and if he had come to grips with his past, Ellroy replied,

> It's true, and I feel very calm and poised underneath it all, but no less passionate or committed to the work. I won't go soft on you, but I feel calm inside. It's not a catharsis in that I can say, 'OK, now this is over with,' but my mother and I will continue on some level that I haven't determined yet. I think my mother's a great character, and I have to say that giving my mother to the world was the biggest thrill of my writing career. It was interesting to write directly about what things meant to me. . . . Here I can say flat out, "This made me, this formed me, this is what I thought about this, this is how I view the world."[5]

Zola's fight against injustice, Woolman's effort to influence change and Ellroy's attempt to solve a mystery have the common ground of early pivotal experience that leads to fierce determination. The following case provides an example of a child who was equally determined to fight intrusion and invasion of her body and to protect herself from harm. The unique aspect of this case is how one of the physical symptoms generated during her experience was incorporated into a behavioral action that worked effectively as a means of self-protection. In her determined effort to protect herself from invasion by remaining pure, purifying herself and by purging, Sarah presents an example of a suffering child who found a way to survive an ongoing dysfunctional and threatening situation in her own obsessively peculiar way.

Case Summary: Sarah

Sarah, a 46-year-old married white female, was voluntarily readmitted for treatment after relapsing to prescription drug abuse. Her admission followed a confrontation by her family physician informing her that the FBI had begun an investigation on her for doctor-shopping for her pain medication. She evasively reported being confused about her medications and said she had been uncertain about what she had taken and not taken. She reported that she may have been overusing her medication to deal with fear and pain. She had been diagnosed with breast cancer that was treated surgically and with chemotherapy and had been in remission for approximately 3 years. She had bilateral mastectomies, spine disease and chronic pain. She had done well while in the hospital but then had difficulty when she returned home, feeling loneliness, fear and lack of support from her husband. She lived at home with her husband in a conflictual relationship; he did not feel she should be on any medication. She had completed intensive outpatient addiction treatment three months prior to current admission. At that time she was in good shape and the medications she was not supposed to be taking were thrown away.

After admission to inpatient hospitalization, Sarah was stabilized. Phenobarbital was used for detoxification. Other medications were continued twice a day for pain. She was then admitted into the intensive outpatient program for a period of eight weeks. Upon review of admission data, many relapse risk factors had already been identified;

chronic pain, family stressors, family history of alcoholism, and post traumatic distress conditions related to an early abusive environment. Sarah had repeatedly relapsed to prescription drug abuse and had been hospitalized numerous times since her cancer diagnosis. She was currently being investigated for drug shopping and was apparently capable of the necessary mobility and mental functioning to carry out this behavior, despite her impairments. She expressed desire for addiction recovery and expressed anger regarding lack of family support. She was told that her cancer was still in remission when she was medically discharged and admitted into the intensive outpatient program.

During Sarah's first week in treatment, her primary concern was to meet with her physician at his office within the facility after each group session. Her initial participation was repeatedly interrupted due to this preoccupation and other setbacks concerning her prescribed medications. Sarah was once again stabilized and strongly encouraged by her physician to focus on substance abuse treatment. She continued to complain that her medication did not relieve her pain sufficiently, but she did appear to be trying to follow his directives.

During the second week of treatment, a pharmacist reported to Sarah's physician that she had tried to obtain pain medication from his drugstore. The physician and the treatment staff conducted an immediate intervention meeting with Sarah. When discussion centered on the possibility of placing her in a restrictive environment, she protested that she was trying very hard, despite appearances, and pleaded for another chance. Rather than discharge her from the program, it was decided that she would be re-instated after signing a treatment contract stipulating strict adherence to all physician/treatment directives, including active AA attendance.

Sarah is an example of a patient who can create many challenges. She suffers chronic pain, needs some level of medication, does not present criteria for inpatient hospitalization and has multiple diagnoses. These considerations were addressed before she resumed treatment participation.

Sarah is small in stature and appears rather fragile. She was very well-groomed and tidy. She looked older than her 46 years; due more to her bearing than her physical appearance. Her dress was tasteful and conservative. She was careful with her hair and makeup, which was also conservative. Her manner was timid and reserved. She walked slowly, just short of a shuffle. Her posture was slightly stooped and she appeared downtrodden. Her features were pleasant and her expression sad, verging on an over-all pathetic demeanor and affect; yet there was a noticeable underlying alertness. She was watchful in her gaze and listened attentively to her peers as if assessing each person while drawing them to her. She responded with compliments and gratitude to each person who gave her an encouraging word. She had a sense of humor. She was not offended by the language or the behavior of other patients. She gravitated toward group members that were flamboyant and rebellious in conduct. She managed to win the confidence and friendship of most of her group, except those who were more self-focused. She appeared to enjoy lively discussion, despite her continued expressed fear of dying, fear of pain and fear of cancer. Her ability to draw people to her, rather than put them off, lay in her ability to generate pathos rather than simply appear pathetic. She made those who were not feeling good about themselves feel needed and important. She was less effective with those who were less vulnerable to this need. For example, her inability to make this work with her family was her greatest frustration.

During the first week after she re-entered treatment, Sarah addressed current problems in process and meditation groups. Primary focus centered on her health concerns, fear of cancer and death. She discussed her initial treatment problem, explaining that her recovery process had been continually sabotaged by constant pain, lack of family understanding, and the extreme fear she experienced every day. Her disclosure and feedback continued in this vein. Although she expressed belief in God and espoused "deep and abiding" spiritual faith, she didn't seem to be able to apply her faith to dealing with her condition. She did receive lots of sympathy from her group peers.

During Sarah's first week of active participation, she revealed that she had been feeling persistent feelings of guilt, shame, anger, fear, worthlessness, worry and sadness since early childhood. This was not surprising, since she initially reported that she had been raised in an abusive home. She said her father verbally and physically abused her mother and that he created a terrifying family environment. Her consistent responses to presented situations indicated that much of her fear during childhood was in relation to her own safety. She described constant feelings of deprivation and insecurity, particularly regarding the future. When describing anger, she used the terms "angry, mad, fury and furious" in response to various presented situations. The physical symptoms she associated with these identified feelings were stomach distress, nausea, pain and crying.

Sarah's disclosure while participating in the "behavior row" (where group members disclose how they think they would respond to a presented situation) were also revealing, and often surprised her peers. In response to situations involving any form of intrusion, abuse and/or threatening behavior, she described patterns of self-protection that began in early childhood that included hiding alone or with her siblings, hiding outside in places where she could watch what was going on inside the house, hiding inside the house in places where she could watch what was going on in other rooms, and constant vigilance for any sign of danger. She described her response to injustice, or to witnessing harm to others, as active hatred, silence, withdrawal and self-deprivation as a form of retaliation. Sarah reported retaliatory planning and action as early as age 6. She would often retaliate by depriving herself of food. Retaliation also involved secretive observation of the person with whom she was angry. She described one event in which, after hearing her mother screaming, she climbed on a chair to watch through the transom of her parents' bedroom door. Barely able to peer through the high window, with her younger sister holding the chair below, she witnessed her father violently sexually abusing her mother. She said she was traumatized by the blood and his instrument of torture, but continued to watch helplessly.

Her disclosure revealed a pattern of stealing as early as age 5. Stealing occurred in relation to hunger and deprivation. She reported stealing from her uncle's garden (he lived next door) while hiding in a secret place in her backyard; a place where she could also watch the house. She said there was never enough food and she and her sisters were often hungry. She consistently reported adventurous behavior in relation to fear and deprivation. This was always done in secret. In front of others, she enacted timid, shy and sickly behavior. She said she was sick much of the time during childhood, but also revealed a pattern of quiet rebellious behavior that was well developed by age 7. Rebellion and retaliation were disguised with an outward appearance of shyness and fragility.

When Sarah disclosed her responses to the presented situations, she would often appear animated and physically changed. This was most apparent when she described retaliation behaviors. The change was so remarkable that group peers were amazed at the transformation in her manner and body language. When describing rebellious actions, she appeared strong and her posture became almost upright. Her facial expression appeared determined and stubborn. When describing vengeful actions, she seemed almost healthy, and spoke with an air of vindication.

Sarah's disclosure in group and written assignments led to her decision to volunteer as focus of group. Her lifespan charts revealed that she had been molested by her father. It was interesting that much of her lifespan chart was written in vague terms concerning the abusive home environment. There was one episode, however, that she wrote about in great detail. It happened at school during Sarah's first grade year.

In Sarah's first grade classroom, there was a girl sitting in front of her who had a pack of crayons. Sarah had none. She described this package of crayons as "beautiful." She wrote, "I wanted them, and I took them!" She described feeling awful about it, but took them anyway — when she thought she would not be seen. The girl suspected Sarah and told the teacher. The crayons were found in Sarah's desk. She was reprimanded and spanked in front of the class. Sarah described feeling hurt, embarrassed and sad. She wrote, "I never forgot it — the shame I brought on myself. It stayed with me all my life and I still think about it all the time." She continued, "I wonder who still thinks of what I did. Every time I see crayons, I think of this."

After a review of her lifespan chart, she was asked if she had quit stealing after this incident. She looked down at the floor, shook her head from side to side and quietly replied, "No." During group process, she admitted that she began stealing when deprived of food. She said she felt compelled to steal the crayons, despite feeling bad about it and knowing it was wrong. The reprimand and humiliation in front of the class did not stop the behavior. She developed better ways to steal without getting caught or being suspected. This pattern was triggered by feelings of deprivation that continued throughout her childhood, diminished during her years of marriage, motherhood and work, and increased after she was diagnosed with cancer and became drug-dependent.

Sarah was scheduled to be the focus of group during her seventh week of treatment. She said that the following experience happened when she was age 6, and that it changed her life forever. She said she was never the same afterward, and that she thinks of this episode at least once a week since it occurred. Her disclosure began with a brief background of her family and environment.

"My father was a hypocrite. He was a respected member of his church and held a position there. In public, especially at church, my sisters and I were expected to be well-behaved. I used to think that if they only knew how bad it was at home, they wouldn't let him in the church. But we knew better than to say anything. We were always on our best behavior outside the home. We were taught to be mannerly, quiet and polite. We were always afraid. At home, he was mean. I tried to stay out of his way. One day, I was trying to get dressed for school. My mother wasn't there. I can't remember why. My father said he would help me. I remember thinking that this was odd. He never helped me with anything. Instead, he started touching me where he shouldn't have. I knew he was not supposed to be touching me there."

Sarah's described feeling response: "I felt, trapped, terrified and angry. I felt ashamed and defiled."

Sarah's described physical response: "I felt nauseated and frozen, unable to move. The nausea began to get worse and I felt pressure in my chest. I started throwing up. Tears came to my eyes and my whole body was trembling. I threw up all over him."

Sarah's described behavior response: "When I started throwing up, he backed away. He began yelling at me and I thought he was going to hit me. I grabbed my stomach and fell to the floor crying. He kept acting mean, but left the room. He was covered with vomit. I had to clean myself and the floor. I was so ashamed. I became so sick that I couldn't go to school. I was sick to my stomach all day. I was left alone. I cried and wished everything would go away. Whenever I was alone with him after that, I would get sick. My father would tell people I was a 'sickly child.' I did everything I could to stay out of his way. One day, he took me in the car and bought me an ice cream cone. I wouldn't eat it. I continued to behave well in public, but I became sick more easily. I didn't like to miss school or I would have been sick more. I often went to school feeling sick."

When Sarah reviewed her pattern of getting sick, she acknowledged that she could easily induce vomiting. She recalled planning to vomit on her father if he ever came close to her again. When she had gotten sick during her father's intrusive behavior that day, it had proved to be an effective means of protecting herself from further intrusion. Fear of another attempt on his part was ever-present. Being sick kept her safe. At school, she was given additional attention and sympathy when she became sick. She also felt safer at school and wanted to do well there. Her one mistake with the crayons had been devastating, because she was caught stealing in a place that provided her some measure of security. She said she could not afford to get into trouble at school again. When people felt sorry for her, she was less likely to be treated harshly.

Sarah said she deprived herself of food when she seemed to be getting healthy. She also deprived herself of food to get back at her father. Food deprivation helped to give her the fragile appearance she began to associate with safety and kindness. She did, however, steal food to eat in private and later would induce vomiting to rid her body of what she had eaten. She also stated that she felt purified when she vomited. Purification became a means of reducing shame and guilt. Her patterns of self-induced sickness, control of food intake and deprivation, stealing, hiding and secretive behavior were well-developed by adolescence.

Rebellion and retaliation were also enacted through this self-harming pattern. Overt rebellion would have resulted in punishment and disapproval. Her covert retaliation actions enabled her to control anger and continue the socially acceptable behavior that helped her thrive at school. Her anger and resentment increased significantly when her parents divorced and her father remarried. She wrote that she "wanted to die" when this happened, and felt "left out, jealous, unloved and very guilty." Her behavioral response to this was to cry, become sick, withdraw and pray, and she still manage to do well at school.

By adolescence she had a well-developed pattern of hyper-vigilant behavior that enabled her to be alert to her environment while maintaining the outward appearance of propriety and even piety. Her piety developed from her pattern of praying. Praying developed from earlier attempts to non-verbally comfort herself. Other internal mental action behaviors began in early childhood when she felt threatened. For example, in her lifespan chart and journal assignments, she writes about "wishing, wanting and hoping" for security, love and happiness during her childhood. Her later descriptions are the same except that she replaces wishing with prayer. Piety became another form of self-protection from intrusion. She wrote; "I decided to keep myself pure for marriage, and I did."

Praying became her primary source of self-comfort. While positive in many respects, her approach to prayer was more wishful thinking than spiritually internalized. During adolescence, she continued to control purification of her body and did remain "pure and chaste" for marriage. She continued to do well in school and began to plan for a future in this environment. She described feeling less guilty when she could keep her body pure. She described adolescence as being hard because, she wrote, "Not only did we (referring to her sisters) have to stay away from our parents, we had to watch out for our bodies."

Sarah wrote that she was determined to be a "clean, decent young lady" when she got married. She became a school teacher and married a man she "loved dearly." She had two children and taught school for over 20 years. Information provided by her family indicated that she was considered a good mother and wife, and that she had an excellent record as a teacher. Although plagued with many minor ailments, she maintained her health well enough to manage her home life and profession. During these years, she suffered the loss of her two sisters (her only siblings) to cancer. Then, she was diagnosed with cancer.

Cancer was the ultimate invasion of her body — an invasion she could not repel or deflect. She could not protect herself or "purify" herself of this condition. When her doctors told her that the cancer had been successfully treated, she began to live in fear of another "attack." Medication helped her cope with what she described as constant worry, fear and pain. She began to abuse prescribed medications from the beginning of her cancer treatment. Medication abuse and depression increased as her obsession with cancer began to create distance between Sarah and her husband and children. The initial support they provided, upon which she had relied, began to diminish. Her husband found it increasingly difficult to cope with her behavior. Sarah began to feel deprived of support and love.

After multiple hospitalizations and repeated relapse, Sarah's relationship with her husband and children disintegrated. Her dependence on the hospital and treatment systems was much like her dependence on the school system. She was adept at visiting several doctors and obtained hundreds of illegal prescriptions. Once her drug-shopping was identified, she was frustrated in her attempts to regain the trust of her physicians and pharmacists. As a result, she became more determined and covertly rebellious. When she was caught again, after treatment admission, she realized that she could no longer manipulate the system; her doctor was wise to her behavior and the FBI was not going to drop the investigation. As a result, her approach to treatment changed and her behavior, while still suspect, became more appropriate.

Sarah's progress began when she tried to approach treatment more honestly. Prior to discharge into continuing care, she was once again diagnosed with cancer. Her worst fear realized seemed to bring forth in her an attitude of compliance and temporary surrender. With determination, she collaborated with staff on a behavioral plan that included a commitment to address her condition without deception or rebellion. Honest disclosure was her most predominant area of change during treatment. Her efforts to identify her most self-harming and deceptive patterns of behavior took courage and fortitude. Sarah's efforts were also recognized by her husband and children. Her relationship with them improved significantly. With their regained support, Sarah faced her grim prognosis with courage. It might be said that Sarah had been courageous most of her life, despite her obsessive, secretly defiant and self-harming approach to self-protection. When her final efforts failed to prevent the intrusion of her body she had battled against all her life, she did the best she could to achieve recovery under the circumstances and continued to attend AA when possible. During the remaining year she lived, she dealt with cancer in a different way, with the support of her family and physician and support from her recovery network.

Note: Had Sarah not been diagnosed with cancer, the prospect of its recurrence would have been the greatest challenge to her recovery.

Notes

1. Zola, E. (1954). *Germinal*, p. 493. (L. Tancock, Trans.). London, England: Penguin Books.
2. Strickland, G. (June 4, 1995). "The Accuser. New York Times Review on Brown, F. (1995)." *Zola: A life*. New York: Farrar, Straus & Giroux. (Emil Zola's (1871-1893) *Les Rougon-Maquart,* his great family saga, appeared in a series of novels intended to follow out scientifically the effects of hereditary and environment on one family, and is the chief monument of the French Naturalist Movement).
3. Woolman, J. (1971). *The Journal of John Woolman and a Plea for the Poor*. USA: Peter Smith.
4. Sawyer, D. (April 1995). Interview for *Prime Time Live*.
5. *The Beatrice Interview*. (1996). Online/interviews/ellroy/ellroy96.html.

CHAPTER VII

A REPEATED REFRAIN:
THE RECURRING MEMORY OF AN EXPERIENCE

He glanced over his shoulder at the open door, where the shadow was still lingering and shivering; and with no conscious repugnance of the mind, yet with the tremor of the belly, he drew near the body of his victim. The human character had quite departed. Like a suit half-stuffed with bran, the limbs lay scattered, the trunk doubled, on the floor; and yet the thing repelled him. Although so dingy and inconsiderable to the eye, he feared it might have more significance to the touch. He took the body by the shoulders, and turned it on its back. It was strangely light and supple, and the limbs, as if they had been broken, fell into the oddest postures. The face was robbed of all expression; but it was as pale as wax, and shockingly smeared with blood about one temple. That was, for Markheim, the one displeasing circumstance. It carried him back, upon the instant, to a certain fair day in a fisher's village: a grey day, piping wind, a crowd upon the street, the blare of brasses, the booming of drums, the nasal voice of a ballad-singer; and a boy going to and fro, buried overhead in the crowd and divided between interest and fear, until, coming out upon the chief place of concourse, he beheld a booth and a great screen with pictures, dismally designed, garishly colored: *Brownrigg* with her apprentice; the *Mannings* with their murdered guest; *Weare* in the death-grip of *Thurtell*; and a score besides of famous crimes. The thing was clear as an illusion; he was once again that little boy; he was looking once again, and with the same sense of physical revolt, at the vile pictures; he was still stunned by the thumping of the drums. A bar of that day's music returned upon his memory; and at that, for the first time, a qualm came over him, a breath of nausea, a sudden weakness of the joints, which he must instantly resist and conquer.[1]

Markheim
— Robert Louis Stevenson

Why are most of our past experiences naturally and regularly relegated to the unconscious as time passes, while others remain accessible to the conscious, sometimes arising spontaneously in our thoughts without provocation? The link between accessible memory and novel experience may be the key to understanding this phenomenon, and it may begin within the first year of life.

In recent years, psychologists have isolated the portion of the brain that responds to novelty. The hippocampus (named after the Greek word for seahorse, which this part of the brain resembles in shape) has been shown to be critical in memory formation. Naturally, an animal could not survive if it were incapable of registering which part of the environment has already been explored or learning from experience those areas inhabited by predators. To do this the animal must first form a memory of its exploration and this task is performed by the hippocampus. Experiments suggest that the hippocampus is necessary for information to be registered. Considerations of reward or punishment do not enter into this; instead, hippocampal function is closely related to the search for novelty and recording information related to survival of novel experiences.

If their hippocampus is destroyed, laboratory animals will return monotonously to areas of the cage where they have already visited, while ignoring unexplored portions of their environment. EEG recordings of the mice or rats in question demonstrate that the greatest discharge rate occurs during large-scale exploratory excursions into completely new environments. In addition, neurophysiological techniques such as single cell recordings of the hippocampus have enabled psychologists to isolate novelty, rather than reward, as the factor that "turns on" the hippocampus to form a memory.

In humans, fully conscious memory does not emerge until 7 to 10 months of age, when the hippocampus is almost fully formed and frontal lobe activity is being "turned on" by the baby's new and ever-changing sensory experiences. By late in the first year, a baby is learning from experience and recording information in relation to those experiences. When children are able to refer to previous events, they have achieved a conscious remembrance of things past. It was not long ago that scientists believed that children could not recall anything prior to the age of three. They now know that memories can be recalled from much earlier, when novel experience is involved.

Edelman[2] assures us that the mind of every individual is unprecedented. The recipe book of the genes does not enable us to predict prenatal patterns, and in any case, after the moment of birth, every single sensory event and every internal thought has a physical impact on one's neuronal network. Thus, who we are is due as much to private history as to genetic destiny. Edelman maintains that the brain is not a computer but something more akin to a complex ecology, like that of a jungle. The dense interconnected tapestry of neurons is not a preordained construction but something that has evolved to cope effectively with *novel circumstances*. A computer program written before the fact would be unable to anticipate the multitude of situations that any organism faces. The outcome of neural development is decided not so much by the genes as by the developmental process that carries out the instruction of those genes. According to Edelman, patterns of connections between neurons are forged by the life we are fated to live — not hardwired, in advance, by genetic design.

According to Restak,[3] for over 25 years human behavior has been explained on the basis of incorrectly interpreted observations of rats and mice, spawning sophisticated rewards and aversion therapies which are spinoffs of operant conditioning experiments. Such explanations have never been satisfactory to anyone who has observed closely the factors that motivate human behavior. Modern advances in psychobiology have re-examined this behavioral paradigm that ignores the greater part of animal as well as human behavior.

Behavior is conditioned by factors far more complex than reward and punishment, particularly when it comes to what may appear to be irrational behavior. In the past, such puzzling behaviors have been written off by facile references to "unconscious processes," like a criminal "wanting to be caught," a "compulsion to confess," etc.. This, of course, provides a handy explanation for inexplicable behavior while at the same time doing away with any need to modify our views of peoples' responsibility.

Recent findings in brain research provide an underpinning for our intuition about the powerful influence that irrational forces appear to have in shaping our behavior and our lives. One brain scientist who has influenced this area is Dr. Paul MacLean, Director of Brain Evolution and Behavior at the National Institute of Mental Health. According to MacLean, the brain is somewhat like an archaeological site, with the outer layer composed of the most recent brain structure, the cerebral cortex, which is highly developed in primates and reaches its greatest level of complexity in humans. Deeper layers of the brain contain structures of our earlier evolutionary forbears, the reptiles and mammals. We are the possessors of a triune brain — not one but three, each with its own way of perceiving and responding to the world.[4]

In the last 25 years, brain scientists have refined their knowledge of the limbic system. Although it occupies only the lowest fifth of the brain, its influence on behavior is startlingly extensive, with all its parts tied bi-directionally to the hypothalamus. Brain and behavior experts have linked this interconnecting wheel arrangement to hormones, drives, temperature control, reward and punishment centers and one part of it, the hippocampus, to memory formation. There is, in fact, a reverberating cycle by which messages can make a full circuit through the five limbic system structures: hippocampus, mammilary body, anterior thalamus, angulate cortex and hypothalamus. Experiments in various animal species have demonstrated that profound alterations in behavior and emotional experiences can be brought about by altering the limbic system.[5]

Recent neuroscientific studies have indicated that early childhood experiences exert a dramatic and precise impact on the neural structure of the brain, physically determining how the intricate neural circuits are established at this peak time in brain development. At the most intense point of a pivotal experience, certain sensory elements (what the child sees, hears, touches, tastes, and/or smells) are captured and stored in memory as vital cues related to the experience. When new sensory stimuli imitates the central element cues of the recorded experience, the associated feelings and physical symptom components will be stimulated, triggering the associated behavior that, with repetition, becomes firmly entrenched in the neuronal structure of the brain.

Accessible memories related to this dynamic provide a window into an individual's early self-perception, perception of others, early influences and environment, and the pivotal experiences that hold vital information about present-day conditions. Memories that emerge spontaneously in the mind, at various times during a life, are the key to identifying the origin of some of the most ingrained patterns of behavior. When problematic and/or obsessive, these patterns can be as frustrating and mystifying to the person enacting them, as they can be to others who are also affected by them.

If we consider our own behavior in this regard, we might easily identify a problem behavior that has been resistant to change. But can we determine how and when it originated? When we cannot stop enacting a behavior that is personally unacceptable, our self-esteem can be negatively affected. We may then reevaluate the need to change and accept the behavior as a character flaw or a less-idealized version of self. But with repetition, our self-regard can continue to diminish, despite efforts to rationalize the undesirable habit.

Why are some behaviors easier to stop or change than others? Why do some patterns of behavior repeat and evolve while others disappear as we mature into adulthood? The answer may lie in memories that are with us occasionally and sometimes repeatedly throughout our lives. They not only hold important clues to the origin of our most habitual behavior, they can help bring about an understanding of self that can facilitate positive change.

During the HRIPTM research, it was determined that every vividly recalled accessible memory provided information that helped to explain the participant's current behavior. Each individual is unique in the experiences that he or she can recall. To dismiss a joyful memory as simply a positive reminder of a pleasant event and focus only on traumatic memories, giving them more value in relation to a problematic condition, is to ignore the fundamental reason for the presence of a memory. The HRIPTM cases consistently demonstrated the significance of each memory (positive or negative) in understanding the current condition of the individual.

When a vivid memory of an experience, involving an intense or extreme emotional and physical response, is triggered by associated stimuli resembling the initial experience, the body, in variable degrees, experiences the same physical and emotional conditions related to that experience. What then propels the behavioral action is not the memory image alone, but the intensity level of the feeling/physical response that is once again generated. The associated behavior, constructed in relation to the initial episode, which has since evolved with each repetition, is recognized by the brain as the effective action related to a specific level of emotional/physical intensity. The compelling nature of behavior driven by this dynamic is the basis for obsessive and/or problematic conditions.

In a nationally televised interview with Barbara Walters in 1994, prior to his retirement at the end of one of the most successful careers in baseball, Nolan Ryan compared his career in sports to the scholastic careers of his siblings. His expression became serious as he began to relate an incident that he credits with altering the course of his life. He said he could remember the experience as if it were yesterday.

The episode occurred at school when he was in the second grade. He described himself as quiet and shy, and suffering from a speech problem. One day, he was sent to his older sister's third grade classroom with a note that was to excuse her from class. The teacher (he could still clearly remember her name) insisted that he enter the classroom and read the note in front of the class. He stuttered in his attempt, and the children in the classroom began to laugh. He was instructed to continue reading aloud until he could successfully read the note. After what seemed like an eternity of humiliation, with repeated attempts and repeated failures, he crumpled the note in his hand and threw it to the floor. He ran from the classroom, the school and the school grounds until he reached the neighborhood park, where he threw a baseball at a tree long into the evening until his anger subsided. He said, "I never cared about school again, since that day."

One incident — and yet the memory arose in his thoughts during a question about education and sports. The emotional pain was still evident as Ryan described the experience in vivid detail. For a man who, throughout his baseball career, seldom gave interviews and was known to be reluctant to share personal information, his revealing disclosure was all the more touching. In Ryan's case, the behavior that was enacted brought him fame and success. He was known to practice relentlessly from dawn to dusk, just as he had that day in the park. Many players half his age wondered at his stamina. He was also known to be a very private and self-contained man. Throughout his career, he rarely gave interviews to the press, until at the close of his long career (while every baseball fan in the country was wishing him well and congratulating him on his extraordinary achievements), he agreed to the interview with Walters, and shared with the country, the pivotal experience that shaped his life. It is interesting to note that Nolan Ryan, shown practicing his pitching with his wife — a large tree in the background — is currently the star of a commercial about arthritis medication.

Behavior constructed to relieve extreme distress does not always result in a pattern that leads to success. For example, a child who throws a rock instead of a baseball and finds some level of relief, will enact the behavior just as relentlessly but with far different results. If the behavior constructed during the experience produces negative consequences and shame and guilt with each repetition, the child's path in life will be much more difficult. But whether the child finds success or failure, behavior patterns stemming from this dynamic create vulnerability because they become infused with the child's core sense of self. A child who becomes reliant on behavior that provides emotional/ physiological stabilization is dependent on behavior that can dominate and alter many areas of the child's development, particularly the development of positive self-esteem.

Studies indicate, for example, that people with high self-esteem often behave quite differently from those with low self-esteem. Research findings indicate that high self-esteem is generally associated with active and comfortable social involvement, whereas low self-esteem is a depressing and debilitating state (Coopersmith, 1967; Rosenberg 1979; Wylie, 1979).[6] Compared with those having low self-esteem, children, teenagers, and adults with higher self-esteem are socially at ease and popular with their peers. They are more confident of their own opinions and judgments and expect they will be more well-received and successful. They are more vigorous and assertive in their social relations, more ambitious and more academically successful. During their school years, those with higher self-esteem participate more in extra-curricular activities, are elected more frequently to leadership roles, show greater interest in public affairs, and have higher occupational aspirations. On psychiatric examinations and psychological tests, they appear healthier, better adjusted and relatively free of symptoms. Adults with high self-esteem experience less stress following the death of a spouse and cope with the resulting problems more effectively (Johnson, Lund & Diamond 1986).[7]

People with low self-esteem present quite a different picture. They tend to be socially anxious and ineffective. They view interpersonal relationships as threatening, feel less positively toward others, and are easily hurt by criticism. Lacking confidence in their own judgment and opinions, they yield more readily in the face of opposition. They expect others to reject them and their ideas and have little faith in their ability to achieve. In school, they set lower goals for themselves, are less successful academically, less active in the classroom, and in extra-curricular activities and are less popular. People with lower self-esteem appear more depressed and express more feelings of unhappiness and discouragement. They more frequently manifest symptoms of anxiety, poor adjustment, and psychosomatic illness.

These contrasts have been noted in studies comparing naturally occurring groups of people who report high or low self-esteem. There is some controversy over whether self-esteem causes these behavior differences, or vice-versa. Scientific evidence, however, is beginning to point to the former (Michener, DeLamater, & Schwartz).[8] This is most evident in relation to pivotal experience. When behavior that is spontaneously constructed to achieve emotional/physical stabilization has problematic characteristics, the child's self- esteem can deteriorate if the behavior repeats and subsequently develops in contrast to, or conflict with, parental and/or societal norms and expectations. This evolving dynamic can also have a direct impact on how the child thrives in his/her environment, and increase emotional vulnerability as the child moves toward adolescence.

Many people suffering chronic addiction describe their first experience with a mood-altering substance as a change from feeling nervous, anxious, self-conscious, fearful, intimidated, awkward and/or inadequate, to feeling "normal." What makes the desire formood-altering substances so compelling is its ability to alter an internal condition that is deficient; for example, its ability to alleviate anxiety or enhance confidence. Those who live in a self that becomes increasingly intolerable, and who suffer an internal condition that becomes (for that child, adolescent or adult) increasingly impossible to regulate, are those most susceptible to substance abuse from the first stage of experimentation.

In these cases, the person is more vulnerable to addiction onset and chronic substance abuse because any absence of the drug is a return to the condition that precipitated its use. It is this underlying condition that is so often unrecognized in the treatment of addiction. In cases where pre-addiction conditions of this nature are *not* present, sustained recovery is more likely because abstinence, in most cases, gradually brings about an improved condition, rather than a return to an intolerable condition.

Cassell addresses this point from a physician's perspective: "When the doctor first sees a patient, much of the illness has already occurred. Yet the facts of the past are as crucial to the clinician's tasks as the facts of the moment. The past must be known in order to recreate the interactions of persons and biology that are the process of the illness. The early symptoms, what happened in the body, the tempo of events, environmental circumstances, and what the person did or did not do now exist almost solely in the memory of the patient. To understand how the patient will behave, act, think, speak, care, and respond, the clinician must know the patient in the past. These facts of the past — 'the history' — are obtained by careful questioning, until what happened and how the patient responded to those events have been recreated within the clinician — until the clinician has experienced the patient's experience. Remember that knowledge and experience are always in a reciprocal relationship — clinicians find the erudition that allows them to make sense of the patient's experiences in their general knowledge of the world, their medical knowledge, and in their knowledge of themselves."[9]

There is often concern that therapeutic processes that address the past are counter-productive because they "trigger" memories that produce emotional upheaval. In some respect, this is true. There are some group or individual session approaches that are not structured to effectively address painful memories. However, if a memory can surface during a therapeutic or group process, it can also be triggered by associated stimuli outside the process. To assume that these memories will remain dormant unless brought to the surface in group or individual therapy is not realistic.

During the course of the HRIPTM research it became evident that the most productive way to elicit information about past experiences held in accessible memory is through a structured approach that focuses on identifying feelings and physical symptoms that are reported to be creating internal distress. The Orchestration Group Process within the HRIPTM* provides a forum for focusing on a person's foremost and current most intolerable and excitable feeling states and associated physical symptoms. When a patient describes these feelings and symptoms, memories often emerge naturally and without provocation. The participant is then expected to record this information in written exercise in preparation for addressing this recalled experience with an investigative and objective approach that is taught within the group structure. The only memories that are addressed are those that are accessibly present. There is no probing for memories that do not arise naturally during the process. During the development of this structured, systematic group process, it became evident that if memory surfaces while describing current problematic states, memory could also occur any time those symptoms were generated outside the process.

* described in Introduction and Prelude

A memory, whether it is stored in the accessible pre-conscious (not yet surfaced), or is surfacing repeatedly in consciousness, represents the central core of a significant experience associated with a specific set of feelings, physical symptoms and resulting behavior. The most basic misconception about the concept of memory is that the images that emerge in consciousness (the vivid center of memory recall) are the disruptive element, when in reality, it is the feelings, physical symptoms and behavioral components that so disruptively churn around the central core memory, which in a sense, is like "the eye of the storm." Whether joyful or sorrowful, stored vivid details that emerge in the mind as memory, represent experiences that created a state or level of intensity that was recognized by the brain as significant. Details representing these pivotal experiences are retained in such a way that, when accessed, they contain vital information about the development and behavior of each individual.

Memories remain accessible for a reason. Memory holds the key to understanding the link between experience and behavior. Obsessive behavior born of childhood experience can begin early and last a lifetime. It can fuel great success and also great failure. It can direct the course of one's life and sabotage it in the process. And, it can function like an illness that may or may not manifest itself in disease, but has the potential to manifest itself in chronic suffering.

Case Summary: William

William, a 51-year-old, married, financially successful land developer, entered treatment for alcohol dependence. He reported a long history of drinking, usually on a daily basis with increased times on weekends. After a previous treatment and an extended period of sobriety, he experienced a relapse. He had been having problems with relapse in his efforts to stay sober for about 7 years. Throughout this 7-year period, his degree of commitment to sobriety fluctuated. He said he drank regularly for most of his adult life. He had attended Alcoholics Anonymous six years previously but did not maintain regular attendance. His reason for entering treatment was that he got drunk in front of his 12-year-old daughter.

During his initial participation, William followed all treatment directives and exhibited cooperative behavior. His manner of speaking was intelligent and articulate. Imposing in stature, he appeared keenly aware of his size in relation to others, as evidenced by his careful approach to his position in the room and within the group. Diffident and polite, he also exhibited caution and hesitation in his responses. He remained distant from most of his treatment peers.

Within the first week of treatment, there was indication that William had a certain level intolerance for others in response to inconsiderate, tardy, immoderate or even slightly inappropriate behavior. While making no verbal comment regarding these actions, his reaction was apparent in his stern facial expression and rigid, tense physical demeanor. His eyes revealed a subtle critical gaze, which when directed at the unsuspecting offender, made its meaning known. He felt less discomfort during group process when order and structure dominated the situation. He described feelings of intense agitation in relation to closed rooms and confined situations. He stated that he felt more comfortable alone and mentioned his desire to "hibernate." He described social situations as anxiety-producing and stated that he felt tense and frustrated when forced into social activities beyond his control. He also resisted disclosure beyond his well-prepared statements. He described feelings of intense discomfort in relation to any form of intrusion or disruption of his plans.

During the course of treatment, William began to reveal feeling and physical symptom responses to a variety of presented situations. He responded intensely to any described experience of unfairness, injustice, embarrassment, humiliation and particularly public embarrassment. He became much more open to the process during these moments, forgetting to keep up his guard. He described his most consistent feeling response as "indignation" and "outrage." His disclosure became more spontaneous and revealing when he was responding to feelings that were triggered by listening to the experiences of his group peers. He also began to increase his peer interactions with those who had disclosed episodes that had produced these reactions.

As treatment progressed, William began to describe distinct and consistent responses to episodes related to injustice or embarrassment. When describing what he might do in response to presented situations, he consistently described how he would use strategies intended to divert the attention from what was occurring, followed by constructive planning to avoid or prevent future repetition of what had occurred. His most intolerable situation involved being the focal point of attention in an embarrassing social situation in which he or another person had been humiliated by his own unintentionally inappropriate behavior.

Because of William's efforts to address the feelings and behaviors revealed in group sessions, he was beginning to make progress. By the fourth week of treatment, he was prepared to share a memory of an experience that he described as present in his thoughts at least once a year, particularly during the time around Valentine's Day. The memory centered on an episode that occurred when he was in the 7th grade during a classroom Valentine's Day celebration. William began his disclosure with a brief background of his family life during his childhood.

William was raised during the mid-1950s. He described his childhood as typical of that era. He had been brought up to be well-behaved, polite and considerate. His parents considered manners "important." He then shared what he considered a significant and relevant earlier memory from age 5. He vividly recalled the intense fear, shame, remorse and bewilderment he felt after his first spanking. The situation occurred when he had not gone home immediately, when he heard his father calling for him, because he wanted to continue playing with his friends. When he did go home, he told a lie to cover up for his impulsive disobedience. He was not believed, because the lie was obvious, and he was spanked. He said he felt confused about why he had so "stupidly" ignored his father's command, and he became keenly aware that disobedience was not worth the hurt and humiliation he felt during and after this punishment. He described the feeling as intolerable.

After that episode, William said he made every effort to behave as his parents expected. By 7th grade, he was tall for his age and aware of his largeness in relation to his peers. He felt comfortable with his size and considered this to be an advantage. He felt comfortable with his peers and had many friends. But that year, something happened on Valentine's Day that changed everything.

William described the classroom and those present in some detail. He recalled the presence of "room mothers" who were working in the front of the classroom, helping the teacher with arrangements. Although everyone was seated at their desks, spirits were high and there was much teasing among the students about "who liked whom" in terms of "Valentine fondness." He remembered that it was a wintry day outside, "the door was closed; everything was closed up."

As the gaiety and teasing escalated, someone shouted that William's "Valentine" was a girl named Jane, who was almost his own size. William said he felt so embarrassed that he responded spontaneously, and just as loudly, by making a disparaging statement about Jane liking a boy who was considered objectionable by the classmates. Suddenly, the room became quiet. William described this moment with the phrase, "God descended and there was silence." Jane appeared humiliated. Her mother, who was there in the classroom working as a room mother, turned and stared at him in anger and disbelief. All eyes were focused on him.

William's described feeling response: "I felt stunned, embarrassed for making a fool of myself, and fear that this situation would be perpetuated. I felt intense self-loathing and guilt because I had hurt Jane. I felt hopelessness, humiliation, fear of my parents finding out, fear of their disappointment, alarmed, fear of what others would think, and fear of not being able to fix it. I felt horrified by what I had done, and stupid."

William's described physical symptom response: "I felt a deep blush, pounding heart, hot, outsized — excessive physical prominence, like a welling up of fullness, ringing in my ears with a steady high pitched reverberating tone, a sinking feeling in my lower chest and stomach, tightness and tension in my lower chest and stomach, like a struggle... trapped, a ringing pitch that lowers then crescendos, peaks, and then trails back down as agitation increases."

William's described behavior response: "I tried to deflect attention from what I said by shuffling things and trading candy. I tried to engage classmates in superficial activity. I tried to make myself less visible. I increased my expectations of myself and swore to never allow this to happen again."

According to William, his behavior significantly changed after this experience. He revealed that he has not, since that day, been comfortable in social situations. From that point on, he began planning and developing strategies prior to and during any situation that had potential for a similar incident. He felt confined and uncomfortable in closed rooms and closed social gatherings. As he grew increasingly hypervigilant in social situations, he became more inclined to be alone. He attributed his verbal mistake regarding Jane to stupidity and spontaneity. It became increasingly important for him to plan more effective strategies for social interactions. He worked to increase his intellectual knowledge and improve his verbal discourse by reading extensively during long periods of solitude. Instead of inspiring self-confidence, his self-expectations grew more demanding along with his expectations of others. He developed an intolerance for anyone who exhibited what he perceived to be ignorant, impulsive, inconsiderate, hurtful and undisciplined behavior. This intolerance, reflected in his attitude and demeanor, made it even more difficult for him to relate to most people. When forming new relationships, his choices were based on increasingly higher standards. His circle of loved ones and friends was confined to those who met these standards.

By young adulthood, William had well-developed patterns associated with the above described feelings and actions. His discipline and hard work led to success in his profession. His marriage to another successful professional placed him in a position where social activity became necessary. Alcohol helped him to relax in these situations. Alcohol also helped him to relax when he was alone. Alcohol dependence developed over the years.

William referred to his wife and two daughters as the center of his life. Despite this, his reclusive behavior and alcohol dependence contributed to his growing distance from his family. If he made any mistake, or felt disappointment in himself in relation to self-expectations, his level of frustration increased to an intolerable degree. He grew more impatient and was easily irritated. He was often caustic and verbally abusive. These actions produced guilt and anxiety, which he alleviated with alcohol and isolation from others. Any form of perceived disapproval or unfair judgment or criticism from others produced a state of rage that William found impossible to control. William viewed loss off control as unacceptable. His inability to maintain control of himself and others became, for him, increasingly unbearable.

It took many years for William to accept that he had a problem with alcohol. He made several unsuccessful attempts to stop drinking on his own. Marital, professional and family problems, related to his alcoholism, were the major factor in his decision to seek treatment the first time. His approach to recovery was sincere and motivated and he said he fully intended to remain sober. When he did not, he became increasingly frustrated, self-recriminatory and reclusive. When he re-entered treatment the second time, he recognized the need to address his behavior as a crucial risk factor to his recovery.

Through his participation in the HRIPTM, William identified behaviors that had developed into patterns prior to the onset of his alcohol dependence. He came to recognized the role of these patterns in his previous addiction relapse and potential relapse risk. The identified behaviors included forming unrealistic self-expectations, excessive planning to avoid social mistakes, hyper-vigilance, reclusiveness, avoidance, phobia in relation to confined spaces, closed rooms and closed social gatherings, and self-defeating verbal aggression that manifests itself in spontaneous bouts of criticism and verbal abuse.

William collaborated with clinical staff to design a plan of positive alternative behavioral action to develop alternative forms of verbal expression and to compete with reclusive and avoidance behaviors. He entered into private therapy to address his phobias and other identified issues. Although he made a commitment to attend AA regularly, there is risk that he will not maintain regular attendance. His sincere desire for recovery and a supportive family are strengths that will compete with his high risk level for relapse.

Note: William's case is a striking example of the power of one pivotal experience. While his earlier pivotal experience at age 5 is tremendously significant, the Valentine's Day episode produced a multitude of patterns that are the primary basis for his high-risk prognosis. His case also demonstrates how an intelligent, sensitive child can respond to an event that might have little effect on another child. William clearly exemplifies the individual nature of perception and response.

Notes

1. Wolf, L. (Ed.). (1995). "Markheim," p. 185. Short story in *The Essential Dr. Jekyll & Mr. Hyde: The Definitive Annotated Edition of Robert Louis Stevenson's Classic Novel. Including the complete novel by Robert Louis Stevenson and in Stevenson's Short Stories.* New York: Plume/Penguin Books.

2. Levy, S. (May 2, 1994) "Annals of Science: Dr. Edelman's Brain." *The New Yorker.*

3. Restak, R.M. (1979). *The Brain: The Last Frontier,* pp. 30-31. U.S.A.: Warner Books.

4. MacLean, P. (June, 1973). "A Triune Concept of the Brain and Behavior." *Zygon/Journal of Religion and Science,* (Vol. VIII) No. 2. University of Toronto Press.

5. *Ibid.*

6. Coopersmith, S. (1967). *The Antecedents of Self-esteem.* San Francisco: W.H. Freeman.
   Rosenberg, M. (1979). *Conceiving the Self.* New York: Basic Books.
   Wylie, R. C. (1979). *The Self-concept: Theory and Research on Selected Topics.* (Revised Ed.) (Vol. 2). Lincoln: University of Nebraska Press.

7. Johnson, K.J., Lund, D.A., & Dimond, M.F. (1986). "Stress and Self-esteem, and Coping During Bereavement Among the Elderly." *Social Psychology Quarterly,* 49, 273-279.

8. Michener, A., DeLameter, J., & Schwartz, H. (1990). "Self and Identity." *Social Psychology,* 2nd Ed.(4). U.S.A.: Harcourt , Brace & Jovanovitch.

9. Cassell, E.J. (1991). *The Nature of Suffering,* p. 266. New York: Oxford University Press.

I do not make films primarily for children. Call the child innocence.
The worst of us is not without innocence, although buried deeply it
might be. In my work, I try to reach and speak to that innocence.
— Walt Disney

Children may not be born with a need or desire for resolution. But from the time of birth, the need for security and attention can create in some children a perception that something is amiss, lacking or elusive. This perception, whether accurate or not, fosters a longing in the child that can be influenced by pivotal experiences that validate this perception. Behavior patterns that emerge from experiences that reinforce notions of deprivation, abandonment or any potential loss of security can be driven by an obsessive desire for resolution.

The research leading to development of the HRIPTM gathered hundreds of case interviews over the years from individuals suffering chronic conditions. Many of these cases reveal memories of uncanny early perceptions of children who felt they somehow did not belong, or were somehow different from their family. The nagging uncertainty that plagues a child who feels this way is not always apparent to parents or guardians. And even when it is, and the child is given reassurance or an explanation, the preconceived notion can persist. The most problematic outcome of this persistence develops when the child begins to rely on resolution-oriented behavior that effectively, but only temporarily, relieves the distress arising from this ongoing condition of insecurity. If the behavior develops throughout childhood into an obsessive pattern in adulthood, the underlying insecurity can be hidden under a facade of behavior that masks the fragile individual beneath. The following notable case exemplifies how even the most successful life can be riddled with insecurity, doubt and uncertainty in relation to this early perception.

Walt Disney was a creative genius who brought joy to children everywhere. Throughout his life, he suffered a recurrent nervous condition aggravated by the stress associated with building a commercial empire. His condition was also aggravated by intense personal doubt stemming from his suspicion, since childhood, that he had been adopted.[1]

Half a dozen times a year, even this long after his death, newspaper organizations telephone, or researchers visit, the archives at the Walt Disney Studio in Burbank, California to confirm stories they have been given about where and under what conditions Walt Disney was born. Some are convinced that they have discovered a skeleton in the Disney cupboard and that Walt Disney was in fact Spanish — and born out of wedlock. . . Stories about his Spanish birth have, in fact, now become so established that until recently a small town in the mountains behind Almeria, in southern Spain, actually posted a plaque on the road leading to the town square announcing: MOJACCA, Birthplace of Walt Disney.[2]

The story in Mojacca itself is that one of the village maidens, Consuela Suarez, became engaged at the turn of the century to a local boy who was killed in Morocco before they could be married. She was already pregnant when news of his death reached her. Thanks to the efforts of the local priest, the baby son Consuela subsequently bore was seen by an American couple who took him off to the United States, and Consuela presently followed. There she signed the papers that enabled her son to be formally adopted and made a U.S. citizen. Only when she came home to Mojacca to die did she reveal that her secret son was now named Walt Disney, the famous father of Mickey Mouse. However, the facts have been proven by the Disney Archives (one of whose functions is to prevent any word of untruth or scandal from being attached to the Disney name and reputation): Walter Elias Disney was indubitably a native American and that Chicago was where he first saw the light of day. His birth certificate, a copy of which can be obtained in Chicago, testifies to that.[3]

Biographer Marc Eliot[4] casts some doubt on Mosley's authorized biography and other previous biographies authorized by the Disney Studio in regard to information surrounding Disney's birth. Eliot spent four years researching the life of Walt Disney. His research and analysis are worth considering in terms of his view on the psychological and physiological impact this issue had on Disney. Whether Walt Disney was born in Chicago or Mojacca is not at issue here — the Disney organization continues to discredit Mojacca as Walt Disney's birthplace. But Eliot's investigation of this matter, which led him to revelatory documents acquired from the Federal Bureau of Investigation, explores intriguing information that sheds light on Disney's obsession with his birth. For example: In 1940, J. Edgar Hoover offered Disney the unlimited services of the FBI to help track down his personal past, in return for Walt's assistance in helping to secure the nation's future.[5]

Disney's concern about his past began in earnest when he attempted to join the army while still a minor. The army, skeptical of his age, requested that he produce a birth certificate. When Walt was informed by the Bureau of Records that no such birth certificate existed, he became greatly disturbed. As far back as he could remember, his father, Elias Disney, had been a patriarchal martinet who believed in excessive physical punishment to enforce discipline. Walt had fantasized, as a child, that his father treated him so badly because he didn't love him, and because Elias wasn't his real father. His worry began, as a boy, during a period when Elias inflicted intense and brutal punishment on Walt and his older brother Roy.

Eliot notes that after the two eldest brothers had had enough of farm life and left home, the burden of work fell to 8-year-old Walt and 16-year-old Roy. Elias used corporal punishment to enforce maximum productivity and thought nothing of taking a switch to his sons, or the fat part of his leather belt, to administer the "corrective" beatings that became a daily part of the boys' routine. At the slightest provocation, real or imagined, Elias would march Roy and Walt to the woodshed and dispense his brutal punishments. In the evenings, following a beating, Walt would often lie awake in bed, whimpering. Roy, older and physically stronger, was able to endure the punishments better than his little brother. He would rub Walt's hurts and rock him to sleep with promises that everything would be all right in the morning. Walt would bury his head in the bend of Roy's elbow and ask if the man who beat them was really his father, or just some mean old man who looked like him and wanted only to frighten and hurt him.

On the rare days he wasn't punished, Walt looked forward to that part of the evening when, after he had gone to bed, his mother would read fairytales to him in her soothing, expressive voice until he slipped gently into sleep. As reassuring as these visits were, Walt remained confused and frightened by Elias's terrifying violence and couldn't understand why his mother didn't stop the beatings.

Walt's father had purchased a forty-eight acre mixed fruit and stock farm in Marceline, Missouri, when Walt was five years old. Despite the hard work and punishment endured under his father's rule, Walt recalled this period as the happiest and most influential of his childhood. During those times, the thing Walt most liked to do was draw pictures. Because paper and pencils were rarely available, Walt improvised, usually with a piece of coal on toilet paper. That was all he needed to pass a free hour sketching the gentle farm animals he considered his only real friends. He later gave the reason why his earliest drawings were never preserved.

> You can guess what I did with them, especially as I ate a lot of green apples in those days," he said. "Anyway, that's all those drawings were really good for — and that's where they went, down the can. Childish scribbles, that's all. The only interesting thing is that I did them at all. I suppose I did them because just about everything around me at Marceline excited me. Even the chores with the birds. Feeding them every day, I got familiar with the shapes and the habits of ducks, chickens, and pigeons. I can't remember I ever made a real pet of any of them, though I did learn their language, and I think they learned to understand me. What I mean is they'd come over when I summoned them by name. There was one pullet I called Martha, who used to come over when I shouted her name and lay an egg right in my hand.
>
> On the other hand, none of the birds meant as much to him as Porker, who became both a challenge and a close friend. "I used to horse around with her a lot," he said. "I guess I really loved that pig. She had an acute sense of fun and mischief, and when she wanted to be, she could be as naughty as a puppy and nimble as a ballet dancer. She liked to creep up, nudge me in the rear, and then sashay off, squealing with delight, especially if she tipped me over. Do you remember the Foolish Pig in *Three Little Pigs*? Porker was the model for him. I did the preliminary sketch from remembering Porker, and I was practically weeping with nostalgia by the time I had finished."[7]

The behavior of drawing, related to the intense feelings of excitement and exhilaration he experienced with animals, became essential to Walt and would not be deterred by lack of supplies, lack of time, lack of money, lack of encouragement, or even by Elias. Walt recalls an episode from his adolescence.

> For instance, I was only fifteen then but already knew I wanted to draw. But when I told my father, he just scoffed at me and said if I was foolish enough to want to become an artist, I should learn the violin; and then I could always get a job in a band if I was in need of money. He tore up my drawings, brought out his own violin, and forced me to saw and scrape at it for hours every day, although he must have known from the squawks I was making I was tone-deaf and would never be any good at music.

In 1917, America entered World War I. Following his brother Roy's example, Walt made up his mind that he too would enlist. When the local recruiter, skeptical of Walt's age, asked to see a birth certificate, Walt wrote to Chicago's Cook County Hall of Records requesting a copy. A week later, by return mail, he received an official-looking document stating that the Hall of Records had no birth certificate for any Walt Disney born on or around December 5, 1901. After several more official inquiries, Walt finally told his parents that he intended to enlist and that he needed a copy of his birth certificate. When they couldn't produce it, he showed them the information he received from the Department of Vital Statistics. Elias insisted it was all a terrible mistake, that of course his birth certificate existed, and he would see about getting a copy. All of this greatly disturbed Walt, whose childhood fantasies that his father couldn't have been his father now reverberated with a deeper, more ominous, resonance. Why wasn't there an accurate record of his birth? What secrets, if any, were his parents hiding from him? Would they ever tell him? Could he ever be sure what they said was the truth? The only thing he was certain of was that he wasn't certain of anything, except that he no longer felt he could trust his parents and never would again, from that time on. This infection of doubt would eat at Walt for the rest of his days, infusing his future films with a feverish passion that would deepen their dramatic themes.[8]

Throughout his twenties, with his brother Roy, Disney worked relentlessly in the face of extraordinary obstacles to establish the studio that would one day become an empire. A self-proclaimed father-figure to his employees, he often ruled with the same relentless expectation of work from his staff that his father exacted from his as a boy. Any form of dissent was felt to be betrayal. By 1931, at the age of 29, and married to his wife Lillian since 1925, he had repeatedly saved his studio from going under. The most recent battle for survival had resulted in the defection of his finest and most reliable animator and friend, Ub Iwercks. The previous year, Roy's wife Edna had given birth to a son, while Walt and Lillian remained childless. It was this gap in his family life, plus his bitterness over the defection, that added to his growing sense of inadequacy. He felt so disgusted with himself after the christening party for his nephew that there was one moment when he seriously contemplated committing suicide.[2] Thirty years later, in his late fifties, Disney reflected on this period in his life.

> I guess I was working too hard and worrying too much. In 1931 I had a nervous breakdown. Each picture we made cost more than we figured it would earn. First we began to panic. Then, I cracked up. I couldn't sleep. I reached the point when I couldn't even talk over the telephone without crying. I was in a highly emotional state.

Two years later, according to biographer Eliot, Walt's symptoms reappeared when he realized that he was about to become a father: Symptoms that had appeared previously during periodic bouts of nervousness and depression now increased dramatically. Privately he was stunned, having long believed that he was incapable of impregnating a woman. Throughout their marriage, Lillian had insisted on (and Walt had agreed) trying every treatment available to increase what had been diagnosed as an unusually low sperm count. The doctors' reports made no mention (if the doctors were even aware) of his problems with recurring bouts of impotence or whether that had anything to do with his apparent infertility. Among the curative treatments Walt submitted to were the packing of his genitals in ice for hours at a time and injections of liver extract directly into his thyroid gland.

When something finally worked and his wife's delivery date neared, Disney increased his already considerable drinking; his chronic cough worsened, and his smoking increased to three packs of cigarettes a day. In addition, his bouts with insomnia extended to weeks at a time, the facial tics and eye twitches from which he periodically suffered returned with renewed intensity, and he obsessively washed his hands several times an hour, every hour.

In December, 1936, Walt was in the final stages of completing his first animated full-length feature film, *Snow White and the Seven Dwarfs*. His studio's financial success was at stake; he had expanded his business and was concerned about staff dissent and rumors of union formation. He was 36 years old and he and Lillian (at her insistence) had just adopted a second daughter. The pressure to complete his film and assume the role of real-life father again caused Disney's nervous condition to flare up. He began staying away from home for days at a time. His facial tics returned, worse than ever, and his smoking went back up to three packs a day. His hair started falling out in clumps, and in one of the few trips he made outside the studio's front gates, he visited the same medical specialist who was treating Gary Cooper's hair-thinning problem.

Disney's classics, *Snow White* and *The Three Little Pigs*, were among the most complex and provocative films to come out of Hollywood, animated or otherwise. Disney's films were often unfettered picture-window views into his inner conflicts and emotions. At the time of the release of *The Three Little Pigs*, it was becoming increasingly apparent to a growing number of critics that Disney's insistence upon creating a perfect world in his films for children reflected nothing so much as what they suspected was his own nightmarish childhood. Eliot comments that while his filmed fairytales may have appeared, at first glance, to be light and dreamlike, upon closer inspection they seemed more nightmares of deconstructed reality in a league with the era's leading neo-Freudian Modernists.

Disney spent much of his adult life trying to discover the truth about his birth. He enlisted the aid of J. Edgar Hoover and intriguing but non-conclusive evidence emerged indicating a link between his father Elias and a Spanish woman named Senora Zamora. Once Disney discovered that he couldn't conclusively prove where, when or even to whom he was born, it was the *possibility* rather than the fact he was adopted or born out of wedlock that haunted him the rest of his life and shadowed many of the characters of his greatest films. Notably, there were the abandoned stepchild left in the woods in *Snow White*; the wooden puppet who longs to be Gepetto's real boy in *Pinocchio*; the forest creature who loses his mother and is separated from his father in *Bambi*; the apprentice in fearful servitude in *Fantasia's* "Sorcerer's Apprentice"; and the baby elephant separated from his real mother in *Dumbo*. Eliot observes that the theme of abandonment also emerges in many of Disney's lesser efforts, with the parentless leader of the Lost Boys in *Peter Pan*; Cinderella and her stepsisters; the homeless street animals in *The Lady and the Tramp*; the adopted dogs in *101 Dalmatians*; and the idealized father/son relationship between Jim Hawkins and Long John Silver in *Treasure Island*. What these films all have in common is their main characters' quests to find their real parents. Those who interfere with that quest, usually symbols of evil authority, complete a recurring dramatic metaphor in Disney's films for the internal struggle between moral conviction and doubt.

Walt Disney died December 15, 1966, at age 65. By the 1960s, Walt Disney Productions had paid off all its debts and had assets worth nearly $80 million in the bank. It was now one of the most prosperous entertainment organizations in the United States. But during all this time, Walt suffered greatly with physical pain and the stresses of running the still-growing Disney empire. One of his closest associates, Ward Kimball, recalls: "There were so many things going on that even Walt, with his historic attention to all details, however small, couldn't find time to cope with any more. Lord knows, he tried. He really was one of the last rugged individualists. . . . His genius was being spread too thin, and we all knew it. And then came the shocking blow: his lungs were being eaten away with incurable cancer. For half of his life, there had been those awful, hacking coughs from chain smoking. His doctors had continually warned him to give up cigarettes and maybe heavy drinking. . . . He was always in a bad temper at these times, and in the studio they began calling him The Wounded Bear. When he really got angry, he would flatten his adversary without a thought, no matter who he was. . . . I still contend," Ward Kimball said, "that the tension combined with trying to keep control of everything that was going on — even though Disney was twenty times bigger than when it started — plus cigarettes and booze made him like a time bomb waiting to go off. He may not have realized a fuse had been lit, but we did."[9]

To many children, Walt Disney's represented a strong, fatherly presence. He seemed to speak from the television or movie screen directly to children. He had a way of connecting with children and his life was a testament to this connection. In his adult life, he presented an image to the world that masked, not only the wounds he suffered as a child, but the emotional, physical and behavioral condition that sabo-taged his wellness in the midst of all his extraordinary success. He once said, "If all the world thought and acted like children, we'd never have any trouble. The only pity is, even kids have to grow up."

The great playwright Eugene O'Neill addressed how image can mask self-destruction. Two of his plays, *A Moon for the Misbegotten* and *A Long Day's Journey Into Night*" address ways in which suffering conditions can be hidden under layers of behavioral disguise. O'Neill's understand-ing of alcoholism is reflected in his work, but he also addresses how behavior that masks one's individual reality is not limited to alcoholics. This theme is unveiled in "individual acts" within the play in which the actors become involved in "acting" in response to one another. O'Neill's ultimate purpose is to reveal slowly and dramatically what is hidden beneath the convincing personas initially presented.

This same dynamic can be observed in individuals with chronic disorder conditions. Superficial realities are often displayed in routines of speech and attitude. Like the principal performers in a play in which they must maneuver their parts surreptitiously, behavior is the marker that creates the acceptable diagnostic illusion. The presented illusion that fits so well into the scheme of modern treatment can be far differ-ent from what lies beneath. Behavior can be misread because people can act entirely different from the way they feel. And, so can children! This is most striking when we listen to the descriptions of behavior people have enacted in response to intense feelings of insecurity, as recalled in vivid childhood recollections.

For example, consider a child who fears being abandoned by his parents, and who without intention, enacts a disobedient behavior that results in a temporary feeling of relief when he realizes that he was punished, rather than abandoned, for misbehavior. When the relief subsides and the fear of abandonment re-emerges to a highly intense degree, the disobedient behavior will be repeated to regain the tempo-rary feeling of security felt after the first episode, even at the expense of being punished. The parents might have difficulty understanding why the child is repeatedly disobedient. Consider another child who fears rejection, and who by pure chance, enacts a behavior that results in praise and a temporary feeling of approval and acceptance. When the relief subsides and the fear once again emerges, the behavior will be enacted to regain approval and acceptance. The child quickly develops a pattern of positive-appearing behavior that is necessary to prevent rejection and insecurity. The first example resulted in punishment; the second example resulted in praise. But both are equally potentially problematic in relation to the child's dependence on the behavior to feel secure. And both can mask the underlying insecurity felt by the child as each develops toward adulthood.

Treatment processes that ignore investigation into the accessible recollections of each individual, often rely on reported information about the individual, or observations of the individual that reflect behavioral facades that have developed since childhood to mask underlying conditions. Khantzian addresses this in his recently published collected works, *Treating Addictions as a Human Process*. He writes,

> I have said little up to this point specifically about character pathology, and yet we know that our patients most often are referred to as psychopaths, sociopaths, and antisocial characters. I believe these labels, so often used pejoratively, describe little that is meaningful or accurate about addicts. Perhaps such descriptions mostly indicate how little we understand character pathology. I suspect that as we study such problems, we shall gain a better appreciation of the relationship between various drive and affect states and the ways in which such states contribute to so-called character pathology and related behavioral disorders such as narcotic addiction. . . . As we more precisely identify such target symptoms and affect states, we shall be in a better position to decide on suitable forms and types of psychological and psychopharmacological interventions.[10]

In-depth investigation targeting symptoms and affect states can help to identify serious underlying conditions that might otherwise remain hidden within, or be understood only as the result of, a categorized disorder such as alcohol dependence. Investigation is often hampered by controversy about whether or not it is important to address the past, and by debate about addressing memories that may be too disturbing to reveal. But this disturbance may be the necessary factor in understanding and addressing chronic disorder conditions that are resistant to standardized methods of treatment.

When a patient in treatment for addiction performs in ways that seem to indicate progress, those who support that person feel hopeful and remain supportive. Expectations rely on the premise that the treatment provided will work for this person because it has worked for so many others. Different individuals are expected to respond the same way and in the same amount of time to the same methods of treatment. Without careful scrutiny, the patient with a complex condition might appear and behave like someone with a less complex condition. This is how a person maneuvers in a world in which fear and insecurity have been the driving factor since childhood. The mask of behavior is worn, not to trick, but to escape the critical light of scrutiny — scrutiny that might reveal a reality that seems too unbearable or shameful to face or to share with others.

Case Summary: Martha

Martha, a 41-year-old single, white, family practice physician, was admitted with suicidal thinking and a sense of utter hopelessness. She decided to "take herself to the emergency room," by calling an ambulance, rather than kill herself, which was her other thought. She said she had gone as long as she could trying to keep up with her responsibilities and no longer felt that it was worthwhile to do so. She described marked feelings of hopelessness and a sense that her life was meaningless. Part of this stemmed from her stated belief that, at age 41, she can no longer have the life she had dreamed of, which included a family and children. She has been single all her life. Her main supports were reported to be her elderly parents, both in their 80s, and one friend.

Martha had suffered increased depression over the course of several months since her discharge from treatment for alcoholism 10 months prior to current admission. Her symptoms also included impairment in her concentration, impaired sleep and continued loss of appetite with an estimated weight loss of 40 pounds. She described an inability to continue her work as a family practice physician, feeling overwhelmed by the responsibilities. She expressed the belief that she momentarily died on the way to the hospital, simply from lack of will to continue breathing. She meant this in the literal sense: she felt that she had expired, then "came back," and described making small noises with her respirations to let ambulance attendants know she was breathing.

She had been under psychiatric care over the course of three months prior to admission. She described the therapy as basically crisis-oriented, and said that her current admission was inevitable.

During her initial participation, after hospital stabilization and transfer into intensive outpatient treatment, Martha followed all directives. She had reconsidered her thoughts about leaving her medical practice and decided to reassume her position there after a period of leave. She expressed commitment to a plan of action that included reestablishing her recovery support network with additional support in keeping with treatment recommendations. She resumed active participation in Alcoholics Anonymous, obtained a sponsor and exhibited cooperative and motivated behavior.

Martha appeared slightly over-weight, despite a recent 40-lb weight loss. She dressed in trendy 60s revivalist clothing. She wore her hair long and wore long, hand-made earrings which she said were her "trademark." In keeping with this style, she wore no makeup. Her manner and affect were serious, concentrated, attentive and inquisitive. At times she appeared skeptical, cynical, amused and condescending. Her interactions with peers were restrained and minimal. Her response was pleasant and polite when approached by others, but she rarely initiated the conversation. Martha gave the impression that she preferred to remain somewhat aloof from members of her group. Her ability to form professional boundaries with patients was incorporated into her involvement with treatment peers. She approached staff members as she would professional colleagues.

During the first week of treatment, Martha revealed that she had become involved with a man she had met during her recent hospitalization. She explained that he had been discharged from the psychiatric unit after stabilization for depression and had resumed his position with a local theatrical company. She explained that he did not have a substance abuse problem and had just been going through a rough period in his life. She said they had been helpful to one another and had developed a bond very quickly. Martha's AA sponsor reminded her that the 12 Step program discourages new relationships during the first year of recovery. This view was reinforced in treatment, but to no avail. Martha insisted that her involvement with this man was the most positive thing she had experienced in years and she was determined to hold on to it. She argued that she was age 41, not 21, and would follow all directives but this one. Her resolve in this matter was stubborn and resistant.

She did exhibit active involvement in both AA and treatment. She arrived punctually, was prepared with completed homework assignments and engaged in disclosure and feedback during meditation and process groups. She addressed current issues surrounding work, finances, aging parents, and concerns about her relationship. She expressed belief in God and stated a need for spiritual connection. She admitted to having felt a void in this area for much of her life.

During the first week of treatment, Martha began describing consistent feeling responses to a variety of presented situations. Her most predominant responses centered around feelings of loneliness and fear. Fear came up in relation to loss and insecurity. Shame and guilt feelings were described in relation to feeling "different from others and set apart from others." She described feeling fear of disapproval and feelings of guilt associated with dishonesty and secrecy. A pervasive feeling of sadness was described in relation to loneliness, potential loss of love, security, family, position and approval. Anger was described in relation to feeling frustrated, powerless and overwhelmed. She associated feeling overwhelmed with hopelessness and despair. Physical symptoms related to these feelings were identified as impaired breathing, tightness in her stomach region and chest, heart palpitations, tension, nausea, anxiety, panic and exhaustion.

During the second week, Martha's response to a variety of presented situations revealed behaviors beginning in early childhood that included vigilant self-protection, negative recriminatory self-dialogue, withdrawal and isolation, skilled verbal expression and aggression enacted to self-protect, to manipulate and control others, and to argue with, defend against and to harm others. Self-harming actions included self-induced physical distress and verbal aggression at self. Self-contained behaviors included secretiveness, dishonesty, mental preoccupation with planning associated with achievement-oriented goals, objectives and high-expectation strategies. Self-punishment actions were described in response to disapproval, mistakes or failures, and criticism from others. Rebellion was described in response to authority and/or control. Isolation and withdrawal were described in relation to pressure and self-imposed expectations.

Martha's treatment progress appeared positive on the surface, but was jeopardized by her efforts to maintain control by resisting concerns about her determination to continue her relationship with the man she had met in the psychiatric unit. Group disclosure revealed that much of her emotional and physical distress revolved around fear of loss. Her parents were advanced in age and she had been fearing for some time that she would be left alone, unmarried and without children. She maintained her belief that she could have a new relationship, and at the same time, make progress in recovery. She argued that her improved health, appearance and motivation reflected the positive nature of her present situation, but this concern continued to be addressed in treatment and with her sponsor. At one point, she did acknowledge that she would be devastated if something were to happen to this relationship.

During the first phase of treatment, Martha avoided addressing adoption issues. In the fourth week, it became evident that early childhood perceptions surrounding her adoption were a contributing factor to her present condition. She said she felt guilty when addressing this issue because she had been raised by loving parents who provided her with every advantage. However, she admitted that intense or extreme insecurity had plagued her since early childhood. She said she was prepared to disclose as focus of group because there was one incident that occurred when she was between ages 4 and 5, that had been in her thoughts at least once a month since the time it happened. Martha began her disclosure with a brief background of her family and environment as it was at the time of the following episode.

Long before she reached the age of 4, Martha was told she was adopted. She knew that her older brother was also adopted. She described her adoptive parents as loving, kind and wonderful people. Her older brother was not "well-behaved" and often "caused problems in the family." She said she did not like him because he upset her parents and this caused her to worry about whether or not her parents would "keep them." She said she had worried about this persistently and could not recall a time when this feeling was not there. To "make up" for her brother's "bad" behavior, she tried to be well-behaved. One day she was complimented for her behavior by visiting relatives, and from then on, she said, she felt more secure when her positive behavior was affirmed by others.

Martha described her family home as lovely and comfortable, "I had a beautiful room and lots of nice things. I didn't play much with toys, but was very curious about books, learning to read and trying to prepare for the day I would go to school. My brother was already in school and he was having problems. I worried about this and wanted to do better than him. It was almost time for me to enter kindergarten when the episode occurred."

Martha's neighborhood was quiet, with few children. She did not play with her brother much because they were "not close, and he was in school." Most of her playtime was spent in the home or in her room, with her mother nearby. Sometimes she played in the yard surrounding their home. One day, she noticed a boy playing in the yard next door. He noticed her too and came into her yard. They were approximately the same age and began playing together. He said he was visiting his aunt. She said she was enjoying this new friendship immensely. They ended up playing behind a large hedge-like apple bush by the basement window. He suggested that they play "doctor." She said she was curious about this, and agreed. He pulled down his pants and then told her she would have to do the same, which she did.

Martha continued: "Then suddenly, from out of nowhere, it seemed, the boy's aunt appeared. She grabbed him by the arm and broke a switch from the bush. She began screaming and waving the switch at me. She called me a 'bad girl.' She screamed that I should 'go to jail' for what I had done. All the while, she held the boy's arm, but directed her anger, blame and threats at me. My mother came running from the house when she heard the screaming. The woman told her that I had been doing nasty things with her nephew and she did not want him ever to play with me again. Then, she dragged the boy away. My mother told me to go into the house and upstairs to my room. She said the matter would be discussed when my father came home from work and that she was expecting him soon."

Martha's described feeling response: "Shock and surprise, and intensely afraid. I felt frustrated and angry at the injustice and overwhelming unfairness. I felt guilty and afraid I would be taken to jail. I felt lonely, alone and hurt, but most of all, deeply ashamed."

Martha's described physical symptom response: "My breath caught when I breathed in and I could not breathe out. I began hyperventilating, shaking, crying; and my stomach was tied in knots. My heart was beating hard and I had palpitations and my face was hot."

Martha's described behavior response: "Inability to speak while hyperventilating, then pleading, apologizing, and complying by going up to my room for punishment. . . . followed by rebellion at myself for not defending myself, and harsh verbal self-criticism, comparing myself to other children who had not been given away by their real parents. I curled up in a fetal position to self-protect, hide, isolate-insulate. I kept biting my nails while waiting for punishment and disapproval. I began planning future cover-up and denial while waiting. Planned lying and denying began from then on. Avoidance and not trusting was planned from then on."

Martha described intense preoccupation beginning that day with securing her position in the family and avoiding mistakes. She said she was not able to eat after the incident, then began eating excessively after her parents appeared to forgive her and assured her that she would not be sent away. She said eating helped to calm her in the aftermath. She stayed near her parents and in the home for several weeks thereafter.

Martha identified insecurity as the basis for the persistent worry she felt prior to the episode she described. She identified the experience as the beginning of a more intensified state of insecurity that included feelings of loneliness, shame, guilt and anger that persisted through childhood and into adulthood, despite accumulated positive achievements.

When Martha started school, she was praised for being "smart" and "good." She described praise as essential to her daily functioning. She would "shrink in shame" at the least indication of disapproval or criticism, and "lived in fear of disappointing." At home, her efforts to be "good" were often sabotaged by "tantrums" she could not control. After a tantrum, she would "do anything" to make up for her outbursts, while secretly punishing herself and then comforting herself alone in her room. She interacted with others at school, but did not bond with classmates or peers, except for an occasional carefully chosen female friend. These friendships were often sabotaged by her "argumentative" behavior. She did achieve respect and admiration for her academic achievements.

By early adolescence, Martha had set a goal to become a professional. At some point during this period, she decided to become a physician, and began a course of intensified study to achieve this objective.

Her weight increased during her teen years. Overweight and self-conscious about her physical appearance, she did not date, but became increasingly temperamental and more reclusive. A scholarship to college and then medical school helped to increase her self-esteem and confidence. She began drinking in college and said it reduced anxiety, increased her ability to socialize and helped her to lose weight.

Martha dated sporadically during this period. She also began buying clothing that disguised her weight, and distracting jewelry that enhanced her appearance. A pattern of binge buying sprees and spending beyond her means began during this period. Her behavior was propelled by the fact that her "new look" worked. She was complimented on her appearance and began to attract male attention. However, the same dynamic that had sabotaged her relationships with female friends now sabotaged her relationships with the opposite sex. She said her relationships with men generated feelings of distrust, competition and worry about being abandoned. As a result, her anxiety and stress would increase to the point where she often instigated conflict that resulted in the relationship ending. But she said she continued to feel hopeful about meeting the "right life partner." Her plan was to complete medical school, begin her career, and then, once established, marry and have a family. She said her life would then be complete.

Martha remained close to her parents throughout these years, but a series of failed relationships, failed professional endeavors, professional and personal conflicts, decline in professional performance, increased dependence on alcohol, fluctuating periods of eating disorder, excessive spending and isolation led to the conditions and events that resulted in hospitalization and treatment.

Martha completed treatment and collaborated on an extensive, well-developed and structured continuing care plan that involves addressing each of her identified patterns with positive alternative actions and additional therapy. While she agreed that beginning a new relationship at this stage of her recovery was an added risk, she refused to consider an alternative and they began living together shortly thereafter. She stubbornly maintained that her efforts in all other areas of her recovery provided ways to address her identified risk factors. She attributed her "rebirth" of commitment to life and recovery to the "after life" episode she experienced in the ambulance prior to hospital admission. She described feeling a new sense of hope and vision toward the future. She continued her active involvement in AA and with her sponsor. She was accepted back into her group practice and began working on a part-time basis. She planned to maintain a limited schedule, despite financial concerns.

This all sounds good unless one considers the nature of her well-established patterns. These identified behaviors that developed into patterns prior to the onset of addiction include: binge eating, hoarding food, preoccupation with weight, nail-biting, self-recriminatory dialogue, skilled verbal aggression, rebellious tantrums, self-contained achievement- oriented behaviors outside the home, excessive efforts to please and secure position within the home; a focus on scholastic achievement to earn love, respect and position; conflictual relationships with others that involve attempts toward intimacy that increase pressure and anxiety, producing verbal criticisms and outbursts, despite her efforts to self-contain. Needless to say, these patterns contributed to repeated loss of relationships, and her unrealistic goals and self-expectations increased internal anxiety and pressure. These behaviors, along with reclusive withdrawal, procrastination, isolation when feeling overwhelmed, binge spending, self-abusive — self-harm ideation and self-harm actions that include holding her breath with intent to die when feeling overwhelmed and hopeless, were all originally constructed to relieve Martha's extreme negative emotional state, but now pose risk to her recovery process, relationships, health, occupation and lifestyle.

During treatment, Martha gained a sense of which specific feeling/ physical symptom responses trigger her most sabotaging patterns of behavior. She recognized her limited ability to cope with stressors that trigger these behaviors. She accepted that she needs to continue to develop positive alternative behavioral strategies to compete with identified patterns, and she agreed that her process of behavioral change requires a life-long commitment — but she remains at high risk and must be clinically considered so in an effort to address her condition with effective continuing care.

Notes

1. Eliot, M. (1993). *Walt Disney: Hollywood's Dark Prince*. New York: Carol Publishing Group.
2. Mosley, L. (1985-1990). *Disney's World*. Chelsea, M.I.: Scarborough House Publishers.
3. *Ibid.*
4. Eliot, *op. cit.*
5. *Ibid.*
6. Mosley, *op. cit.*
7. *Ibid.*
8. Eliot, *op. cit.*
9. Mosley, *op. cit.*
10. *Ibid.*
11. Khantzian, E.J. (1999). *Treating Addiction As A Human Process*, p.37. Northvale, New Jersey/London: Jason Aronson Inc.

CHAPTER IX

A DRAMATIC ARIA: INDIVIDUAL BEHAVIOR RESPONSE
EVOLVING FROM PIVOTAL CHILDHOOD RELATIONSHIPS

> The mere sight of his father who had hated him from his childhood, had been his enemy, his persecutor, and now his unnatural rival, was enough! A feeling of hatred came over him involuntarily, irresistibly, clouding his reason. It all surged up in one moment! It was an impulse of madness and insanity, but also an impulse of nature, irresistibly and unconsciously (like everything in nature) avenging the violation of its eternal laws.[1]
>
> *The Brothers Karamazov*
>
> — Dostoyevsky

Pivotal experiences involving the most important relationships in a child's life are profoundly influenced by the complexity of the relationship, particularly when ongoing dysfunction surrounds the experience. The child depends on the parent or guardian for security, protection and guidance throughout the developmental years. This dependency, when coupled with fear and insecurity within that dependency, creates a conflicting and confusing dynamic that sabotages healthy development and lays the groundwork for problematic behavior.

The following examples were chosen because they provide a historic window into lives that have been affected by fear and insecurity during the developmental process. The concluding case summary, taken from the HRIPTM research, represents one of the many documented vivid recollections of chronic patients who reported similar experiences. Many patients suffering chronic addiction and other behavioral disorders report family histories of alcoholism. Family dysfunction that includes physical, sexual and/or verbal abuse are highly represented in the early lives of many of these individuals. HRIPTM research findings noted the significance of early childhood perception in relation to these situations, and to situations where recognized abuse factors were *not* an issue but the child somehow developed a perception of threat or insecurity. The prevalence of arousal experiences that provide a means of solace, pleasure and escape from fear and insecurity will also be addressed in this chapter.

Ludwig von Beethoven is considered by many to be the greatest composer of all time; but his life was tragically unhappy, except for the joy he found in his music. Beethoven's grandfather was a famous court composer and musician; his father was an alcoholic. His mother was loving but she couldn't protect him from his father's control. His father abused him verbally and physically, and forced him to play piano from very early childhood, punishing him if he played poorly. Beethoven was sometimes locked in the basement. His father would often come home late and drunk; he would wake up Ludwig to play for his drunken friends. Despite this, Beethoven felt an exhilaration while playing, even in the midst of the suffering he endured at the hands of his father.

While another child might have rebelled against music and resisted practice, Beethoven played and obsessively practiced, and found in his music a joyous realm beyond his abusive environment. However, rebellion did emerge in relation to others. Increasingly isolated in practice, and influenced by his relationship with his father, an explosive temperamental pattern of behavior developed. This pattern evolved along with his musical skill and genius, sabotaging his social interactions, and later, his personal relationships throughout his life.

Beethoven's father wanted another Mozart. Mozart was the premier musician of this time period. Beethoven was a prodigy, but no Mozart. Yet something extraordinary was born in the passion he felt while playing. When he was still in his teens, he visited Mozart and played for him. Mozart predicted his greatness, but the two never met again. When Beethoven's mother died, he had to assume financial responsibility for his father and siblings. Beethoven was bitter and his disposition worsened after this event. He was often bad-tempered and subject to explosive outbursts. At the same time, he was also very sensitive, passionate and disciplined when it came to his music. This conflicting dynamic continued to escalate.

When Beethoven started going deaf, he invented ways of playing that helped him hear sound and vibration while trying to keep his deafness a secret. When he could no longer do this, he tried many unsuccessful cures. Finally, he fell into a state of despair and withdrew from the world for a while. Then, in the depths of his agony, he found another way to the joy he could only attain in his music, and he rose again through it as a composer. Of all the musical gifts he gave to the world, his "*Ode To Joy*" is perhaps his greatest testament to this experience.

In 1783, when Beethoven was eleven years of age, he wrote the following in a letter to the Prince Elector Max Friedrich:

> Most Illustrious!
>
> From my fourth year music started to become the foremost occupation of my youth. So early acquainted with the gracious Muse who tuned my soul to pure harmonies, I grew fond of her — and as methought ofttimes, she in turn grew fond of me. Now, I have reached already my eleventh year; and ever since during hours of solemn inspiration my muse did whisper ofttimes into my ears: "Try once to write down the harmonies of thy soul!" Eleven years of age — I mused — how would I look as an author, and how might the men of Art respond to it? I grew almost timid. My muse, however, commanded, — and I obeyed and wrote. . . .[2]

Experiences of this nature can alter the course of a child's life in a positive or negative direction, depending on the behavior associated with experience. Obsession that arises from need or desire to enact the behavior can also change life direction from a positive course to one of self-destruction. When conflicting dynamics and coexisting patterns of positive and negative characteristic develop and coincide, at certain points, one may outweigh the other and overwhelm the intention of the individual. Patterns that continue in this vein, to a dramatic and catalytic degree, produce an ongoing battle for emotional survival.

It may even appear that the battle is won if the seemingly positive patterns bring about achievement and recognition, so that the "good" outweighs the "bad." This outweighing is often facilitated by additional experiences that propel the positive dynamic. When success occurs, negatives can be rationalized more easily. People often overlook or make excuses for the problematic behavior of successful individuals. But the fluctuating nature of success can produce even more insecurity in the person who has come to rely on success to achieve some level of security. A healthy emotional foundation that has not been able to develop fully, and that remains vulnerable at the very core of the individual, does not suddenly grow stronger because one has achieved success. This person will be particularly vulnerable when additional stressors occur or accumulate. A slight shift or alteration in pressure can easily create an imbalance that triggers obsession in both the positive and negative patterns. Obsessive actions intensify when an effort to achieve functional balance is most needed.

Behavior that is constructed and repeated for relief of suffering and/or the replication of exhilaration can manifest as patterns that infiltrate the developmental process of a child and continue into adulthood. Because of the evolving nature of these patterns, they can appear at times as a phase that disappears only to reappear in a more developed manifestation. To understand exhilaration, consider the child who experiences ongoing suffering, and then by chance experiences an episode of pleasurable arousal that produces excitement, joy, happiness, ecstasy. This child will be strongly compelled to repeat the action that produced this feeling. Despite consequences, the child who is in most need of this feeling, is the child, and then adult, who will endure pain, punishment and even humiliation to feel this way again.

The great Russian writer Fyodor Dostoyevsky provides a striking example of this in his description of his experience before having an epileptic seizure. In 1867, writing to the critic Nikolai Stakhov, he explained:

> For a few moments before the fit, I experience a feeling of happiness such as it is quite impossible to imagine in a normal state and which other people have no idea of. I feel in harmony with myself and the whole world, and this feeling is so strange and so delightful that for a few seconds of such bliss one would gladly give up ten years of one's life, if not one's whole life.[3]

He later incorporated his experience into his Christ-like hero in *The Idiot* (the character with whom John Lennon identified). "In the moments before an attack (as his epileptic Prince Myshkin explains), his heart and body seem to wake up to vigor and light, and he was filled with joy and hope and ecstasy. There would be an instant of harmony and beauty to the highest degree. These instants were characterized by an intense quickening of the sense of personality."[4]

Hippocrates (460-380 B.C.) wrote that epilepsy was a brain disease, and that "pleasures, joys, laughter, and jests as well as sorrows, pain, griefs, and tears originate in the brain." But Dostoyevsky understood and wrote about the nature of extreme conditions. It may be said that he traveled the infinite orbit between heaven and hell with as much consciousness as rarely another poet and dramatist before and after him.[5]

Fyodor Mikhailovich Dostoyevsky was born October 30, 1821, in an apartment attached to the Hospital for the Poor in Moscow, where his father, who had previously been an army surgeon, was the attending physician. His father was described as a petty-minded man who ruled his family with rigorous discipline. Young Fyodor was noted for his irascible nature, slightly effeminate interests and strong attachment to his mother, who tried to protect her children from their father. Her early death left Fyodor and his siblings at the mercy of this unloving man.

Shortly thereafter, Fyodor and his older brother were sent to Army Engineering College. Here Fyodor's life was unbearable; his literary bent and artistic interests made him the scorn of his fellow students. A classmate reported that he "always held himself aloof, never took part in his comrades' amusements and usually sat in a corner with a book." His morbid self-consciousness was further aggravated by his father, who had retired to a disorderly life on his estate and refused to provide his son with a regular allowance. On one occasion, Dostoyevsky sent his father a letter reviling him for his neglect; before the elder Dostoyevsky was able to reply he was murdered by his serfs.[6]

His father, a member of the lower middle class, aspired to a more aristocratic title when he purchased his small estate in Tulsa Province. Little is known of how he treated his serfs on the estate; however, immediately following his death, the story circulated that the old man had been brutally murdered by the peasants. Naturally, the family did all it could to hush up the affair, but the suspicion lingered the older Dostoyevsky had indulged his propensity toward being a martinet as he reigned supreme on his estate, and the serfs had risen in anger and butchered their cruel taskmaster. It is interesting to note how close this is to the theme of the brutal patricide that dominates Dostoyevsky's last novel, *The Brothers Karamazov*.[7] It is a family tradition that the first of his epileptic seizures, from which Fyodor was to suffer throughout his life, occurred at this time.[8]

Following his examinations at the Engineering School, Dostoyevsky was made a second lieutenant. However, without "money to buy civilian clothes," he resigned his commission to devote himself to literature. His first novel, *Poor Folk* (1846), was highly praised and he was regarded as the most promising of the younger novelists. For the next two years he became part of a literary society and too hastily published some novels that were badly reviewed. His associations included a small group of young men stirred by revolutionary events in Western Europe. They regularly met to read censored books and discuss forbidden ideas. Some of them were fervent Socialists of the Utopian school. They formed no revolutionary plans, though they freely criticized the arbitrary measures of the government. In the discussion about serfdom, Fyodor always insisted that emancipation must come by the lawful path, by decree of the Tsar. As to Utopian communes, he declared that, to him, life in such a commune would be more terrible than in a Siberian prison.

On April 23, 1849, he was arrested with other members of his circle and confined in the Petropavlovsky prison. On the December 22nd of that year, the prisoners were led out to Semyonovsky Square, the death sentence was read to them, they were given the Cross to kiss, the dagger was broken over their heads, and the first three were stood up before the palisades for execution. Dostoyevsky was in the second group. Then, suddenly, "retreat was sounded, those bound were brought back, and it was read to us that his Imperial Majesty had granted us our lives." The Tsar had wished to teach the young men a lesson. One of them went insane. What Dostoyevsky experienced is indirectly recounted by a character in his novel, *The Idiot*:

> He said that those five minutes seemed to him to be a most interminable period. . . . He seemed to be living in these minutes so many lives that there was no need as yet to think of the last moment, so that he made several arrangements, dividing up the time into portions: one for saying farewell to his companions — two minutes for that; then a couple more for thinking over his own life and career and all about himself; and another minute for a last look around. . . . Having bade farewell, he embarked upon those two minutes which he had allotted to himself. . . . He wished to put it to himself as quickly and as clearly as possible, that here was he, a living, thinking man, and that in three minutes he would be nobody; or if somebody or something, then what and where?" He fixed his eyes on the gilded spire of the church, and could not tear them away from the ray of light. He got the idea that these rays were his new nature. But the

most dreadful thought of all was: "What if I should not die now? What an eternity of days would be mine!" And all this became such a burden on his brain that he could not endure it, wished they would shoot him quickly and be done with it.[9]

His four-year term in the Siberian forced-labor camp, plus several years in the Czar's semi-barbaric outpost, may have been a slightly better fate than death, but an execution that was carried out all except for the final shots of the firing squad had a horrifying effect on Dostoyevsky and his comrades. The Czar's cruel joke, coupled with the notorious filth, vermin and inhuman conditions of his penal colonies, took their toll on Dostoyevsky's health. In prison, he reported, he "lived like a person buried underground." Perhaps the only real benefit he derived from all this experience was a long period of contact with the worst forms of criminality and brutality, found among his fellow prisoners. All this is carefully described in his autobiographical work, *House of the Dead*, in which he gives the raw facts about those prison years and shows how he came to know the darker side of human existence so well. In his pre-prison work, *The Double*, we can see the makings of a writer who was groping for answers to the true motivation behind human behavior. In *The House of the Dead* and all later works, we see a writer who has been given unique insight into this behavior.[7]

Dostoyevsky transcended the limits of psychic life and revealed spiritual depths and distances that lie beyond. He uncovered a volcanic crater in every being, under the layers that psychologists had explored and illumined by the light of reason and brought under rational norms. The eruption of those underground volcanoes fills Dostoyevsky's work. It takes a long time for this latent force to collect its revolutionary energy; the enclosing earth becomes more volcanic while on the surface the soul keeps its old equilibrium in submission to the ancient laws — then, suddenly, there is an explosion, like dynamite. Man in that mood tears himself away from the social order, rejects the rules, and enters the universe in another dimension. "The worst thing of all," he wrote to Maikov, "is that my nature is too passionate and unrestrained. I always go to extremes; I have exceeded the limit all my life.". . . It was a gift of Dostoyevsky's to be able to grasp and present man in all his passionate excited activity, and the reader himself is carried along by the hurricane. These upheavals are hidden in the depths of man's being;

Dostoyevsky's art was to express the underground disturbances of human nature, whose dynamic pressure continually throws existing things into confusion, as Berdyaev observes.

Stakhow, who knew him intimately, writes of him: "All his attention was upon people, and all his efforts were directed towards understanding their nature and character. People, their temperament, way of living, feelings, thoughts, these were his sole preoccupation."

Dostoyevsky was more than anything else an anthropologist. His work is an anthropology-in-motion in which things are seen in such an atmosphere of flame and ecstasy that they have meaning only for those who are themselves involved in the tempest. He leads us into the pitch darkness of man's innermost recesses — and there a glimmer of light must be found.[11]

This search for light in the midst of human darkness is presented by Dostoyevsky as possible, but not always attainable. He understood the individual nature of human conditions. He had experienced extremely traumatic circumstances in group settings and he knew that during such experiences, each person involved responds in distinctly individual ways (both internally and externally). All of Dostoyevsky's major characters live at certain moments with such intensity that scores of pages are required to record all that they experience. His focus on "intense experience" measured the scope, depth, levels of intensity and extremities that take place during an experience. In his novels, he demonstrates through his characters how, under certain circumstances and extreme conditions, goodness and evil converge. The conditions and behaviors that arise from this state were those he battled firsthand throughout his life.

For example, despite recognition from the immediate popularity of his written work, he rarely, if ever, was able to enjoy his success. He suffered constantly from a violent form of epilepsy, anxiety, and the debt that accompanied his chronic gambling. He had turbulent love affairs and exhibited other rash, impulsive, high risk behaviors, such as refusing to taking his seizure medication; all possibly related to regaining feelings he described as "happiness," and "seconds of bliss." His otherwise suffering condition was made worse when these patterns of behaviors escalated during periods of desperation and self-induced poverty.

Because of financial obligations, he signed ruinous contracts with publishers that forced him to write at abnormal speed such works as

Crime and Punishment (1866) and *The Gambler* (1867). His success as a novelist enabled him to satisfy some of his creditors, but this so enraged others that he was forced to leave St. Petersburg to escape indictment. Dostoyevsky's position after his flight from Russia was a desperate one. He had borrowed 3,000 rubles from an editor as an advance on a projected novel, and lost the money at the roulette tables. He borrowed another 1,000 — and lost them too. And yet, despite more gambling losses, mounting debt and increased illness, his four years in exile were among the most productive of his life, because he came to depend completely on his writing. "Now," he wrote to his wife from Saxon-les-Bains, "the novel, the novel alone can save us, and if only you knew how much I rely on it. Be sure that I will achieve my aim and be worthy of your respect. Never, never shall I gamble again."[12]

And in his desperation, he wrote from this perspective, and found within himself the strength to produce works of monumental brilliance. Many of the characters in his novels are men and women with twisted minds — some plainly abnormal, others oscillating between saintliness and licentiousness — and the poor, the despised, the misunderstood and happy have hardly ever been portrayed by other writers with as much insight and sympathy as by Dostoyevsky.[13]

Upon his return, praise and respect mounted with each written accomplishment as he began a gradual rise to prominence, which continued until his death. When he died in St. Petersburg in 1881, enormous crowds attended his funeral: men and women from all walks of life; statesmen of high rank and downtrodden prostitutes, illiterate peasants and distinguished men of letters; army officers, priests, students and learned scientists. A grateful nation came together as one to honor and pay solemn tribute.

He was revered was not only because he was one of Russia's most famous men of letters. He was loved as a noble and lofty man, a prudent teacher and inspired prophet whose thoughts pointed toward heaven. He had measured the depths of man's quivering heart with all its struggles, sins, and tempests; its riddles, pains and sorrows; its unseen tears and burning passions. And he understood the seeds of good and evil within himself and wrote novels with heroes who discovered the extremes of each within themselves. This understanding of all that is human was translated into a literary voice that touched people at the core of their being — that taught us that we all have these capabilities in the right set of circumstances — but that there is hope in the knowledge that we also have within ourselves the undying seeds of joyous resurrection. His concern for understanding human nature is perhaps the most important aspect of Dostoyevsky's art and one that marks it for immortality.

Dostoyevsky's life experiences and written work are relevant to understanding behavior that is constructed under extreme conditions because it emphasizes the role of individual perception. He repeatedly addressed the important fact that what others perceive as truth may not coincide with one's own reality. "Reality," he wrote in his notes, "is the most important thing of all. It is true," he goes on, "that my conception of reality may be different from the conception of other people."[14] Behavior that may be impossible to understand from one person's perspective has meaning to the person who is enacting the behavior.

A child's reality can be distorted by individual perception, and a child's perception of an experience can increase the intensity of the experience. Perception is influenced by age, circumstances, hereditary and/or environmental influences, stage of development and the child's uniquely individual perspective. This perspective may be based on what the child has seen, heard, believes to be true and even imagines to be so. For example, an adult may appear like a giant to a three-year-old, and cartoons may seem as real as people. If a child perceives something to be real, whether it is true or not, that reality will be associated with the response it generates. If a child experiences extreme fear in response to a perception, the behavioral response that reduces that fear will be constructed and registered in the brain in relation to that perceived reality. If a child perceives that he or she cannot endure or survive what is being experienced, that reality will be perpetuated in a behavioral response that becomes associated with survival.

Survival perceptions are generated during highly intense/extreme states that are experienced as a psychological and physiological attack on the system. The child may believe he will die from what is happening or would rather die than endure what is happening. The very young child's limited understanding of death and dying can produce added terror, and in some cases, strong attraction to an internal, safer place. Some children withdraw inwardly, and silently contain the disturbing impact of their perception; but the impact on the child's emotional and physical well-being and behavior can be monumental, because it is not easily recognized by others and therefore remains unaddressed.

It would be difficult to find a more profound example than the life of Franz Kafka. The childhood perception revealed in his famous book, *Letter To His Father*, and the stunning disclosure found in his diaries and letters, demonstrate with extraordinary depth and clarity how one child responded to his father.

Franz Kafka is recognized as one of the most original and complex figures in modern literature; his work has been praised by such writers as Thomas Mann and Herman Hesse. Yet when he died, he left a note asking that all of his writings be burned.[15] He is often taken for a metaphysical, prophetic or even a religious writer, who had supernatural insight into events that followed his death, particularly during the war in Europe. His fables are interpreted to fit later historic phenomena as if he had had a window into the future. What is often missed in these interpretations is his basic understanding of the human condition at its most extreme level of suffering. It matters not when or where this suffering takes place but that suffering does exist to this degree. And the origin and basis for this suffering does not necessarily arise in a specific historic or phenomenological context, but rather in one's perception of oneself in that context. This point is crucial in understanding Kafka. Whether he was writing about a singing mouse, an enigmatic ape, an impenetrable castle, a deadly contraption, the Great Wall of China, a creature in a burrow, fasting as an art form, and, most famously, a man metamorphosed into a bug, he was writing from his own experience. His ability to translate that experience into words that explain man's struggle to transform in the midst of human suffering is less an enigma than a uniquely individual and brilliant interpretation of that struggle.

Kafka was born in Prague, July 3, 1883, the son of Hermann and Julie Kafka. He had three surviving younger sisters: Valli, Elli, and Ottla. His father was a self-made middle class Jewish merchant, who raised his children in the hopes of assimilating them into the mainstream society of the Austro-Hungarian Empire. The official ruling language of the empire was German, so Franz attended German grammar school (Volksschule am Fleischmarkt), and later the German Gymnasium (Altstädter Deutsches Gymnasium). He finished his Doctorate of Law in Prague, studying at the German-language university (Die deutsche Universität) there. He initially gained employment at a private insurance firm *Assicurazioni Generali* and then with the *Arbeiter-Unfall-Versicherungs-Anstalt für das Königreichs Böhmen in Prag*. His Job at the Worker's Accident Insurance provided him with a steady income and "regular" office hours, so that he could dedicate his evenings to writing. His diaries contain continuing accounts of his restlessness and sleeplessness as he would work all night writing, only to return to the office for the next day of work, thoroughly exhausted. Although he spoke and wrote Czech fluently throughout his life, his literary work was all completed in German.

He is known to have started writing at an early age, but all of his earliest attempts were later destroyed. His first published work came in 1907, and he continued to publish throughout the next seventeen years, but most of his works were published posthumously by his friend Max Brod.

Kafka's relationship to his father dominates all discussions of both his life and his work. See his *Brief an den Vater* to get a feel for the relationship between the thin, intellectual, and awkward Franz, and the robust, loud, and corporal Father. The ideas of "father" and "family" permeate the fabric of many of Kafka's texts, either directly as in *Das Urteil* or *Die Verwandlung*, or more abstractly as in the cases of his two novels *Der Proceß* and *Das Schloß* (which remained unpublished during his lifetime).[16]

Kafka died of tuberculosis in 1924, a month short of his 41st birthday. He did not live to see human beings degraded to the status and condition of vermin eradicated by an insecticidal gas. If he was able to imagine man reduced to an insect, it was not because he was prophetic. It was his own status and condition that Kafka knew. He believed himself to be "apathetic, witless, fearful," and also "servile, sly, irrelevant, impersonal, unsympathetic, untrue. . . . from some ultimate diseased tendency." He vowed that "every day at least one line shall be directed against myself." He wrote, "I am constantly trying to communicate something inexplicable. Basically it is nothing other than . . .fear spread to everything, fear of the greatest as of the smallest, fear, paralyzing fear of pronouncing a word, although this fear may not be fear but also a longing for something greater than all that is fearful."[17]

In *Letter To His Father*, Kafka recalled:

There is only one episode in the early years of which I have a direct memory. You may remember it, too. One night I kept on whimpering for water, not, I am certain, because I was thirsty, but probably partly to be annoying, partly to amuse myself. After several vigorous threats had failed to have any effect, you took me out of bed, carried me out onto the *pavlatche*,* and left me there alone for a while in my night-shirt, outside the shut door. I am not going to say that this was wrong — perhaps there was really no other way of getting peace and quiet that night — but I mention it as typical of your methods of bringing up a child and their effect on me. I dare say I was quite obe-dient afterward at that period, but it did me inner harm. What was for me a matter of course, that senseless asking for water, and then the extraordinary terror of being carried outside were two things that I, my nature being what it was, could never properly connect with each other. Even years afterward I suffered from the tormenting fancy that the huge man, my father, the ultimate authority, would come almost for no reason at all and take me out of bed in the night and carry me out onto the *pavlatche*, and that consequently I meant abso-lutely nothing as far as he was concerned.[18]

This "extraordinary terror" is described in detail, with all the asso-ciated physical symptoms, in a letter Kafka wrote to his great love, Milena Jesenska, to whom he wrote his most passionate letters. Milena was a beautiful, politically committed, enormously talented journalist. She took an early stand against the rise of Hitler, and as the head of an opposition newspaper, was arrested in 1939 and sent to the Nazi con-centration camp in Ravensbruck. Milena died in the camp three weeks before D-Day.[19] Kafka's letters reveal a love story characterized as an agony of despair, bliss, self-laceration and self-humiliation. Their love was essentially a letter-love, like the love of Werther or Kierkegaard.

Kafka's indecisiveness, which stemmed from his paralyzing fear and perception of his own "nothingness," affected every relationship and every life-decision to a paralyzing degree. When trying to move forward toward marriage in his relationship with Milena, he writes of his struggle to make the decision to meet her in Vienna:

But this isn't yet the climax of what is astonishing. It consists in the

*"Pavlatche" is the Czech word for the long balcony in the inner courtyard of old houses in Prague. (Ed.)

fact that if you wanted to come to me, if therefore — musically judged — you were willing to renounce the whole world in order to step down to me, to such depths that from your vantage point you would see not only very little, but actually nothing, that you for this purpose — strangely, strangely enough — would not have to climb down but would have to reach *beyond* yourself in a super-human way, *beyond* yourself so powerfully that in doing so you might perhaps be torn to shreds, stumble, disappear (and I, no doubt, with you). (pp. 110-111.)

It follows, perhaps, that we are now both married, you in Vienna, I to my Fear in Prague, and that not only you, but I too, tug in vain at our marriage. (p. 107.)

As it is, I have no one, no one here but the Fear, locked together we toss through the nights. (p. 100.)

You've noticed, perhaps, that I haven't slept for several nights. It's simply the 'fear'. This is really something which deprives me of my will, tosses me about as it likes, I no longer know up from down, right from left. (p. 99.)

You say, Milena, that you don't understand it. Try to understand it by calling it illness. It's one of many manifestations of illness which psychoanalysis believes it has uncovered. I don't call it illness and I consider the therapeutic part of psychoanalysis to be a hopeless error. All these so-called illnesses, sad as they may appear, are matters of faith, efforts of souls in distress to find moorings in some maternal soil; . . . Such moorings, however, which really take hold of solid ground, are after all not an isolated, interchangeable property of man, rather they are pre-existing in his nature and continue to form his nature (as well as his body) in this direction. And it's here they hope to cure? (pp. 217-218)

In my case one should imagine 3 circles, an innermost one A, then B, then C. The center A explains to B why this man has to torture and to distrust himself, why he has to renounce (it's no renunciation, that would be very difficult, it's only having-to-renounce), why he may not live . . . . To C, the acting person, nothing is any longer explained, it only takes orders from B. C acts under MOST severe pressure, in a cold sweat of fear (is there any other sweat that breaks out on the forehead, cheek, temple, scalp — in short, all round the whole skull? This is what it's like for C.) Thus C acts more from *fear* than from understanding; he trusts, he believes that A has explained everything to B and that B has understood and handled everything correctly." (pp. 217-218.)[20]

Continued from *Letter To His Father*:

That was only a small beginning, but this feeling of being nothing that often dominates me (a feeling that is in another respect, admittedly, also a noble and fruitful one) comes largely from your influence. Father, understand me correctly: in themselves these would have been utterly insignificant details, they only became depressing for me because you, so tremendously the authoritative man, did not keep the commandments you imposed on me. Hence the world was for me divided into three parts: one in which I, the slave, lived under laws that had been invented only for me and which I could, I did not know why, never completely comply with; then a second world, which was infinitely remote from mine, in which you lived, concerned with government, with the issuing of orders and with the annoyance about their not being obeyed; and finally a third world where everybody else lived happily and free from orders and from having to obey. I was continually in disgrace; either I obeyed your orders, and that was a disgrace, for they applied, after all, only to me; or I was defiant, and that was a disgrace too, for how could I presume to defy you; or I could not obey because I did not, for instance, have your strength, your appetite, your skill, although you expected it of me as a matter of course; this was the greatest disgrace of all. This was not the course of the child's reflections, but of his feelings.[21]

The diaries, letters, writings, and biographies of Kafka reveal an internal view of obsessive behavioral disorder that disrupted and eventually overwhelmed to the point of self-deprivation and debilitation. Kafka's descriptions of his early experiences with his father are remarkably clear in their implication and recriminatory tone in his perception of these early influences as detrimental to his development.

Eternal childhood. Life calls again.
October 18, 1921

I don't believe people exist whose inner plight resembles mine; still, it is possible for me to imagine such people — but that the secret raven forever flaps about their heads as it does about mine, even to imagine that is impossible.

It is astounding how I have systematically destroyed myself in the course of the years, it was like a slowly widening breach in a dam, a purposeful action. The spirit that brought it about must now be celebrating triumphs; why doesn't it let me take part in them? But perhaps it hasn't yet achieved its purpose and can therefore think of nothing else."

October 17, 1921[22]

December 23. Saturday. When I look at my whole way of life going in a direction that is foreign and false to all my relatives and acquaintances, the apprehension arises, and my father expresses it, that I shall become a second Uncle Rudolph, the fool somewhat altered to meet the needs of a different period; but from now on I'll be able to feel how my mother (whose opposition to this opinion grows continually weaker in the course of the years) sums up and enforces everything that speaks for me and against Uncle Rudolph, and that enters like a wedge between the conceptions entertained about the two of us.

Diaries, 1911[23]

— Franz Kafka

There are few who are able to describe their pivotal experiences with such a brilliant literary voice. But like Kafka, many children who suffer fear and insecurity speak out in problematic behavior long before they speak out in words. The following case is an example.

Case Summary: Donald

Donald, a 44-year-old white male accountant, was admitted into the hospital for depression. He had a history of embezzlement and alcohol abuse. The major precipitant for his current depression was that he was caught embezzling from his second employer while he was on probation for his first embezzlement charge. He had embezzled about $4,500 from his second employer over a period of 50 days, prior to admission. His employer had confronted him and gave him a choice — either Donald would get help, or the employer would press charges. Donald chose to come into the hospital for treatment. He reported having had fluctuating periods of sobriety for ten years after he had completed a brief addiction outpatient treatment program. During this 10-year period, he said there were several episodes of relapse. He had begun drinking 4 or 5 beers a day, approximately two years ago. Both of his embezzlement episodes occurred while he was drinking.

His first embezzlement occurred when he was working for the County, and continued over a period of one year. He said he did not feel he was able to provide for his wife in the manner her father had. He said he needed money for a renovation of their kitchen. When he got caught, his wife and her family cut him off. He moved into the basement of his parents' home. An older man, who was a neighbor, befriended him and help him with his legal problems. When this man died, he began embezzling from his most recent employer. He has since been fired.

Donald's initial assessment and psychological evaluation recommendations addressed his need for sobriety and regular AA attendance, while pointing out that his avoidant personality style might present obstacles to this type of interaction. He was admitted into the intensive outpatient addiction treatment program.

During his initial participation in treatment, it was evident that Donald was not comfortable in group or social situations. He exhibited cooperative behavior but hesitated to initiate any involvement that was not necessary. Solemn and silent, he moved slowly from one task to another as if carrying a great burden. He appeared surprised by any individual attention and seemed to be relieved when it was over.

His initial group disclosure was contained and limited. He stated that he wanted to change and to begin a new way of life, but appeared unmotivated.

Donald had a large build and in stature he appeared weighted down. His shoulders stooped. He was moderately overweight, which was evenly distributed and gave the impression of bulk rather than obesity. There was a heaviness to his manner and movement, which was slow and lumbering. He was pallid in complexion and fair in coloring. His eyes and mouth were slightly down-turned, giving the impression of sadness and pathos. There was a gentle quality in his affect that offset what might otherwise have seemed an apathetic attitude. There was something in his persona that made him seem approachable, rather than distant and not interested. It appeared as if he wanted attention, but was so uncomfortable when he got it that he could hardly respond to it. As a result, his involvement began awkwardly and his quiet discomfort eased gradually over a period of weeks.

Donald's first group disclosure centered on legal problems and the probability that he would receive a prison sentence. He avoided discussion about family issues, stating that his support system was his treatment group. He brought up the question of why he now felt some hope for change. He said this hope had come to him when he realized that his past life had been a series of failed efforts. He said he did not fear prison because it could be no worse than the prison of his life — and there, he would not fail to live up to the expectations of others. During this disclosure, his expression changed from his normally passive affect to one that revealed anger, frustration and an air of rebellion. This was the first indication that he was not as defeated as he first appeared to be.

Donald was a reluctant 12 Step Program participant. He said he found meetings stressful and invasive. He explained that he found it difficult to approach anyone about becoming a sponsor, needed more time for this, and was not comfortable with the entire process.

During the first week of participation, Donald began to reveal feeling and physical symptom responses to a variety of presented situations. His consistent responses indicated that he had been feeling frustrated and inadequate since childhood. He repeatedly identified futility, embarrassment, anger and frustration as recurrent and ongoing throughout his life. He stated that as a child, he had often felt different from others, and stupid. He believed himself to be an underachiever and that all of his efforts were in vain. Physical symptoms identified in relation to these feelings were described as intense-to-extreme pressure in his stomach, chest and throat.

Donald's written assignments revealed that he had minimal recollection of his early childhood prior to elementary school. When he began attending school, he wrote that he could recall feeling "sort of weird, funny looking and odd." He described feeling lonely and resentful during this period, and stated that he was extremely shy.

During the second week of treatment, Donald revealed consistent behavioral responses to a variety of presented situations. He identified self-contained, self-recriminatory and isolating behaviors as present since childhood. The first indication of obsessive behavior was revealed when he described repetitive thought processes that he admitted were relentless and self-hurtful. He said he had not associated his internally verbalized self-punishment to symptoms of depression. When he began to recognize the self-abusive nature of his thinking and self-talk, he was able to acknowledge the negative impact this behavior had on his self-worth and functioning. Donald recalled harshly criticizing himself regularly as a child. He cited report-card grades as a major cause of self-recrimination because he tried so hard to make good grades. When he fell short of this goal, he berated himself for being "stupid."

Donald's disclosure did not come easy. At first, he was hesitant to give his most immediate response, and initially reported that he resented being expected to respond from a personal perspective. As he made progress through this difficult initial period, he became more motivated and admitted to gaining insight from repeatedly looking at how he might react to presented situations. He said he had come to realize that much of his life was spent trying, without success, to live up to the unrealistic expectations of others, and that his own self-expectations were built on the expectations of others. This realization occurred during the fourth and fifth weeks of treatment. During the fifth week, he volunteered to share, as focus of group, an experience that occurred when he was age 16.

Donald began by explaining that the episode he was about to share had been preceded by a multitude of similar experiences that occurred since he entered first grade. He said he chose the episode because it stood out in his memory, and because he had tried so hard to be successful that particular school year. He added, "I've thought of it at least a couple times a month since it happened."

At age 16, Donald was living with his parents and two older sisters. He said that. from the time he entered school, he was aware that he came from a family of high achievers and that his father expected him to work hard to make good grades. He explained that he did try very hard, but somehow fell short of making all A's and B's. He excelled at spelling, but recalled one occasion when he lost an "important" spelling bee by one letter. "It was if everything in the room stopped. I can still see the face of my father fall in disappointment, in reaction to my failure."

The same held true for baseball. He was good in some areas, but couldn't run fast enough. He joined the band and did very well on the trombone, but froze during a performance that his father attended. After each "inadequate performance," his "failure" was the subject of family dinner conversation that evening. Success was expected. When this did not happen, errors were scrutinized in detail. As his elementary school years went by, it became increasingly difficult for Donald to motivate himself to try harder.

During the 7th grade, he was heavily reprimanded for receiving a D on his report card. He recalled, "If I could just maintain a decent level of performance, I could at least keep the heat off." From that point on, he pushed himself to work harder and by high school had his grade level up high enough to make the National Honor Society. Unfortunately, he missed it by one grade and this failure led to the following episode.

"I remember the sun coming into the room with a yellowish, orange glow. It was the month of May. The evening was warm. Dad, mother and my two sisters and myself were sitting around the dinner table. My father brought up the subject of the honor roll. I was constantly being compared to the son of friends of my parents. His name was Johnny. My father asked if I had heard that Johnny made the National Honor Society. He asked if I had also made it. I simply replied, 'No.' My father didn't realize how close I had come. It didn't matter because coming that close and not making it was just 'not making it.' You either made it or you didn't, and I didn't. My father responded by repeating my words with a questioning tone, 'No?' And then asking, 'Why not?' I could hear the frustration and disappointment in his voice. My sister Lisa was snickering."

Donald's described feeling response: "I felt anger, frustration, embarrassment, futility, stupidity, and that I was born to be an underachiever. I felt intense pressure."

Donald's described physical symptom response: "I felt like steam was welling up inside of me. I felt energy in my gut moving up. The steam felt hot as it moved up. I also felt a sinking feeling. My throat became constricted and there was ringing in my ears. Tears began to well behind my eyes."

Donald's described behavior response: "I kicked my sister under the table to get her to stop snickering. I used my body to grip the chair and stared at the center of the table. I requested that I be allowed to be excused. I asked in an appropriate manner. I was told that I would first have to do my chores, which I did. Then I retreated to my room, opened the window and went outside on the roof to listen to the sounds, away from everything inside. I sat there and kept going over and over in my mind what I had done wrong. I kept obsessing about the situation. I recriminated myself for not making the National Honor Roll. I cried."

Donald's pattern of harsh self-judgment and obsessive self-recrimination began before this episode, but accelerated after this episode. His motivation and efforts never again reached the level that precipitated this experience. Although he continued to enact appropriate behavior in respect to others, he became more determined to cover up his mistakes and failures. In an individual session that followed this group disclosure, Donald revealed another experience that he had been thinking about.

"This incident had seemed minor to me before, but now it doesn't. I was in the fifth grade, standing with a group of friends, waiting for the school bus. There was a sweet gum tree at the bus stop. Two other boys and myself started throwing sweet gum balls into the street. We weren't really hurting anything or throwing them at anyone. It was just something to do. Someone in the group ran to tell the school principal, who came out to the bus stop and held us there to reprimand us for this behavior. As a result, we missed the school bus. The principal told us that we each had to tell our parents what we had done and why we missed the bus."

"When I arrived home and my father asked me why I was late, I lied. Then, the mother of one of the other boys called and told my father what had happened. This harmless incident turned into a nightmare. I was punished as if I had done something horrible. It was as if I had disgraced the whole family. I remember reprimanding myself for not thinking quick enough. I decided that I had to get better at covering up even minor mistakes. There was no room for error. I didn't think about not doing anything wrong again, just making sure no one found out about it. I think my lying and covering up for myself began there. It just took me a long time to do it well enough to keep it hidden for so many years."

Donald went on to describe what occurred prior to his first embezzlement. He said his father-in-law cast a large shadow over his marriage. His wife constantly reminded him that he did not provide for her the way her father had — and this reminded him of the way his parents had compared him to Johnny. He said it didn't help that his in-laws lived only two blocks away and got involved in every aspect of their married life. "I was making a good income but was always expected to do better and move forward in my job. One time, I was late on the house payment and it was as if I had taken our children out and slaughtered them in the public square."

He admitted that he was drinking on a regular basis by then. He explained, "alcohol greatly relieved the pressure I was feeling every day." He recognized that it was becoming a problem because it was depleting his already inadequate income. When his wife wanted the kitchen remodeled, the pressure increased because he knew he would be scrutinized for this lost income. He began embezzling to cover this shortfall. "I didn't embezzle because I was drinking. I embezzled to *cover up* my drinking, although I do acknowledge that if I had not been drinking, I wouldn't have come up short." Embezzling was not the first dishonest behavior he had enacted to cover up his mistakes; but it was the first time money was involved. Once money *was* involved, it was incorporated into a pattern of dishonesty and deception that had been developing since childhood; it overtook his positive efforts toward achievement and was repeated each time he felt inadequate and threatened. His pattern of positive effort, however, has the potential to emerge again with encouragement and reinforcement because it persisted until he was age 16.

The insights Donald gained into the origin of his most vulnerable feeling states, their accompanying physiological symptoms and corresponding behavior patterns, helped him to understand their role in his substance abuse and relapse. His recognition of relapse risk potential, fueled by obsessive self-punishing recrimination and dishonesty, helped him to collaborate on a positive alternative behavioral plan that was incorporated into his approach to addiction recovery. Behavioral development planning that addresses his pre-addiction condition is essential to his progress and his continued participation in his AA support group.

Donald is currently serving a two-year prison sentence. His wife obtained a divorce. He writes regularly about his efforts with behavioral and spiritual development. He is involved in an Alcoholics Anonymous support group in prison. His letters indicate significant change in his attitude toward himself. He also writes regularly to his father.

Notes

1. Dostoyevsky, F. (1952). *The Brothers Karamazov*. (C. Garnett, Trans.) Originally published 1880. Chicago, IL: William Benton.
2. Beethoven, L.V. (1933). *The Symphony of Life: Letters by Ludwig von Beethoven*, p.13. (Trans. U.L. Steindorff.). Los Angeles, California: U.S. Library Association, Inc.
3. Margarshack, D. (1955). "Translator's Introduction" in Dostoyevsky, F. *The Idiot*. (D. Magarshack. Trans.), p.8. Baltimore, Maryland: Penguin Books. Dostoyevsky's great work addresses the dual nature of man and man's individual perception of reality. Individual perception in relation to experience is central to this masterpiece.
4. Brewster, D. (1927). Introduction to Dostoyevsky, F. *Crime and Punishment*, p.v-vi, ix. New York: Grosset & Dunlap. Dostoyevsky, F. (1963). *Crime and Punishment* (M. Scammell, Trans.). Reprint from original serialized edition published in St. Petersburg, Russia (1866). New York, New York: Washington Square Press.
5. Berdyaev, N. (1965). Dostoyevsky, p.21. (Living Age Book/Meridian Books). Cleveland, OH: The World Publishing Company.
6. Biographical Note, Fyodor Dostoyevsky, 1921-1881. (1952) *Britannica Great Books*, p. v: 55-10358. University of Chicago: William Benton
7. Seammell, M. (1963-1969). Introduction to: Dostoyevsky, F. *Crime and Punishment*, p. ix. First published serially in Russian in *Russky Vestnik*, St. Petersburg (1866).
8. Biographical Note, Fyodor Dostoyevsky, 1921-1881. (1952) *Britannica Great Books*, *op. cit.*
9. Brewster, *op. cit.*
10. Seammell, *op. cit.*
11. Berdyaev, *op. cit.*
12. Margarshack, *op. cit.*
13. Hubben, W. (1948). Editor's Introduction. Dostoyevsky, F. (1948). "The Grand Inquisitor on the Nature of Man." In: *The Brothers Karamazov* (C. Garnett, Trans.). Indianapolis, IN: Bobbs-Merrill Educational Publishing. Dostoyevsky addresses the danger of scientific pursuit that does not recognize man's need for spiritual faith. His explanation of the faithless who pray for miracles when faced with extreme disaster is relevant to exploring changes in behavior that emerge under extraordinary conditions.
14. Margarshack, *op. cit.*
15. Crawford, D. (1973). *Franz Kafka: Man Out of Step*. New York: Crown Publishers, Inc.
16. "Constructing Kafka" (April 1997). Kafka Internet website.
17. Ozick, C. (January 11, 1999). "The Impossibility of Being Kafka." *The New Yorker*.
18. Kafka, F. (1966). *Letter to His Father* (E. Kaiser & E. Wilkins, Trans.). New York: Schocken Books.
19. Buber-Neuman, M. (1988). *Milena: The Story of a Remarkable Friendship*. Translated by Ralph Manheim. New York: Schocken Books Inc.
20. Kafka, F. (1953). *Letters to Milena*. Edited by Willy Haas. Translated by

Tania and James Stern. New York: Schocken Books, Inc.

21. Kafka, F. (1966). *Letter to His Father, op. cit.*

22. Kafka, F. (1949). *The Diaries of Franz Kafka, 1914-1923* (M. Brod, Ed., M. Greenburgh, Trans.). New York: Schocken Books.

23. Kafka, F. (1948). *The Diaries of Franz Kafka, 1910-1913,* (M. Brod, Ed., J. Kresh, Trans.). New York: Schocken Books.

What passion of hatred can it be which leads a man to lurk in such a place at such a time! And what deep and earnest purpose can he have which calls for such a trial! There, in that hut upon the moor, seems to lie the very centre of that problem which has vexed me so sorely. I swear that another day shall not have passed before I have done all that man can do to reach the heart of the mystery.[1]

Diary of Dr. Watson
— Sir Arthur Conan Doyle

There is a unique intelligence generated when curiosity is stimulated in children. In the documented cases reported in the HRIPTM research, curiosity was described as a feeling state, ("I felt curious" or "I became curious") in response to puzzling episodes or events. Overwhelming curiosity can be experienced as intense arousal — a *disturbing* arousal state that can lead to searching, seeking, questioning, exploring, and other mental and physical investigatory actions that develop into patterns of behavior. Obsession arising from curiosity engages the behavior to a relentless degree.

When a child has an experience that is not understood and that generates curiosity, the behavioral reaction is constructed to, not only satisfy curiosity, but to address the state of disturbance generated. When the behavioral response (asking questions, seeking an explanation, trying to mentally "figure-it-out") is only minimally effective, curiosity can become persistent as the desire to understand develops into a preoccupation. Preoccupation and the associated behavior can evolve to include other puzzling questions that arise in association with the initial experience, if the mystery remains unsolved. The behavior pattern can expand to include other situations that generate curiosity, creating multiple obsessive quests for understanding and resolution.

In years past, when a problem existed in the family, children were often given no information about family problems, particularly when those problems involved addiction or mental health. In matters of birth, death, illness, divorce, abuse, change, absence, separation, religion, war and other life occurrences, many children were "left in the dark," with no clear explanation or any effective resolution to their feelings and observations. In today's "age of enlightenment" regarding the need to inform and communicate with children, there are still many who have not had the opportunity to understand the events of their lives in a way that has brought about healing resolution. Those who deal with this lack of resolution with behavior that is obsessive, self-destructive and/ or destructive to others, represent a need to understand this condition more fully. Through the life of one extraordinary man who exemplified this condition, this chapter addresses this issue of *mystery* in relation to behavior.

Sir Arthur Conan Doyle, the creator of Sherlock Holmes, was greatly affected as a youth by the circumstances and *mystery* surrounding his father's "mental health condition" and repeated hospitalizations. When he later became a physician, Doyle began writing detective stories. He wrote them from a medical and a scientific perspective, and as a result, became a pioneer in "the art of investigation" and its relation to the study of human behavior.

Doyle was keenly aware of the role of investigation in understanding human conditions that precipitate illness and crime. He also wrote from painful personal experiences that, once addressed to some degree through his fictional characters, he continued to address to an obsessive degree that went beyond the logical scientific methods employed by the most important character he created, Sherlock Holmes. Throughout his life, whether solving a fictional crime, investigating a real-life crime, or extolling a belief that was to eventually undermine his reputation, his investigative approach to life and even the *after-life* was continuous and undeterred until his death.

Doyle was a man blessed with talent, imagination, creativity and gentlemanly charm. Volumes have been written about Sherlock Holmes, but only about a dozen respected biographies have been written about Doyle. His son, Adrian Doyle, writes that his father was fortunate to have had two genuine biographies — by Dickson Carr and Dr. John Lamond. After a rather scathing commentary on what Adrian describes as "perverted" theories surrounding the legends of Holmes and Watson, he writes;

But the man who wishes to discover the truth, and by that I mean the real design that lies behind the Holmes stories, will find it in his power to do so. It is not necessary to swat up the stories until one can quote them verbatim by the paragraph — instead, he will study Holmes in conjunction with the life and accomplishments of that greater form that looms behind him, the figure of Holmes's creator. All the evidence is there. In Dickson Carr's *Life*,[2] and let us remember that Carr alone had entrée to Conan Doyle's gigantic collection of biographical papers and to his surviving associates and that every statement therein is drawn from the solid facts and not from any chosen conception of its author, in that fine book we find ourselves face to face with the first great truth — that Holmes was to a large extent Conan Doyle himself. Incidentally, and it stands to their credit in view of my father's reticence, this fact was recognized almost from the first by the police chiefs of the world who, speaking or writing from America, France, Germany, China, India, or Egypt, paid him tribute. The exception was, of course, Scotland Yard whose silence put to shame even that of the immortal Colonel Bramble. Scotland Yard owed too much to Conan Doyle and its always painful to acknowledge large debts.[3]

Adrian Doyle recognized his father in Sherlock Holmes because of his knowledge of him and the experiences they shared. He recalls, "What significant fragments crop up in one's memory as one looks back. The very English face of Major W — ; the fog of tobacco smoke in my father's study, all cluttered up with weird objects; the incident of the missing dumbbell which by rolling under an old cupboard touched off a train of thought in Conan Doyle's mind that resulted in the missing dumbbell of *The Valley of Fear*."[4]

Adrian attributes the tendency of others to inaccurately describe his father to Doyle's reticence about sharing the intimate details of his life. This is substantiated in his biographical information. Arthur Conan was careful when it came to self-disclosure. He was self-protective, rather than defensive, and even more protective of his own father. He reveals little personal data beyond the facts. However, his fictional stories reveal much and demonstrate his strong desire to fight injustice, right wrongs, vindicate the innocent, investigate the seemingly obvious beyond what is too easily accepted, and solve mysteries surrounding those who are without defense.

Doyle's investigatory inclinations were not confined to solving mysteries through his legendary characters, Sherlock Holmes and Dr. Watson. He personally investigated several true cases that he considered to have been miscarriages of justice. The best-known example is that of George Edalji,[5] a country lawyer who was sentenced to seven years in prison, in 1903, for mutilating cows and horses at night. Doyle was convinced of Edalji's innocence, especially after testing his eyesight and determining that it was so poor that he could not possibly have made his way across rough country fields in the darkness. It then took several years of intensive effort to convince the establishment of Edalji's innocence and to obtain his release.

Conan Doyle also rose to the defense of Oscar Slater, an individual of questionable morals, who was sentenced to death for the brutal murder, in 1909, of an old woman in Glasgow. His death sentence was commuted to hard labor for life. Doyle studied the evidence and concluded that it was circumstantial and in good part erroneous. He agitated for many years on behalf of Slater, presenting his objections to officialdom and publishing a book on the subject.[6] Slater was finally exonerated in 1928.

These cases were both unusual in that, without Doyle's interest and investment of time, it is doubtful that either would have been vindicated. Arthur Conan Doyle also had the courage to challenge a formidable system, improbable odds, and public opinion, and did so with relentless investigation and Sherlockian logic. He also exhibited compassion for victim and criminal alike, which was reflected in Sherlock Holmes. For example, Holmes reacted sympathetically to the murderer, Jefferson Hope,[7] and promised to keep secret the confession of another villain-hero, John Turner,[8] who had killed Charles McCarthy, "a devil incarnate."

This tenacious and independent behavior would continue to evolve along with an esteemed reputation that would later be tarnished by an interest in spiritualism that became an obsession. When this occurred, his behavior appeared so strange and illogical, that his reputation was harmed and his friendships were strained to the breaking point.[9] He was ridiculed in the press, ignored by colleagues, and generally thought to be off-balance — all of which came about as he attempted to support and vindicate those who believed as he did. This happened because, beyond adopting a deep and abiding faith in spiritualism, he also publicly and emphatically supported questionable evidence regarding the existence of *fairies*.

It wasn't until the discovery of *The Doyle Diary*,[10] a remarkable sketchbook and personal journal written by his father, Charles Altamont Doyle, that his motives became more clearly understood. The book, which came to light in 1977, was written during his father's confinement at the Sunnyside insane asylum in the year 1889. It was reproduced as, *The Doyle Diary: The Last Great Conan Doyle Mystery*, with an introduction by Michael Baker entitled, "*The Strange and Curious Case of Charles Altamont Doyle.*"

Reading through Charles' beautifully illustrated *Diary*, one steps into the strange and whimsical world he created while confined at Sunnyside. The diary contains page after page of softly colored drawings, depicting images of elves and fairies intermingling with familiar images, nature, political satire and family likenesses (most often his wife Mary). The images reflect an "Irish" mentality, created by a man of Irish descent, who had been described as a dreamer. With this influence, he would not necessarily have had to be insane to create such a world, but from another perspective (the perspective that surrounded him) it was viewed as such.

Charles Doyle lived in an era when insanity was often used as a cover for problems considered much more disgraceful. Asylums housed a multitude of conditions that erroneously fell under the broad category of "mental illness." People who acted strangely could be committed and confined for years for behavior deemed socially inappropriate. Family members were often discouraged from discussing the matter and little explanation was afforded to those who were curious about the committed person's absence. It is then understandable, how the absence of the central figure in a household could become a mystery for the eldest son, who was expected to fill this vacated role long before he felt capable of assuming that responsibility and burden.

As a result of his father's repeated hospitalizations, young Arthur was left in the unenviable position of wage-earner and spiritual guide to the members of his impoverished family. And, although his own autobiography, *Memories and Adventures*,[11] would lead us to believe that he held his father in considerable respect, there are clues in his fictional work which tell us that his subconscious mind held other, more violent, inclinations. In *The Stark Munro Letters*,[12] the narrator (thinly disguised, but clearly Doyle himself) recalls his father urging him to find regular employment, since he is in the grip of a terminal illness:

> Of course I could only answer that I was willing to turn my hand to anything. But that interview has left a mark on me — a heavy ever-present gloom away at the back of my soul, which I am conscious of even when the cause of it has for a moment gone out of my thoughts. I had enough to make a man serious before, when I had to face the world without money or interest. But now to think of my mother and my sisters and little Paul all leaning upon me when I cannot stand myself — it is a nightmare.

Michael Baker's introduction to *The Doyle Diary* includes an amazing account of the Doyle family history. Baker's investigation reveals much about the mystery surrounding Charles Doyle, and the effect this mystery had on his son, Arthur Conan.

Charles Altamont Doyle was born in 1832 and died in 1893 at the age of 61. Charles' father, John Doyle, whose family originated from Dublin, was the celebrated political caricaturist of the Regency period known under the pseudonym of "HB." His mother was Marianna Conan, the sister of Michael Conan, an artist, critic and journalist working on both sides of the Channel. His elder brother Dicky was a renowned illustrator and his three other brothers, Francis, James, and Henry were talented artists. Although they were well-known and regarded as peers to the artistic and literary luminaries of this Victorian era, the Doyles lived an austere and secluded existence. John brought up his family as strict Catholics. Despite this social reserve, in the space of three generations, the Doyles were the only family in the British Empire to have five separate members in the *Dictionary of National Biography*.

Charles Doyle's name was not among them, although, like his brothers, he had been trained as an artist. In 1849, at age 17 (and not of his choosing), he had been sent to Edinburgh to take up a post as assistant to the surveyor in the Scottish Office of Works, where he held a position of some responsibility. Six months later, he met Mary Foley — who was also Irish and Catholic. In 1855, they married and proceeded to have ten children, seven of whom survived. Arthur, the fourth child but first boy, was born in 1859. Charles remained in his position at the Scottish Office for the rest of his working life. The family reputedly struggled to makes ends meet. Charles's health began to deteriorate and he retired. It was at this time that he began periodic residence in "convalescent homes." Baker notes the sketchy evidence regarding Charles in the Conan Doyle biographies.

> Despite the considerable light shed upon Doyle by his son's biographers, I was puzzled by a number of questions and discrepancies. On the surface it seemed obvious that here was a talented artist who was unable to face up to the disappointments of exile in Edinburgh, a humdrum civil servant's job and the demands of a large family; he had simply physically and mentally deteriorated under the strain. Yet as Holmes would have been quick to point out, nothing is more deceptive than the obvious. None of this explained why Doyle was sent to Edinburgh in the first place. Moreover, what exactly was his job and what were the circumstances of his departure from it? What was the true state of his condition which necessitated retirement to a "convalescent home?" I had been able to deduce that Doyle's health was probably beginning to give anxiety at the time Arthur was leaving school in 1875, and it was generally agreed by the biographers that he had entered a nursing home by 1879. But what was the matter with him? Was the "home" also an asylum? Was it Sunnyside, indeed? Above all, why had such a promising artistic talent of undeniable skill and originality, surrounded by a family of reputation and influence, never received an equal share of the world's recognition?[10]

Baker's exhaustive and extensive research led him to the following discoveries: Charles Doyle died on October 10, 1893, in the Crighton Royal Institution, Dumfries. Cause of death was given as epilepsy of "many years" standing. Prior to Crighton, Doyle had resided at Montrose Royal Lunatic Asylum. Baker commented that it was quite normal practice to admit epileptics to mental asylums during this period and that that could account for Doyle's early retirement. The medical authorities at these institutions did not permit access to their records but were prepared to give a general picture of Doyle and his condition. Crighton confirmed that Charles was not only epileptic, but he was also was diagnosed with alcoholism. Crighton's institution included several detached residences such as Maryfield, which catered to a dozen or so patients, or Hannahfield, which housed a few elderly gentlemen "whose cases are considered chronic, and who lead there a quiet life amid surroundings suitable to their peaceful condition."

Charles had been admitted to Montrose Royal in May 1885 from a nursing home called Fordum House, which specialized in the treatment of Alcoholics. His admission had followed an incident at home in which he had managed to obtain drink, had become violent and broken a window, and had then tried to escape. He was accordingly admitted to Sunnyside, which was within Montrose, under a detention order, though he subsequently became a paying patient. Baker notes that it is a point of interest that Charles's epilepsy appeared to develop only *after* his admission to Montrose Royal and it was suggested that this condition may have been symptomatic of his alcoholism.

It was during his residence at Sunnyside that Charles produced a sketchbook that revealed his remarkable talent for naturalistic art. His extensive notes were penciled in neat handwriting, providing a record of his varying moods from day to day during the year of 1889. The sketchbook also revealed a melancholy disposition and a sharp wit. He stated that it was only the "Scotch Misconception of Jokes" which branded him as mad.

His devout Catholicism, evident in his recollections of childhood (*Diary*, p. 15) and allusions to the Ursulines (p.47) combined with this condition to produce an almost obsessive preoccupation with death, especially death as a deliverance from his fate. This was captured in his drawing "Well Met" (p. 55), where he humbly greets the skeletal, scythe-carrying figure of Death ("I do believe that to a Catholic there is nothing so sweet in life as leaving it," reads the caption). His drawings (pp. 15, 26, 46) also indicate outrage at the British treatment of the Irish. Most relevant, however, in relation to Arthur Conan's behavior, are the fairy and elf-like creatures that populate the sketchbook pages with captions such as "I have seen a green lad just like it," (p.22) influencing further speculation about Charles' sanity and a plausible predominate motive for Arthur's later obsessive attempt to prove their existence. His father's words in the sketchbook almost seem prophetic in this appeal; "I would have thought, however, that it would be the duty no less than the pleasure of refined/Professional Gentlemen to protect men like myself — than otherwise — and not endorse utterly false conceptions/of sanity or Insanity to the detriment of the life and liberty of a harmless gentleman."(p.87)

Arthur had always considered his father the greatest artist in the family. In his biography, he compared his father's pictures to Blake's.

He described his father as "a tall man, long-bearded and elegant; he had the charm of manner and courtesy of bearing which I have seldom seen equaled. His wit was quick and playful. He possessed, also, a remarkable delicacy of mind which would give him moral courage enough to rise and brave any company which talked in a manner which was coarse. . . . He was unworldly and impractical and his family suffered for it."[13]

Doyle's attempts to rehabilitate his father's memory did not begin until after he had become the enormously successful author of Sherlock Holmes. Through these stories, he created mysteries that could be solved. From a Freudian perspective, this literary form of disclosure was fitting to Doyle's era. In his Freudian analysis of Holmes, K. Jones writes, "The nightmares that dogged young Arthur Conan in those early years led him to strengthen the bond with his mother, whom he once described as 'the quaintest mixture of the housewife and the woman of letters, with the high-bred spirited lady as a basis for either character.' Throughout Holmes's stories walk a procession of intimidated and exploited women possessing both the practicality and immense moral strength and spirituality of Doyle's mother: Violet Hunter of *The Copper Beeches,* Violet Smith of *The Solitary Cyclist,* Helen Stoner of *The Speckled Band,* and numerous others. Each is willing to confront the powers of darkness, each possesses considerable fortitude, and each draws from Holmes a considerable reservoir of warmth and admiration."[14]

Jones continues, "Their foes are invariably lecherous, scheming, cold, and mercenary. They exist to be destroyed, and about each is a suggestion of the nightmare world which Doyle had so clearly suppressed. The theme of innocence seduced is one which haunts the Holmes stories, and it is hardly surprising that revenge features so largely in the sixty plots that make up the Canon. From the fertile brain of Sir Arthur Conan Doyle was summoned an avenging angel. More than any other form of literature, the crime story provides a catharsis for those unresolved feelings and emotions which we carry with us from childhood in the shape of memories and dreams. To writer and reader alike, there is a freedom to kill and be killed, to crucify and resurrect until the phantoms that beset us are finally laid to rest."

There existed in this avenging angel, however, a compassion and understanding that allowed mercy to intervene. If Doyle was, in fact, able to express his frustration, anger and even rage toward his father in these stories, then it appears that he also came to some level of understanding and forgiveness as a result of this catharsis. In Holmes, Doyle created a person of superior intellect who suffered from addiction to cocaine. The complexity of Holmes suggests a level of vulnerability that made him very human, despite Watson's exasperated assertion that he was "an automaton — a calculating machine."[15] However, it was also through Watson that worry and concern could be expressed. For example, during the early years of their friendship Watson confronts Holmes's abuse of cocaine:

> "But consider," I said earnestly. "Count the cost! Your brain may, as you say, be roused and excited, but it is a pathological and morbid process which involves increased tissue-change and may at least leave permanent weakness. You know, too, what a black reaction comes upon you. Surely the game is hardly worth the candle. Why should you, for mere passing pleasure, risk the loss of those great powers with which you have been endowed? Remember that I speak not only as one comrade to another but as a medical man to one for whose constitution he is to some extent answerable."[16]

Throughout their years together, Watson attempted to treat Holmes's addiction. He recognized that, although he had helped Holmes to "slowly" achieve recovery from the "drug mania," there was always the potential for relapse. It would be nearly impossible to create the concern that Watson had for Holmes in *The Adventure of the Missing Three-Quarter*[17] without intimate knowledge of this condition and the worry that accompanies it.

> Things had, until now, been very slow with us, and I had learned to dread such periods of inaction, for I knew by experience that my companion's brain was so abnormally active that it was dangerous to leave it without material upon which to work. For years I had gradually weaned him from that drug mania which had threatened once to check his remarkable career. Now I knew that under ordinary conditions he no longer craved for this artificial stimulus, but I was well aware that the fiend was not dead but sleeping, and I have known that the sleep was a light one and the waking near when in periods of idleness I have seen the drawn look upon Holmes ascetic face, and the brooding of his deep-set and inscrutable eyes. Therefore I blessed this

> Mr. Overton, whoever he might be, since he had come with his enigmatic message to break that dangerous calm which brought more peril to my friend than all the storms of his tempestuous life.

Doyle's insight regarding the worry, dread and frustration felt by those who witness addiction in others made it possible for him to translate into fiction a reality that is easily recognized by those who have fully experienced it. The brooding that begins with no warning; the deadly calm that penetrates the atmosphere in pervasive and all-consuming waves of tension; and the wall — the thick impenetrable wall — that shuts out the most genuine caring. Like a sudden shift toward self-destruction that bears no resemblance to logic and reason, this growing tempest pulls those who are near it directly into "the eye of the storm," that then becomes for those who are pulled in, their own central nightmare of recollection. Arthur Conan Doyle wrote from this "inside" perspective and those who, like myself, read his stories again and again, are drawn to Holmes because he questioned rather than accepted, and found resolution in the end.

Doyle knew the overwhelming power of addiction. He recognized that it could sometimes reign supreme over the finest and most intelligent mind when certain conditions and/or circumstances were present. He also understood obsession as equally powerful and distinct, in that addiction and obsession may coincide, intertwine, accelerate and regress, presenting both negative and positive characteristics, and that one may be a catalyst for the other and/or symptomatic of the other. Holmes was obsessive in his approach to investigation, as were his most diabolical adversaries in their approach to crime. And the Watson he created, documented these observations, not with the unemotional detachment Holmes encouraged him to develop, but with feeling and a caring concern that was an intrinsic part of Doyle's nature.

Conan Doyle was familiar with the new science of psychology as it was developing in the 19th century. He incorporated into Holmes his extensive knowledge of problem solving, memory, perception and divergent thinking. He was also conversant with such controversial fields of study as graphology, phrenology and physiognomy. In Watson, he created a pioneer in psychiatry and an expert on mental disorders. His treatment of Holmes's drug dependency reflected his counseling skills as well as a sophisticated understanding of psychological theories.

There have been correlations between the work of Sherlock Holmes and the research conducted by two famous psychologists, Sir Cyril Burt and Sir Francis Galton. It has been concluded that Holmes possessed an understanding of psychology that was unparalleled in England during the Victorian Era.[18]

While much has been written about the later influences of Dr. Joseph Bell, Sir Henry Littlejohn, and Sir Robert Christison on Doyle during his years at medical school in Edinburgh,[19] Doyle himself indicated a further debt to two previous writers of detective fiction: Edgar Allen Poe and Emile Gaboriau. "Gaboriau had rather attracted me by the neat dovetailing of his plots, and Poe's masterful detective, M. Dupin, had from boyhood been one of my heroes."[20]

This influence from boyhood was remarkable in channeling the direction of his life. But it was the mystery surrounding his father that propelled this direction. It distracted his focus from his medical practice to writing, and then prompted him to involve himself in solving the "real life" cases of those who appealed to him to prove their innocence. Through Holmes he wrote, "It's every man's business to see justice done."[21] As Doyle matured, the injustice he began to perceive in relation to erroneous judgments regarding his father drove him to move beyond the limited efforts of others to see that justice was done.

Sherlock Holmes, upon entering a crime scene, would never make conclusions based on "what *appears* to be probable," without investigating every component of the crime scene and the individual accused, even when confronted with a situation such as; a man standing over a dead body, holding a bloody knife, in a room with all doors and windows locked and no other apparent means of escape. Holmes would consider the immediate assumption of this man's guilt to be "poor detective work indeed!" Not until everything inside and outside was investigated, and everything leading to the crime was explored, would he consider the probabilities. And yet, as Doyle knew well, the very opposite sometimes occurs in diagnosing mental illness and addiction.

The combined role of physician/detective was recently addressed in this present era in an interview with former Surgeon General, C. Everett Koop. Remarking on the serious lack of physician-time spent patients, he stated:

When I was a young surgeon in the 1940's, whenever a magazine had a poll asking readers, "What profession do you admire most?" the No. 1 answer was always medicine. Now, I don't think we'll ever crawl back to the top spot. I don't know when the difference came. During my childhood, physicians were held in awe. I wanted to be a doctor from the age of 6, so I paid great attention to physicians — they were gods among men to me. When the family doctor drove up to your house for a house call, you knew the healing had begun. Many times he would sit down at the kitchen table and have a cup of coffee.

These doctors were interested in the whole person. They knew that if someone was having psychosomatic troubles, it could be because of the alcoholic spouse or the child who was delinquent. I have often told my medical students that you learn more in one house call with a patient's family than you can in 10 office visits.

Years ago, doctors listened more. We didn't have the myriad tests we have now. The art of diagnosis was to listen to the patient's history and put it together as a detective would.[22]

Sir Arthur Conan Doyle created stories that repeatedly demonstrated that there is a propensity to miscarry justice when hasty speculation is based on what appears evident or obvious. Through his fictional character, Sherlock Holmes, he created a hero that vindicated the innocent by means of thorough investigation.

Although Doyle was admittedly influenced by the earlier detective stories written by Edgar Allen Poe and Emile Gaboriau, an advanced investigative branch of literature was fully developed in China several centuries before Poe or Doyle were born. Imperial/Confucian culture lasted in China for about 2,100 years (from 200 BCE to 1900 CE). Midway through the Han dynasty, about 2000 years ago, Chinese bureaucracy was as sophisticated as that of modern Western governments. And although Imperial/Confucian culture had its weak points, any system of human government that can survive for as long as the Chinese managed must be considered a brilliant success.[23] In this culture, it was understood that a good mystery not only explains the human capacity for the best and worst of human behavior, but also explains the circumstances and the society that surround the crime. A typical Chinese murder mystery would be written in as many as ten volumes, examining every detail surrounding the case. The investigation would involve obtaining as much information about the suspect as possible, including the childhood history, family and ancestral background, and social environment. The central figure in Chinese detective stories is the district magistrate. From early times until the establishment of the Chinese Republic in 1911, this government official united in his person the functions of prosecutor and detective, judge and jury.

Each village or section of a town had a warden who was responsible for knowing who lived in his area and what they did. Districts were ruled over by judges/magistrates who in turn reported to provincial magistrates, who in turn reported to the Imperial court. If a person was accused of a crime, the law permitted the judge to put the questions to the defendant under torture, provided there was sufficient proof of his guilt. *It is one of the fundamental principles of the Chinese Penal Code that no one can be sentenced unless he has confessed to his crime.* If, however, a person should die under this "great torture," as the Chinese called it, and it should be proved later that he was innocent, the judge and all the court personnel concerned would receive the death penalty.

To prevent such a mistake, a full investigation of the accused could take months. Every aspect of his life, including a visit to the village of his birth, interviews with family, neighbors and friends, interviews with the local judge and authorities, a review of all incidents during childhood that might reveal previous problems and/or an exhibited tendency toward the behavior enacted during the crime, was important to the final decision. But the motivation was clear. Without it, a more immediate verdict and execution would most certainly have prevailed.

When a current condition or set of circumstances is viewed as the most important causal relationship to the problems arising from it, it may seem more efficient to address the problem with solution-focused treatment or a specific period of confinement. However, if the causal factors are intrinsically part of the developmental process of the individual, approaches that simply deal with the "here and now" have the potential to be sabotaged by the past. High addiction relapse rates and criminal recidivism statistics remain a costly and constant reminder of the destructive impact of repetitive behavior.

Behavior patterns linked to experiences that propel a child into extreme dimensions can dramatically and sometimes irreversibly influence life-course. The obsessive nature of these patterns evolves over a period of time that, when measured and examined in relation to a person's lifespan, demonstrate in their persistence and complexity why they are resistant to treatment. As a pattern evolves, there may be periods of regression when the behavior is not repeated as often and periods of obsession when the repetition escalates. Obsessive periods often emerge when the person with the problematic pattern(s) experiences difficult periods such as puberty and adolescence, life-changing events that produce stress, anxiety, pressure, grief, and other conditions such as addiction or addiction withdrawal.

Obsessive periods can emerge in the most successful individuals. When this dynamic is present in its most accelerated form, achievement, fame, power and wealth are no prevention or match for the destructive snowball effect that can develop. When studied in successful individuals, a broadened context can be established that gives perspective to the challenges of those who have less successful lives and who are struggling with obsessive patterns. When this dynamic is present within an otherwise seemingly positive lifestyle, it demonstrates that even the most extraordinarily successful or notable person can suffer bouts of obsession that stem from early experience.

In Arthur Conan Doyle's life, a distinct alteration in his behavior occurred after the loss of his son. It was also around this time that he had a strange re-connection with his father that led him deep into the world of the occult and rekindled his obsession for resolving injustice; particularly the injustice suffered by his father. Doyle's attempts to rehabilitate his father's memory left an impression not merely of youthful judgments mellowed by age but of a determination to vindicate a life which had been, to all intents and purposes, a failure.

Doyle had always been interested in the occult. After his son's death during WWI, he took up spiritualism as a serious cause. He even claimed to have made spiritual contact with his father. In 1924, at his own expense, he published *The History of Spiritualism*.[24] Prior to this, in 1922, he had publicly supported the authenticity of the controversial Cottingly Fairy Photographs[25] (which were later proven fraudulent) to be evidence of the existence of fairies, and authored a book on the subject.[26] If he could prove that fairies existed, then his father could no longer be considered to have been insane on the basis of his belief in them. (By the end of his life, Doyle had written a dozen books and many newspaper articles on life after death.) He spent the following years on grueling lecture tours throughout the world, including his first visit to the United States. By the end of 1923, he had traveled 50,000 miles and addressed nearly a quarter million people. He eventually became the President of The World Federation of Spiritualists.

Doyle's obsession with spiritualism led to a chasm in his friendship with the famed magician, Harry Houdini. While Doyle rigidly adhered to his belief in the spirit world, Houdini exposed one fraudulent medium after another to prove that the spirit world did not exist.

Several sources indicate that Houdini's interest in escape was stimulated by a rare book that he acquired when he was still a struggling young magician. The book was entitled *Revelations of a Spirit Medium, or Spiritualist Mysteries Exposed — a Detailed Explanation of the Methods Used by Fraudulent Mediums,* by A. Medium. The book had a profound effect on Houdini because it revealed the "real work" of mediums — how, under cover of darkness or within their "spirit cabinets," they could release themselves from rope ties, metal "spirit" collars, and knotted and sealed bags. Houdini used the escape from tied wrists and a knotted bag in the course of "metamorphosis," the only segment in his early magic act that concerned itself in any way with escapes. Exposing fraudulent spiritualists was a subject that became an obsession only later in his life, during the time of his relationship with Arthur Conan Doyle.

Although Houdini initially visited mediums with Doyle in an attempt to communicate with his (Houdini's) dead mother, he quickly observed their trickery and exposed one after the other until he and Doyle could no longer find a common ground on the subject. Their private disagreement led to a public battle. Houdini openly taunted Doyle for his beliefs. Doyle responded with an angry newspaper article, prompting Houdini to threaten to sue for slander. However, after Houdini's death, Doyle said, "We were great friends. . . . We agreed on everything except spiritualism."[27]

Houdini had been his adversary, but their once mutual respect remained in Doyle, stronger than the rift between them. His forgiving remarks are reminiscent of Sherlock Holmes's remarks about Professor Moriarty. Holmes understood that if he (Holmes) had turned his hand to crime, he would have been a great criminal mastermind; "It is fortunate for this community that I am not a criminal."[28] But his following defense of Moriarty, in response to a remark by Watson, raised his great adversary above mere criminal status. The defense also includes reference to libelous action.

But in calling Moriarty a criminal you are uttering libel in the eyes of the law — and there lie the glory and wonder of it! The greatest schemer of all time, the organizer of every deviltry, the controlling brain of the underworld, a brain which might have made or marred the destiny of nations — that's the man! But so aloof is he from general suspicion, so immune from criticism, so admirable in his management and self-effacement, that for those very words that you have uttered he could hale you to court and emerge with your year's pension as a solution for his wounded character. Is he not the celebrated author of *The Dynamics of the Asteroid*, a book which ascends to such rarefied heights of pure mathematics that it is said that there was no man in the scientific press capable of criticizing it?"

He is the Napoleon of crime, Watson. He is the organizer of half that is evil and nearly all that is undetected in this great city. He is a genius, a philosopher, an abstract thinker. He has the brain of the first order. . . . You know my powers, my dear Watson, and yet at the end of three months I was forced to confess that I had met an antagonist who was my intellectual equal. My horror at his crimes was lost in my admiration of his skill. . . . Never have I risen to such a height, and never have I been so hard-pressed by an opponent. He cut deep, and yet I just undercut him.[29]

In the midst of his own obsession and perhaps not consciously mindful of it, Doyle understood Houdini, and thus could be forgiving to his friend at the time of his death. The behavioral path that brought these two men together in friendship, and then separated them, also brought each of them worldwide fame and legendary status. So it is only fitting that this chapter flow into the next (which focuses on Houdini) without interruption, in order not to separate them once again.

Notes

1. Doyle, A.C. "Extract From the Diary of Dr. Watson." The Hound of the Baskervilles. In: The Complete Sherlock Holmes, p.732. New York: Doubleday & Company, Inc.
2. Carr, J.D. (1949). The Life of Sir Arthur Conan Doyle. London: John Murray. Considered by Adrian Doyle to be one of the best biographies of his father.
3. Doyle, A.C. (1955). Introduction by Adrian Conan Doyle. A Treasury of Sherlock Holmes, p. vii. Garden City, New York: International Collectors Library
4. Doyle, A.C. (Jan. 1888). The Valley of Fear. Holmes first makes reference to the existence of Professor James Moriarty in Watson's account of this case; some commentators (Nicholas Meyer included) have maintained that the professor was in fact harmless and that Holmes suffered an acute form of paranoia, using the professor as a symbol for his persecution.
5. Doyle, A.C., "The Case of George Edalji: Special investigation by Sir Arthur Conan Doyle." Daily Telegraph, (London) (1901) Part 1 Jan. 11, Part II, Jan. 12.
6. Doyle, A.C., (1912). The Case of Oscar Slater. London: Hodder & Staughton.
7. Doyle, A.C. A Study in Scarlet. Originally published in: Beeton's Christmas Annual 1887, with an Introduction by Catherine Cooke and Publisher's Note by Edgar Smith. Reprinted in 1960.
8. Doyle, A.C. 'The Boscombe Valley Mystery." The Adventures of Sherlock Holmes. In: The Complete Sherlock Holmes. (Vol. I). New York: Doubleday & Company.
9. Carey, A. (October, 1998). Houdini's Duel with Doyle in, "Harry Houdini: Best of a Vanishing Breed." Biography Magazine.
10. Baker, M. (1978). Introduction to The Doyle Diary: The Last Great Conan Doyle Mystery, with a Holmesian Investigation Into the Strange and Curious Case of Charles Altamont Doyle. Facsimile of the author's diary-sketchbook. US and Canada: Paddington Press. Library of Congress Cataloging in Publication Data. A facsimile of Charles Altamont Doyle's diary-sketchbook came to light in 1977, having been stored in a country retreat near Minstead, England; it had been sold by the Doyle family in 1955. The book, a major find, was written by Sir Arthur Conan Doyle's father during his confinement in a mental asylum.
11. Doyle, A.C. (1924). Memories and Adventures. London: Hodder & Stoughton.
12. Doyle, A.C. (1894). The Stark Munro Letters. A semi-autobiographical account of Doyle's experiences as a young doctor.
13. Doyle, A.C. (1924). Memories and Adventures, op. cit.
14. Jones, K.I. The Freudian Holmes. Jones quotes T.S. Blakeney, who wrote, in 1932: "The psychoanalyst has yet to plumb the depths of his (Holmes's) subconscious mind" and that what was needed was a "deep investigation of the man's personality." Contributions to this branch of Holmesian studies have come not only from established Sherlockians but also from professional psychiatrists. Whatever one's own prejudices in the matter, it remains true that Freud's methods are still useful, and especially so in the field of literary analysis. It should not be forgotten that some of Freud's most illuminating work was in the field of art and literary interpretation.
15. Doyle, A.C. (1892-1927). In: The Complete Sherlock Holmes (Vol. II), p.96. New

York: Doubleday & Company, Inc.

16. Doyle, A.C. The Sign of Four. In: *The Complete Sherlock Holmes* (Vol. I), p. 89. New York: Doubleday & Company, Inc.

17. Doyle, A.C. (1892-1922). "The Adventure of the Missing Three Quarter." The Return of Sherlock Holmes, in *The Complete Sherlock Holmes* (Vol. II), p.622. New York: Doubleday & Company, Inc.

18. Kellogg, R. "Sherlock Holmes and the Origins of Psychology." Richard Kellogg received his doctorate in educational psychology from the University of Rochester (N.Y.) in 1970. He has lectured and written frequently on the Holmesian literature. He teaches psychology at Alfred State College (State University of New York) in Alfred, New York.

19. Bramwell, B. (1923). "The Edinburgh Medical School and Its Professors: My Student Days (1865-1869)." *Edinburgh Medical Journal*, 30:133-156.

20. Doyle, A.C. (1924). *Memories and Adventures, op. cit.*

21. Doyle, A.C. (1892-1927). "The Crooked Man." Memoirs of Sherlock Holmes. In: *The Complete Sherlock Holmes* (Vol. I). Garden City, New York: Doubleday & Company, Inc.

22. Koop, C.E. (March 21, 1999), "Medicine Man." Section heading: "Trailblazers of the Century." *People Magazine*. C. Everett Koop was U.S. Surgeon General from 1981 to 1989.

23. Van, Gulik, R. (Translation with Introduction and Notes) (1976). Author: Anonymous. *Celebrated Cases of Judge Dee (Dee Goong An): An Authentic Eighteenth Century Detective Novel.* New York: Dover Publications, Inc. Chinese magistrates like Judge Dee were men of great moral strength and intellectual power, and at the same time refined literati, thoroughly conversant with Chinese arts and letters. It is a curious fact that "Judge Dee" was already introduced to Western readers more than 150 years ago. The fifth volume of the monumental work *Memoires concernant l'histore, les sciences, les arts etc. des Chinois,* published in Paris in 1780 and one of the first Western source books with reliable information on China, gives in the section "Portraits des celebres Chinois" a brief biography of Judge Dee, which bears the title "Ty-Jin-Kie, Ministre." (Gulick, 1976).

24. Doyle, A.C. (1975). *The History of Spiritualism* (Vols. I-II), (A facsimile of the 1924 ed.). New York: Arno Press. This book represents an example of Conan Doyle's obsession with the after-life and his total dedication to what he termed "psychic religion". This behavior, which contradicted his scientific background, dominated his later years, and cost him his reputation, provides an example of behavior not grounded in logic and reason that has its roots in Doyle's early experiences and his relationship with his father.

25. Cottingly Photographs. In 1917, two English girls produced photographs of what they claimed were fairies in their garden. A heated national debate ensued over the existence of fairies and whether the photographs had been faked. In July, 1998, one of the celebrated photographic fakes sold at auction in London for close to $35,000. In 1917, Elsie Wright, 15, and her cousin Frances Griffiths, 10, had created the creatures' bodies and diaphanous wings using hatpins and colored cutout drawings, and then played with photographic techniques such as superimposing images. Sir Arthur Conan Doyle believed the photographs proved that "ectoplasmic thought

forms" were coming from the girls' psychic auras. Elsie said they felt too sorry for him to confess the hoax. The women admitted the joke in 1982, although Frances maintained that one picture was of a real fairy.

26.   Doyle, A.C. (1922). *The Coming of the Fairies*. New York: George H. Doran Company. Conan Doyle's extraordinary book examines a number of cases where people had claimed not only to have seen fairies but to have photographed them as well.

27.   Cary, A. (October, 1998). "Harry Houdini: Best of a Vanishing Breed." *Biography Magazine*.

28.   Doyle, A.C. (1892-1927) "The Adventure of the Bruce-Partington Plans." His Last Bow. In: *The Complete Sherlock Holmes* (Vol. II), p. 913.

29.   Doyle, A.C. (1892-1927). "The Tragedy of Birlstone." The Valley of Fear. In: *The Complete Sherlock Holmes* (Vol. II), pp. 769-770. Garden City, New York: Doubleday & Company, Inc.

> The easiest way to attract a crowd is to let it be known that at a
> given time and a given place someone is going to attempt something
> that in the event of failure will mean sudden death.
> — Harry Houdini

The seeds of behavior that can astound, shock and confound
might be rooted in a transcendent experience that sends a child into a
state that combines intense exhilaration and distress. If a child experiences something that creates an internal condition of arousal that sur-
passes anything felt before, even if shock, fear, pain or other symptoms
of distress are involved to some degree, the compelling desire to re-
experience this state by replicating the events that caused it will not be
deterred by the distress symptoms; rather, these components will become associated with intense arousal and inextricably linked to the
behavior that is constructed to replicate the experience.

Fascination, mesmerization, shock, astonishment, curiosity, wonder, amazement, fear and terror are some of the childhood reactions to
horrific scenarios and images. When the reaction generates extreme
feelings and physical symptoms that combine the thrilling aspects of
arousal with the terrifying or painful aspects of suffering, the constructed behavioral response becomes potentially problematic when
the child is driven to repetition by a compelling desire to re-experience
the state.

While many children have a fascination with scary monsters and
violent scenarios depicted in television, film and computerized programs, not all children have an extreme response to these visual images.

Also, a child who becomes fascinated with violence and horror is not always responding to media exposure, although the media is a major contributor to problems in this regard. Family violence, unusual situations, accidents, natural occurrences and even a child's individual perception and imagination can produce frightening experiences and extreme responses.

When a child does have an experience of this nature and becomes unnaturally intent on enacting specific actions involving violence and/ or horror, there is cause for concern. Behaviors originating from this dynamic may at first seem harmless. The behavior may be enacted in secret or blatantly exposed. Once the behavior becomes a pattern necessary to the child, it has the potential to evolve through adolescence into adulthood.

That very dynamic can be found in the remarkable life of Harry Houdini. His friend, Sir Arthur Conan Doyle, created a legendary fictional figure known throughout the world. Houdini became a *real* legendary figure, achieving worldwide fame of mythic proportion. In the year 1920, he was at the peak of his career and was justly proud that his name had become an accepted part of the English language. That year *Funk and Wagnall's New Standardized Dictionary* carried the following entry: *Hou'di-ni, 1. Hu'di-ni; 2., Harry (4/6 1874-) American mystericist, wizard and expert extrication and self-release, B. hou'di-nize, vb. To release or extricate oneself from (confinement, bonds, or the like), as by wriggling out.*[1] Recently, investigator and psychic James Randi, appearing on a PBS documentary on Houdini, concluded: "I've had people actually ask me whether Houdini was a real person or whether he was like Sherlock Holmes, a fictional creation. To get to a point where people don't know whether you were real or not, that's fame beyond fame."[2]

Houdini was born Erich Weiss on March 24, 1874. Though he claimed throughout his life that Appleton, Wisconsin was his birthplace, he was really born in Budapest, Hungary. In his autobiography, he wrote:

> My birth occurred April 6th, 1874, in the small town of Appleton, in the State of Wisconsin, U.S.A. My father, the Rev. Dr. Mayer Samuel Weiss, at that time received an annual salary of $750 (£150). Some of the leading actors in the congregation, thinking he had grown too old to hold his position, supplanted him for a younger man, and one

morning my father awoke to find himself thrown upon the world, his long locks of hair having silvered in service, with seven children to feed, without a position, and without any visible means of support.

We thereon moved to Milwaukee, Wisconsin where such hardships and hunger became our lot that the less said on the subject the better.[3]

Houdini's reinvented birthplace was one of many attempts to gain the security and acceptance his father had lost, but his innovative and seemingly fearless behavior led him to fame and success his father could not have imagined. His feats set him apart because he was willing to endure tremendous pain and suffering while risking his life beyond the norm for his "profession." He once said, "My brain is the key that sets me free." He continually tried to improve his mind and spent years creating an extensive personal library. He was especially pre-occupied with his health. He swam and had massages regularly, didn't drink or smoke, and was evangelical about his diet. But within his brain, evolving obsessions driving behaviors he depended on for security and success, competed with all his efforts toward self-enrichment and self-care.

Other magicians have been killed trying to duplicate Houdini's feats, but he appeared to thrive on danger. On occasion, escapes left him mangled, bruised and bloody. He broke, injured and sprained almost everything in his body. After one performance, his foot was almost amputated and, during another, his arms were almost paralyzed. His magic entailed not only extraordinary risk, but extraordinary pain. His greatest feats were nothing short of "modern miracles of near-biblical proportions," writes biographer Kenneth Silverman. "Magicians know pretty much how other magicians do their tricks, but they still don't know how Houdini did what he did."[4]

While biographical data on Houdini and his magic is voluminous, accurate information surrounding events in his childhood often include fictional embellishment of his legend by himself and others. Houdini was reluctant to discuss the unpleasant details of his family's impoverishment, but often eager to exaggerate other facts to enhance his achievements and reputation. There are, however, many biographical consistencies and two intriguing incidents that indicate a probability of pivotal experience that may be the origin of some of his most bizarre and life-risking behavior.

Magician Doug Henning, who was greatly influenced by Houdini, writes, "Most professional magicians, including myself, first became fascinated with magic by seeing and being astonished by another magician, and Houdini was no exception. This likely happened when his father, Rabbi Weis, took the young Houdini to a stage performance of a traveling magician named Dr. Lynn. Dr. Lynn's magic act featured an illusion called 'Palegensia.' In this illusion, he pretended to administer chloroform to a man, and then after tying him in place inside a cabinet, Dr. Lynn proceeded to dismember the man with a huge butcher knife, cutting off legs and arms, and finally (discreetly covered with black cloth), the man's head. The pieces were then thrown into the cabinet and the curtain was pulled. Moments later, the victim appeared from the cabinet restored to one living piece, seemingly none the worse for the ordeal."[5]

While Doug Henning astutely speculates on the importance of this experience, it is notable that he bases his belief on discovering that, "Many years later Houdini purchased this illusion (reportedly for $75) from Dr. Lynn's son and presented it during the last two years of his show, without chloroform, playing more for laughs than shocks. It is significant that, at an early age, Houdini had been fascinated with this particular illusion literally embodying the theme of death and resurrection, for this was the motif that reoccurred in all Houdini's performances throughout his career."

It is also notable that this illusion contained a horrifying visual display of dismemberment and cruelty that, during the performance, the young Houdini was reported to have believed to be real until the mutilated person was once again restored to wholeness. The effect of this kind of visual violence, whether on stage, television, movie screen or in real life, is a current concern and a subject for debate in relation to youth violence. Gauging from Houdini's response to Dr. Lynn's display of horror, his experience appears to have been instrumental in creating his obsession with viewing and collecting visual displays of grisly horror.

Biographer Ken Silverman writes, "Houdini was fascinated by mutilation. He had a gruesome collection of photographs; in one of them, [we see] some of the prisoners in Asia who were beheaded, and the heads are sort of lying around the fields like cabbages. . . . But Houdini's strongest obsession was death. After a schoolhouse burned down, he traveled out of his way to view the charred remains of the young victims." While Houdini's "collection" did not pose a threat to others, it does demonstrate how early visual experience can lead to obsessive behavior linked to that experience.

Another reported childhood incident may have led to his most self-harming, life risk behavior. Silverman continues, "There's a story that when he was young, he was swimming in the river. He was seven years old, and almost drowned. That story always fascinates me because so many of Houdini's greatest stunts are really underwater escapes. Perhaps that experience so much scared him that he spent a lot of the rest of his life trying to be sure he could overcome it and survive it."[6] Houdini was also interested in helping others survive in water. He held a patent for a style of diving suit. The innovation was granted U.S. Patent Number 1,370,316 on March 1, 1921. The improved construction of the suit was a direct result of Houdini's interest in underwater escapes. The patent reads:

> The invention relates to deep sea diving suits or armors, and its object is to provide a new and improved diver's suit arranged to permit the diver, in case of danger for any cause whatever, to quickly divest himself of the suit while being submerged and to safely escape and reach the surface of the water. Another object is to enable the diver to put on or take off the suit without requiring assistance.

The study of Houdini's water tricks helps to explain why his feats are nearly impossible to duplicate. Few magicians are willing to risk the point of death to the degree that Houdini did. In 1912, after spending five years in his basement workshop secretly developing what he considered "the climax of all my labors," he began performing the Chinese Water Torture Cell illusion. And although it certainly included pre-planned methods of survival, he often appeared to come so close to death that many in his audience were terrified; all the while the stage orchestra played *Asleep in the Deep*.[7]

Houdini was in the middle of a U.S. tour in the fall of 1926 when he began to experience severe stomach discomfort. He refused medical treatment, because that would have meant missing some shows. It is suspected that Houdini was suffering from the onset of appendicitis. He was tired, and unusually accident-prone. In Albany, NY, his ankle broke as he was being lifted into the Water Torture Cell. In pain, he continued to perform. A few days later, in Canada, he allegedly was punched in the stomach by a university student who was testing Houdini's well-known ability to withstand blows to the body. That punch may or may not have been the cause of Houdini's ruptured appendix. Houdini collapsed on stage in Detroit and was admitted to the hospital, suffering from peritonitis. On October 31, he passed away. His last words were, "I'm tired of fighting."

> "My dear fellow," said Sherlock Holmes as we sat on either side of the fire in his lodgings at Baker Street, "life is infinitely stranger than anything which the mind of man could invent. We would not dare to conceive the things which are really mere commonplaces of existence. If we could fly out of that window, hand in hand, hover over this great city, gently remove the roofs and peep in at the queer things which are going on, the strange coincidences, the plannings, the cross-purposes, the wonderful chain of events, working through generations, and leading to the most outré results, it would make all fiction with its conventionalities and foreseen conclusions most stale and unprofitable.[8]

Could another such "wondrous" chain of events have shaped the infamous Jeffrey Dahmer, and propelled his obsession with consuming his victims and storing their gruesome remains in metal containers? In one of many interviews given by his father shortly after Jeffrey's trial in 1994, Lionel Dahmer recalled an intriguing episode involving himself and Jeffrey. During the interview, Lionel shared his grief, confusion and method of coping with the notoriety surrounding Jeffrey's arrest, trial, and subsequent conviction in a multiple murder case that shocked the country. Much of this shock stemmed from media news reports after the arrest. Few could forget the sight of the men of the task force in their protective overhauls, carrying out from Jeffrey's apartment the large metal containers that held the severed remains of his victims.

During the course of the interview, Lionel touched on many areas of Jeffrey's childhood and adolescence, and their family life, as he shared how he had puzzled over what could have been responsible for Jeffrey's madness. He revealed that his former wife, Jeffrey's mother, had taken medication during her pregnancy; and while this could be a factor, there was no real evidence to support any of his suspicions. With a puzzled expression, Lionel then stated, "But there was one thing I do remember that stands out in my mind." One incident had, since the arrest, surfaced in Lionel's thoughts as a recurrent memory. The incident occurred when Jeffrey was approximately 5 years old.

Having discovered the source of an unpleasant odor that was permeating the house, Lionel crawled underneath the building and extracted the remains of several dead animals that were rotting in the crawlspace. Jeffrey was playing nearby. Lionel placed the carcasses and bones in a metal bucket, and crawled under the house again to make sure he had gotten everything. When he emerged from the crawlspace, he said he was startled to see Jeffrey standing over the bucket and staring into it as if mesmerized. He seemed totally unaware of his father's presence as he continued to stare. He then began picking up various bones from the bucket. As he held the bones in his hands, he kept repeating the word "fiddlesticks" over and over. Lionel said he still thinks of that incident because it was so strange.

> What could Jeffrey have been feeling during that experience? What were the feelings and physical reactions taking place that produced what appeared to his father to be a state of mesmerization? What did the word "fiddlesticks" mean to him? What was going on in his mind during the experience? His father said never knew what to make of this curious episode or why it remained significant in his memory. He described it again in the following Crime Library report on the Dahmer case entitled, "Why?"[5] As in the earlier interview, the incident is given only minimal attention in the over-all analysis of Jeffrey's behavior, except for Lionel's persistent comments on its significance. The report questions;
>
> Why does a Jeffrey Dahmer happen? How does a man become a serial killer, necrophiliac, cannibal and psychopath? Very few convincing answers are forthcoming, despite a spate of books that propose to understand the problem.
>
> Many of the theories would have you believe that the answers can always be found in childhood abuse, bad parenting, head trauma, fetal alcoholism and drug addiction. Perhaps in some cases, these are contributing factors, but not for Jeffrey Dahmer.[9]

The Crime Library reports: Jeff Dahmer was born in Milwaukee on May 21, 1960, to Lionel and Joyce Dahmer. He was a child who was wanted and adored, in spite of the difficulties of Joyce's pregnancy. He was a normal, healthy child whose birth was the occasion of great joy. As a tot, he was a happy bubbly youngster who loved stuffed bunnies, wooden blocks, etc.. He also had a dog named Frisky, his much-loved childhood pet.

Despite a greater number than usual of ear and throat infections, Jeff developed into a happy little boy. His father recalled the day that they released back into the wild a bird that the three of them had nursed back to health from an injury: "I cradled the bird in my cupped hand, lifted it into the air, then opened my hand to let it go. All of us felt a wonderful delight. Jeff's eyes were wide and gleaming. It may have been the single happiest moment of his life."

The family had moved to Iowa, where Lionel was working on his Ph.D. at Iowa State University. When Jeff was four, his father swept out from under their house the remains of some small animals that had been killed by civets. As his father gathered the tiny animal bones, he said:

> Jeff seemed "oddly thrilled by the sound they made. His small hands dug deep into the pile of bones. I can no longer view it simply as a childish episode, a passing fascination. This same sense of something dark and shadowy, of a malicious force growing in my son, now colors almost every memory."

The following case example contains aspects of points made in this and the previous chapter. Curiosity, mystery, horror and a small child's perception are at work here. The pattern that evolved, if observed, might have seemed harmless in the beginning, but the impact it had on Harriet's life was quite harmful.

A "Singular" Case in Point: Harriet

Harriet, a 67-year-old widowed white female, was admitted into treatment voluntarily, stating, "My brother thinks I'm drinking too much, but I'm not." She had been living alone in her deceased parents' home for three years. She said she had taken care of both parents off and on prior to their deaths. She reported that she had a stroke in 1964 and again in 1995 and has had some slurred speech secondary to the stroke. She complained of difficulty going to sleep, sleeping sporadically 5 to 6 hours a night. She reported a 25-lb weight loss in the last three years. She admitted to drinking a 12-pack of beer and a fifth of liquor a month. On admission, she denied any withdrawal symptoms. She had attended AA in the past and had completed a 14-day inpatient program 10 prior to admission. Since that time, she said she drank whenever she felt depressed. She described recent bouts of depression with loss of memory. She described episodes of binge drinking of 2 to 3 weeks with alcohol. She reported having blackouts. Psychological testing indicated that she was capable of continuing to live independently, and that despite minor speech impairment from the two strokes, there was no indication of dementia or cognitive impairment. Depression appeared to be a major factor in her alcohol abuse patterns.

Harriet's initial attitude toward treatment was positive and she appeared motivated. However, her approach to program involvement was more in keeping with social club or church group interaction and attendance. Harriet had only pleasant things to say about herself, the staff and group peers. During the morning meditation, she fervently expressed belief in God and devotion to her church. She also brought humorous readings that were not relevant to her substance abuse or spirituality. They were often, in fact, surprisingly a bit "off-color." This contradiction, in terms of appropriateness, was the first indication that Harriet could become confused about priorities within a specific context. Her psychological testing results had also indicated limitations in this area. While she excused this behavior by saying that she liked to make people laugh and "see the humorous side of life," there were other signs of confusion in relation to treatment goals and objectives and life-situation realities.

Short in stature and several pounds under her previous, fairly heavy weight, she appeared frail but not unhealthy. Her grooming was impeccable. Her makeup and dress were colorful but not beyond what would be considered suitable at her church. Her facial expressions were cheerful, lively and alert, her manner and demeanor charming. She would have been a delightful presence in certain social settings and appeared to view treatment as one of them. There was a sense of wonderment about Harriet; she often appeared to be not quite clear about what was happening. She gave the impression that, whatever the situation and despite her confusion, she would attempt to make things better or make every effort to avoid unpleasantness.

During the first week of treatment, Harriet addressed current issues surrounding her admission. Her initial approach to therapy group process was to express sympathy toward her peers after listening attentively to each disclosure. She would then try to cheer everyone up as group concluded. Disclosure concerning her own problems was limited to positive and optimistic statements such as, "I'm just so happy to be here with all you lovely people," or "I'm sure, with the help of God and the wonderful people who are helping us, we will all find success and happiness." Group members had little to say in response to these pronouncements, except to sometimes look at one another with raised eyebrows. She was simply accepted by them as someone who did not fully grasp the reality of her situation or theirs. No one in her group wanted to hurt her feelings.

During the second week of treatment, Harriet's disclosure became more revealing as she began to identify feeling and physical symptoms in response to a variety of presented situations. She consistently described "confusion" as her most probable response. When Harriet imagined herself in a situation that she identified as frightening or potentially dangerous, she said she would have "wondered" what was happening, why it was happening, what she should do, and then would have become more confused as the situation worsened. She identified physical symptoms of chest pain, rapid heart beat, difficulty breathing and shakiness associated with these responses.

During the third week, Harriet's disclosure revealed cause for concern. In response to any situation involving disruption, danger or conflict, she repeatedly described various ways she would try to avoid whatever was happening, or try to "make it better." Harriet said she would apologize for things she had not done, if it would make things better. If she made a mistake, she tried to make up for it by doing extra work, or giving away her possessions. She allowed other people to take advantage of her rather than to see them upset. She consistently tried make others feel better at her own expense. She also put herself in danger by allowing herself to be overpowered by more dominant personalities. Her only form of self-protection in the past was found in close relationships with family members with whom she strongly bonded.

Harriet described feeling unsure and afraid, from an early age, whenever she was alone. She had been devoted to her parents. Her sister had been her most constant companion. Reliance on these close family members began in childhood and continued into her adult life and marriage. She often put her own welfare aside to attend to those she loved and needed. She said she would do anything to make them happy. Her pattern of using humor to cheer up her companions began at a very early age, when she wanted to amuse her sister. Her consistent response to the presented situations, in terms of what she would have done at various age periods, was to run to her sister. She had one older brother with whom she did not form a close relationship.

Harriet's treatment progress began when she was able to reveal her intense fear of being alone. In written assignments and group disclosure, she also revealed that she was currently being intimidated by her brother and did not know what to do. When Harriet was widowed in her mid-fifties, she took care of her parents until their death. Although she had inherited only one-third of the house and property deed, her parents had assured her that she could live in the family home for the rest of her life. Harriet said this was understood and accepted by her siblings. Her sister, who was married and lived nearby, had been a constant source of support during this period. When her sister died suddenly, one year prior to Harriet's admission to treatment, her brother tried to convince her that their parents' wishes were not legally valid.

Until the sister's death, her brother had lived with his wife and children in another state. Harriet said he somehow acquired her sister's one-third share of the deed. With proof of two-thirds ownership, he unexpectedly returned to the family home, moved in with his family, furniture and belongings, and took control. Overpowered and confused, Harriet said her drinking and depression increased. She was now convinced that her brother was trying to force her out and planned to do this by having her declared incompetent. While Harriet admitted abusing alcohol since the death of her parents and sister, she said her condition had worsened dramatically after her brother moved in to her home.

Psychological testing had shown that Harriet was not cognitively impaired, and was capable of living independently. Until entering treatment, she had tried to avoid a confrontation with her brother and "prayed that he would go away." Confusion and anxious prayers increased as her fear and anxiety escalated. Harriet described this same dynamic when recalling childhood responses to fearful situations. With her sister's death, she lost her closest companion and ally. In place of her sister, Harriet substituted reliance on alcohol to relieve her fear, loneliness and grief.

When Harriet shared this situation with her group, she received supportive feedback. Bolstered by the obvious concern of her peers, she became more allied with the group. As a result, she began to express feelings of anger and frustration. She explained that she did not want to leave her home and hated how her brother and his wife "brought in all their furniture without even asking." She described her housekeeping as tidy and that she did a "good job" caring for the home. She said they were trying to push her out despite her efforts to be nice to them.

Harriet appeared to gain confidence with each disclosure and group support. During her fourth week of treatment, she surprisingly volunteered to share an experience she recalled from approximately age 3. She said she thought of it often and remembered the episode as if it had happened yesterday. She said the memory came into her thoughts whenever she felt confused and afraid.

Harriet began with a brief background of her family and home environment at the time of the experience. She lived with her parents and a sister who was two years older, and one older brother. Her father was a salesman who traveled much of the time. Her mother ran a boarding house that catered to many traveling salesmen. Harriet, unlike her siblings, was not yet old enough to assist her mother with minor boarding house duties. Harriet said she felt much love for her family and was eager to help her mother in any way she could. Until the day of the episode, she had only been allowed to follow her sister and watch her perform her assigned housekeeping tasks.

One morning, Harriet woke up earlier than her sister. She went downstairs and entered the kitchen alone. Her mother was placing biscuits in the oven. Harriet remembered the noise of the percolating coffee pot. Her mother turned, looked a bit surprised to see Harriet standing there alone, and asked if her sister was still sleeping. Harriet replied that she was. Her mother then asked Harriet to run up the stairs and wake up one of the boarders — a man named Jack. His room was the first door to the right on the upstairs landing.

Harriet recalled feeling so pleased to be given this job that she ran immediately to the stairway and hurriedly climbed up to the landing. She remembered reaching up to the doorknob and using both hands to turn it slowly. When the door opened, she could see the man lying asleep in the bed. She recalled, "I can still see him lying there with his hand resting against the rounded metal headboard." When the door opened further to widen her view, she was startled to see a leg lying on a chair by the window. The leg still had a sock and shoe on it, and a strap at the top. She said it looked real.

Harriet's described feeling response: "I felt frightened and confused. I could not understand why his leg was on the chair. I wondered if it fell off or why it was cut off of him. I wondered if he was hurt and if I should wake him. I felt scared about what to do, and more confused."

Harriet's described physical symptom response: "I began breathing fast. My heart was pounding and I started shaking all over."

Harriet's described behavior response: "I didn't wake Jack. I ran down the steps to my mother. I asked her to help me and told her what happened. She took my hand and led me back up the steps. I didn't want to go, but I didn't want to disobey my mother. I was still shaking when she led me into the room and woke up Jack. She told him in a very kind way that his leg had frightened me. He sat up and started to tell me a story about how he lost his real leg and had to have a new one made. I knew my mother expected me to be kind to Jack. I accepted his story and went with my mother back downstairs. I was still confused and didn't really understand what he had explained. I left my mother to run to my sister, wake her up and tell her what had happened. I never wanted to be away from my sister after that. My sister wanted to see the leg. On several occasions, we quietly opened the door when we thought Jack was sleeping, just to look at the leg. We were both afraid of Jack. We treated him very nice after knowing about his leg because we decided that he would not harm us if we were very nice to him. We didn't tell anyone about our secret habit of looking at Jack's leg. I would never have done this without my sister. We used to talk about the leg before we went to sleep at night. One night I dreamt about the leg. I still think about it and sometimes dream about it."

Harriet's description of her feeling and physical symptom response to the experience was almost a perfect replication of the most predominant feelings and physiological responses she had been describing in relation to her present condition. Her described behavioral response to the experience helped to identify the origin of her strong security attachment to her sister, and the beginning pattern of giving the appearance of accepting an explanation, and behaving obediently, while still in a state of confusion. Once her appearance of acceptance begins, despite distress, she behaves in a kindly and agreeable way; if then her emotional/physiological distress continues or escalates, her confusion persists. In her childhood situation, her mother had attended to her and gave her an explanation about Jack's leg. But although Harriet did not fully understand the explanation, she pretended to because she did not want to displease her mother.

By then going to her sister, she was no longer alone in the state of distress that persisted and she found relief in this secure attachment. Her feeling of security relied on this form of attachment throughout her life. When Harriet's husband, parents and sister died, her entire her foundation of security was gone. She had no experience dealing with difficult situations alone and often became confused and afraid.

When Harriet was not in a distressed state, she was competent, rational and functional. She demonstrated this during psychological testing. But, when she was intimidated or frightened by something she did not understand, she was not functional. When she began abusing alcohol to calm her fears, initially it helped her to regain functioning. As her alcohol abuse increased, she became less able to function and think clearly. With abstinence, Harriet regained this ability, but was still vulnerable to high stress situations. She was certainly willing to follow all treatment directives, but her initial approach to treatment clearly demonstrated that Harriet could cover-up her anxiety and confusion with the appearance of obedience, much like her approach to the situation with Jack. As a result, her clarity of purpose was often clouded.

Her pattern of secretive collusion with her sister, replaced by her relationship with alcohol, presented risk for relapse. The secretive behavior she had enacted with her sister is significant in that together, they were willing to investigate repeatedly a situation they considered frightening. Alone, Harriet would not have ventured back to Jack's room to look at the leg. With her sister, she defied the rules. With alcohol, she was perfectly capable of doing the same to defy her then-current frightening situation, while covering up her drinking with the appearance of recovery.

Harriet's disclosure and written assignments helped her to understand more about why she becomes confused and about the conditions that trigger this state. She gained understanding of her need for a solid support system of people who are aware of this, and she recognized that she needs to develop realistic dialogue with her support group.

During Harriet's last week of treatment, there was concern about pending legal proceedings involving her brother and her home. Her efforts to come to terms with the reality of her situation had helped her to enlist the aid of an attorney and to permit treatment staff to communicate with him on this matter. She also addressed these issues with her 12 Step support group and her church group. Harriet continues to progress at moderate-to-high risk. On her own, she is still very fragile. She is aware that it is vital that she maintain a structured support system that is aware of her condition. Her competency relies on her continued abstinence and recovery. Her brother is still formidable and will benefit if she relapses. The court case was in progress at last report.

Notes

1. Henning, D. & Reynolds, C. (1977). *Houdini: His Legend and His Magic.* New York: Times Books

2. PBS Documentary (1999). *Houdini: The American Experience.* New Content 1999 PBS Online/WGBH.

3. *The Unmasking of Robert-Houdin* (1908). Houdini Historical Center of the Outagamie County Historical Society, Appleton, WI.

4. Silverman, K. (1996). *Houdini!!!: The Career of Ehrich Weiss.* New York: Harper Collins.

5. Henning, D. & Reynolds, C., *op. cit.*

6. Silverman, K. *op. cit.*

7. PBS Documentary (1999). *Houdini: The American Experience.*

8. Doyle, A.C. (1892-1927). "A Case Of Identity." *The Adventures of Sherlock Holmes. In: The Complete Sherlock Holmes* (Vol. I). Garden City, New York: Doubleday & Company, Inc.

9. Dahmer website: *Crime Report.*

Hollywood Director Tim Burton was drawn to directing *Sleepy Hollow*, the film adaptation of Washington Irving's gothic 19th century fairytale about Ichabod Crane and the Headless Horseman, for very personal reasons. As a kid growing up in Burbank, he'd while away the hours in darkened theaters, watching mind-warping triple bills of *Scream Blacula Scream*, *Dr. Jekyll and Sister Hyde*, and *Jason and the Argonauts*. *Sleepy Hollow* was a throwback to those flicks, the kind that made him want to be a filmmaker in the first place. "I always remember how grateful I was to see them because they let you work through things," says Burton. "They were a catharsis." Listening to him riff off the therapeutic powers of *Scream Blacula Scream*, it is hard *not* to wonder: when a kid finds catharsis, redemption, even his basic sense of well-being watching schlock horror, what kind of freakish misfit does he grow up to be? "I don't consider myself strange at all," Burton replies. "In fact, early on in my career that point of view made me quite sad, and that was the inspiration for *Edward Scissorhands*. I'd always wonder why people are treating the monster badly — from King Kong all the way up. They treat it badly because they see it as different.[1]
Nashawaty, 1999.

When children feel different from other children, and when this difference is reflected in the behavior of others with teasing and cruelties that would be intolerable for most adults, they are especially vulnerable to externalized and internalized problematic conditions. Illness, disability, injury and other conditions that set a child apart from the norm are also influenced by how others respond to these conditions. Children who have a perception or reality of difference that results in ongoing experiences that produce highly intense to extreme feelings of loneliness, separation, powerlessness and hurt are children who suffer.

Behavior patterns that evolve from ongoing suffering during development years can take on characteristic, personality, dual or multiple dimensions and may be enacted with the skill and artistry of a master. It is not uncommon to create an imaginary friend during early childhood, but the child who discovers this ability in response to an extreme state of distress and then repeats the mental action when the state is again generated, will become reliant on this constructed creation. If the internal mental action produces comfort and pleasure to the suffering child, the mental actions will work to produce an external replication of what has been imagined. This occurs because the creation becomes essential to the child and develops along with the child. Once he has discovered the ability to create another dimension of reality, a child may construct multiple creations in response to a variety of ongoing experiences, or continue to rely on the one dimension that continues to be effective as it evolves in relation to the child's needs.

Two writers who have written extensively on the concept of dual-personality or dual-self are Fyodor Dostoyevsky and Robert Louis Stevenson. Dostoyevsky's fantastic work, *The Double*,[2] faintly represents studies in split personality that give us the extraordinary "doubles" of his great novels. Robert Louis Stevenson's understanding of duality in the individual began early. When he was only three years of age, he is supposed to have said, "See, mother, I have drawed a man. Shall I draw his soul now?"[3]

In his later years, Robert Louis Stevenson lived as a patriarch in the South Seas and was known as Tusitala — "The teller of tales." But it is in his writings of early childhood recollections that his own story unfolds as a stunning example of the powerful influence of experience on behavioral development. He understood the child's ability to use imagination to travel to distant realms despite the physical confines of illness. Through his own experience, he came to know and write about how this separation could transform an otherwise intolerable situation into an escape to adventure and a means of freeing the "soul."

While Stevenson's creative ability most probably stemmed from his genetic makeup, his experience as a sickly child often confined to bed surely had a direct influence on his developing mind and behavior. A powerful influence within Robert Louis' experience was his nurse-maid, Allison Cunningham, whom he called Cummie. Cummie, the fiercest of Covenanters, thought card playing, theaters, and novels were wicked. At the same time, she had her own very vivid sense of language, which she expressed in dramatic readings of Bible texts and especially of Pilgrim's Progress, a book that left a deep imprint on the child's imagination. Stevenson, conscious of his debt to her, dedicated A Child's Garden of Verses to Cummie. Even as an adult, he continued to send her affectionate letters. "Do not suppose," he said in one of them, "that I will ever forget those long, bitter nights, when I coughed and coughed and was so unhappy, and you were so patient and loving of the poor sick child. . . . Indeed, I wish I might become a man worth talking of, if it were only that you should not have thrown away your pains."[4]

During these long days and nights, his imagination was fed by Cummie's vivid descriptions until it soared with strength and freedom in the shape of characters that were able to pursue lives of adventure. This separation from the bounds of his physical confinement to the mental freedom of his imagination was a behavior that evolved along with his extraordinary talent. His unique understanding of man's ability to create duality in relation to emotional survival underlies his insightful classic, *Dr. Jekyll and Mr. Hyde*.[5]

This simple moral tale still stands as the most vivid and beguiling portrait of our divided selves. "I had long been trying to write a story on the subject," Stevenson said, "to find a body, a vehicle, for that strong sense of man's double being which must at times come in upon and overwhelm the mind of every thinking creature." And the inspiration finally came to him in a dream that produced all the basic plot elements for *The Strange Case of Dr. Jekyll and Mr. Hyde*. Henry Jekyll is torn, as we all are at times, between his "good" self and his "bad" desires. He calls it his "dual nature" and describes how "both sides of me were in dead earnest. I was no more myself when I laid aside restraint and plunged in shame, than when I labored in the eye of the day, at the furtherance of knowledge or the relief of sorrow and suffering."

Stevenson took just six days to put together something so insightful and perceptive that it anticipates by decades Freud's and Jung's writing on the subject. He understood, from the depths of his own experiences, that in this duality, both good and evil could be explored and released.[6] This is best reflected in the following closing stanza of a poem that Stevenson sent to his cousin, Katherine de Mattos, along with a copy of *Dr. Jekyll and Mr. Hyde*, and is central to its theme. The dedication to Katherine, with whom he was particularly close, was written January 1, 1886.

It's ill to loose the bands that God decreed to bind;
Still will we be the children of the heather and the wind;
Far away fro home, O it's still for you and me
That the broom is blowing bonnie in the north countrie.

When family members provide information regarding a patient who has been admitted into addiction treatment, it is not unusual for the patient to be described as a "Dr. Jekyll and Mr. Hyde." Verbal and physical aggression, unleashed during drinking bouts or other drug use, are commonly attributed to the substance involved. The substance is therefore blamed for a divide in personality that supposedly would otherwise have remained intact. But when aggressive behavior pre-exists substance use and continues to emerge during abstinence, the underlying condition propelling the behavior responsible for this divide in personality may have been developing for years. A problematic and evolving behavioral condition rapidly advances and becomes more visible when the system is affected by addiction, abstinence or additional life-changing experiences. When a divide in personality has been evolving since childhood, it can emerge in many forms other than the behavior characterized by Jekyll and Hyde.

The following is a remarkable example of this dynamic and one that demonstrates how behavior born of childhood suffering can fuel the most imaginative forms of creation, expression and personality.

Magdalena Carmen Frida Kahlo was a Mexican artist born on July 6, 1907 in Coyoacan, three years before the beginning of the Mexican Revolution. She was to become famous for her self-reflective, Surrealist paintings. Frida's father was a Hungarian Jew and notable Mexican photographer. Her mother was of Spanish and Indian descent.

Shortly after Frida's birth, her mother became pregnant again and was unable to breastfeed. Because of this, the infant was suckled for a time by an Indian wet nurse. Years later, Frida painted the wet nurse as the mythic embodiment of her Mexican heritage. Frida also later described her feelings toward her mother as ambivalent. Although she was not very fond of her mother, she loved her father very much and they were extremely close. She recalled that she contracted polio at the age of six and her father took care of her during a nine-month recuperation period. As a result of the disease, Frida was left with a deformed leg and foot and was often referred to as "peg-leg Frida." Carlos Fuentes described her as a child:

> Frida: "A prancing, cheerful child stricken by polio and stung by the peculiar Mexican capacity for malice, for ridiculing the other, especially the infirm, the imperfect. Beautiful little Frida, the striking

child of German, Hungarian and Mexican parenthoods, little Frida, with her bangs and billowy ribbons and huge headnots, suddenly becomes Frida the peg-leg, Frida *pata de palo*.[7]

As a means of protecting herself from ridicule for her atrophied leg, Frida became eccentric by dressing in costume-like, camouflaging clothes and mainly played with boys. She would continue throughout her life to invent her own distinct way of dressing, later adorning herself with elaborate antique jewelry and intricate hair-dos accented with decorations. Additionally, Frida developed an imaginary friend who was able to dance, rather than limp as Frida often did. This imaginary friend became a confidante with whom Frida shared her "secret problems (Herrera[8])," and later immortalized in her paintings as "another Frida."

The following poem is among the most intimate and revealing of Kahlo's diary. A private memory of a cherished childhood fantasy first written in small scratchy words in blue ink, and then again with determination in a larger brown scrawl that underscores the importance of this recollection. Her poem tells a detailed story of her "descent" into a make-believe world where she found her imaginary friend (a narrative that resembles the adventures of Lewis Carroll's Alice). During her ventures "through" the glass window, Kahlo finds ineffable freedom and security, feelings associated with the comforting assurances of a mother. One of the two Fridas may well be the child who is sustained by a mother's reassurance, while the other, realizing her autonomy, knows she is beyond consolation. The child Kahlo makes her own way, while keeping in touch with her other self.[9]

Origin of the Two Fridas

'Memory'
I must have been six years old
when I had the intense experience of
an imaginary friendship
with a little girl . . roughly my own age.
On the window of
my old room,
facing Allende Street,
I used to breathe on one of the top panes.

And with my finger I would draw
a "door"........
Through that "door"
I would come out, in my imagination,
and hurriedly, with immense happiness, I would
cross all the field I
could see until I reached
a dairy store
called PINZON... Through
the "O" in PINZON I en-
tered and descended impetuously
To the entrails
of the earth, where
"my imaginary friend"
always waited for me. I don't
remember her appearance or her
color. But I do remember her
joyfulness - she laughed a lot.
Soundlessly. She was agile.
And danced as if she
were weightless. I
followed her in
every movement and while she
danced, I told her
my secret problems. Which
ones? I can't remember. But
from my voice she knew all about my
affairs. When I came
back to the window, I would enter
through the same door I had
drawn on the glass. When?
How long had I been
with "her"? I don't know. It could
have been a second or thousands of
years... I was happy. I would erase
the "door" with my
hand and it would "disappear." I ran
with my secret and my
joy to the farthest corner
of the patio of my house, and
always to the same place,
under a cedron

tree, I would shout and
laugh Amazed to be
Alone with my great happiness
with the very vivid memory of
the little girl. It has been 34 years
since I lived that magical
friendship and every time
I remember it it comes alive and
grows more and more inside
my world.
                    PINZON 1950.
                    — Frida Kahlo[10]

At the age of fifteen, Frida's prose poem "Memory" was published
in *El Universal Illustrado*. She had high school art classes but received no
special art training while she was young. She liked art books and enjoyed drawing very much, but never studied under anyone famous or
had any kind of specialized learning. Once she was old enough, Frida
began a paid apprenticeship in engraving with Fernando Fernandez.
Another great influence was the American photographer, Tina Modotti.
Modotti provided Frida with her introduction into the art world and
introduced her to the famous Mexican muralist artist, Diego Rivera.

Frida entered the National Prepatory School in 1922 with the
hope of studying medicine, something very uncommon for women of
her time.[11] She was recognized as talented, accepted by the other students, and progressed well for almost three years. Then the course of
Frida's life was once again changed forever by an experience that resulted in severe physical injury.

In September, 1925 a streetcar crashed into the fragile bus she was
riding, broke her spinal column, her collarbone, her ribs, her pelvis. Her
already withered leg now suffered eleven fractures. Her left shoulder
was now forever out of joint, one of her feet crushed. A handrail crashed
into her back and came out through her vagina. At the same time, the
impact of the crash left Frida naked and bloodied, but covered with
gold dust. Despoiled of her clothes, showered by a broken packet of
powdered gold carried by an artisan. Will there ever be a more terrible
and beautiful portrait of Frida than this one?[12]

At the age of twenty-two, Frida married Diego Rivera. Together
they fought for the ideas of Marxism and enjoyed shaping one another's

art. Their marriage was volatile and there was a series of mutual affairs. Due to the accident, Frida was unable to carry a child, which caused her much sorrow. But her work began to be respected and well-known from the time of her first show at the Julien Levy Gallery in New York in 1938.

Exposing intimate aspects of herself, a large number of Frida's paintings were self-portraits. It is said that Frida painted herself as a type of catharsis, trying to release all of the sorrow associated with her illnesses and inner tragedy. Similarly, by painting self-portraits, Frida was able to project her pain onto "another Frida," the one she painted on the canvas. In doing so, Frida relieved herself from the burden of dealing with all of her agony on her own.[13] Fuentes describes Frida's life of pain living in the midst of the Mexican Revolution as representative of human pain in a world where horror persists and human spirit prevails.

> Frida Kahlo is one of the greatest speakers for pain in this century that has known, perhaps not more suffering than at other times, but certainly a more unjustified and therefore shameful, cynical and publicized, programmed, irrational, and deliberate form of suffering than ever. From the Armenian massacres to Auschwitz, from the rape of Nanking to the gulag, from the Japanese POW camps to the nuclear holocaust in Hiroshima, we have seen pain, we have felt horror, as never before in history. The bloodshed of the Mexican Revolution is small beer indeed next to the executions ordered by Hitler and Stalin. Frida Kahlo, as no other artists of our tortured century, translated pain into art. . . . She suffered thirty-two operations from the day of her accident to the day of her death. Her biography consists of twenty-nine years of pain. From 1944 on, she is forced to wear eight corsets. In 1953, her leg is amputated as gangrene sets in. She secretes through her wounded back. She is hung naked, head down, from her feet, to strengthen her spinal column. She loses her fetuses in pools of blood. She is forever surrounded by clots, chloroform, bandages, needles, scalpels. In *The Broken Column* or in *Tree of Hope*, Kahlo portrays herself as this flayed skin, this bleeding, open skin, cut in half like a papaya fruit. As she lies naked in a hospital bed in Detroit, bleeding and pregnant, Rivera writes, 'endurance of truth, reality, cruelty, and suffering. Never before had a woman put such agonized poetry on canvas. . . .' For what she lives is what she paints. But no human experience, painful as it may be, becomes art by itself. How did Kahlo transform personal suffering into art, not impersonal, but shared?[14]

Frida Kahlo died on July 13, 1954. Her extensive diary exemplifies her extraordinary ability to reveal both her joy and suffering to the world, her obsessive need to express this through her talent for language and art, and her unique understanding of the physical relationship to this passion. Throughout her life, she was confined to bed much of the time. But she devised ways to set up her tools and brushes so she could still paint, even when lying down.

Kahlo and Stevenson's lives demonstrate how behavior arising from experiences related to their illness, confinement, disability and childhood suffering, resulted in heroic efforts and gifted expression. The obsessive need and desire fueling behavior to success beyond impossible odds is the same dynamic that drives behavior toward the most destructive outcomes.

Case Summary: Jackie

Jackie, a 30-year-old white, single female, was voluntarily admitted into treatment due to a relapse that occurred over a 24-hour period after a period of approximately 6 months of sustained abstinence. She was currently unemployed and on Social Security disability. She had a past psychiatric history of several hospitalizations for depression, dissociative identity disorder, and alcoholism. She had also been diagnosed with borderline personality disorder and post-traumatic stress disorder. She had been in addiction treatment ten times in the past seven years, and relapsed after each treatment. She attended Alcoholics Anonymous and had periods of sustained abstinence and active involvement. She had an AA sponsor who reportedly had helped her during her six months of sobriety prior to the latest relapse.

Jackie reported sexual and physical abuse from her mother and older brother as a child. She was currently living with a female partner, who also had psychiatric problems. She described this relationship as difficult but, for the most part, supportive. Prior to recent unemployment, she had been working part-time through Vocational Rehabilitation (when she was not hospitalized). Her mental status upon admission was alert, oriented and cooperative. She spoke in a voice suggestive of a hearing impairment which she, in fact, did not have. She also used some hand gestures suggestive of the American Sign language which she studied in the past. She exhibited no other abnormalities of speech or behavior. Her appearance was masculine. She was wearing a cowboy hat, blue jeans and a work shirt. She appeared anxious and said she had been having nightmares, flashbacks and could not "really sleep." She said she had been "on guard" most of the previous night. She reported visual hallucinations of crows flying at her. She associated these images with her sexual abuse. Her intelligence was estimated to be normal and average.

Prior to relapse she had been experiencing depression, flashbacks and changing personalities. She and her female partner had been in much conflict over her participation in AA. Her partner was jealous of Jackie's new set of friends and her sponsor at AA. She reported increased nightmares and flashbacks due to the impending Mother's Day, which she reportedly associated with childhood abuse. Two weeks prior to admission, she reported increased alcohol cravings to ward off nightmares and flashbacks and to alleviate stress related to conflict with her partner. She described sleeping one to two hours at night and feeling very tired, but afraid to close her eyes because of visual flashbacks of sexual and physical abuse. She had one overdose attempt in her past, but decided to come into treatment to avoid repeating this behavior. She attributed this decision to "James," whom she referred to as one of her "alter" personalities.

During her initial participation in treatment, Jackie appeared disturbed, agitated and detached. She was cooperative but not entirely focused on treatment. She explained that she was not sure she could "go through it again." She said the conflict in her relationship was resolved because the relapse had convinced her partner that AA attendance was necessary. She identified her most troublesome problem as inability to concentrate due to sleeplessness, flashbacks and nightmares.

Jackie was medium in height and overweight, but appeared strong and sturdy in build, with dark eyes and hair, a fair and freckled complexion and pleasant features. She dressed in masculine clothing, with a flair for costume. She often wore cowboy accessories and sometimes referred to herself as "Jesse James." She reported having many "alter personalities," each with a different name, specific age and gender. She appeared to dissociate when uncomfortable or distressed, which occurred often during the first week of treatment. At other times she exhibited a social and friendly manner with her treatment peers. She could very quickly change from personable and interested in others to appearing detached and unaware of her surroundings. She occasionally exhibited hostility in the guise of a personality she referred to as "Black Sheep." She preferred to discuss treatment issues with staff rather than peers during group sessions.

During her first week in treatment, Jackie exhibited diversionary and sometimes disruptive behavior. She appeared to occasionally dissociate during group process. She was encouraged to try to participate as actively as possible. It was initially difficult to determine if she would be able to participate effectively. She expressed worry about addressing painful memories. She said she was working through some of her worst memories with her therapist and would rather not address them in treatment. It was explained to her that the purpose of the HRIPTM process was not to focus on her painful memories, but to identify feelings, symptoms and behaviors associated with lifespan experiences still accessible in memory, whether painful or *otherwise*, in order to determine if they were a factor in her addiction relapse. In her case, the *otherwise* proved to be prophetic in relation to some of her most dangerous and sabotaging patterns.

Since she had already acknowledged that memories were the basis for her nightmares and sleeplessness, it was suggested that it might be helpful to her and her therapist if, during treatment, she could identify the most predominant feelings, physical symptoms and behaviors in her present life in relation to feelings, symptoms and behaviors associated with past events. She said this made sense to her and from then on she was more present and attentive during group.

Jackie's extensive experience as a patient in addiction treatment within a psychiatric hospital environment was evident in her masterful understanding of the system. The psychiatric hospital setting in which the HRIPTM program was conducted, included addiction treatment and preliminary detox, if needed; it then phased from inpatient to intensive outpatient addiction treatment. Jackie was involved in intensive outpatient treatment, outdoor therapy classes, exercise classes in the evening, and art therapy classes several times a week. She was acquainted with every member of the hospital staff, including in administration. The art therapy assistant reported with concern that Jackie had been waiting outside for her after work and had left notes on her car. She said she felt nervous about this and blamed herself for giving

Jackie extra attention in class. The outdoor clinical director's office was filled with art works that Jackie had made in art therapy class and had presented to her as gifts.

If it were not a summary, this report could contain hundreds of examples of Jackie's ability to manipulate the system and monopolize hospital staff. She was, at times, very charming, likable, thoughtful, attentive, endearing, spontaneous, caring and childlike. She revealed several "personality alters" that were introduced at any given time. She also exhibited intimidating, watchful, dramatic, destructive, rebellious and disruptive behavior that generated attention to her case and ensured her continuing patient status. This observation is not made to diminish the severity and complexity of her condition. Her condition was symptomatic of the extreme abuse she experienced as a child. However, the behaviors enacted to bring about attention, security, disability benefits, and inclusion in a system that requires a severe level of illness and/or life-threatening behavior for each readmission, stemmed from an experience that did not involve abuse at all.

This experience was identified as a result of her more attentive and productive participation. When Jackie began describing what it was like to dissociate, instead of appearing to dissociate during group process, she also began to reveal consistent feeling responses to a variety of presented situations. She said dissociating was like disappearing into herself and becoming invisible; her most consistent identified feelings precipitating these occurrences were fear of entrapment, confinement, abandonment and death. She described intense and persistent guilt and shame in relation to a childhood perception of herself as "bad" or "evil." She repeatedly described feelings of anger, frustration, irritation, rage and desperation as present since childhood. Physical symptoms associated with these feelings were described as extreme agitation in her stomach area, "knots in my stomach," muscle tension, a lump in her throat, trembling, sweating, increased heart rate, extreme anxiety and "feeling like I'm dying or suffocating."

During the third week of treatment, Jackie revealed consistent behavioral responses to a variety of situations. She repeatedly described behavioral actions that included hiding within herself, withdrawal into self, going to a place or places within, self-protection by detaching from the external world and hiding in corners, closets and contained areas, aggression when interrupted while trying to enact self-protective behaviors, destruction of property, use of explosives, fire-starting, verbal and physical aggression toward others that included use of weapons, self-abuse that involved cutting her arms and other self-inflicted wounding, choking herself, high-risk driving, obsessions with hanging and with fire, suicide attempt with overdose, binge eating, excessive spending, retaliation planning and action, and stalking.

Jackie's effort in group was beginning to increase her motivation to continue making progress. She appeared less depressed and more involved; she exhibited less detachment and less disruptive behavior, and was even helpful to new group members. She was not encouraged to present as focus of group because of her early concerns about addressing abuse memories that were being addressed with her therapist. Instead, she was encouraged to review her lifespan experiences in written assignment and to pinpoint specific areas related to how she managed to excel in sports throughout elementary school and high school and complete almost three years of college despite an abusive home environment.

Jackie's work on this assignment resulted in the identification of a significant event in her life that was still vividly present in her memory. The incident had never before been addressed in treatment because she previously considered it a positive experience, not relevant to her condition. She identified the episode as one of the "happiest" experiences of her life. She was in the 2nd grade and almost 8 years old when it happened. She was encouraged to volunteer to share this experience as focus of group.

When she began her disclosure, Jackie did not include a brief background of her family and home environment during the period of the episode. She said she would rather not refer to that and instead concentrated on the experience as it happened. She proceeded by describing herself as a quiet kid who had difficulty at school. She said she had trouble concentrating, paying attention, being confined in a classroom, and reading. She liked "playground activities and playing ball games." She described games as her favorite activity at school. She said her behavior in the classroom was often addressed by the teacher.

On that particular day, she was in trouble for not having her homework and for daydreaming in class. When the teacher criticized her in front of her classmates, she said she responded by putting her head down and placing her arms over her head. She explained, "The teacher continued to harass me and tried to pull my head up, so I pushed my desk over on her foot. She sent me to the principal's office. I almost ran out of the school, but knew I would be beaten at home if I were found, so I went to his office. I had to wait for a long time before he opened the door. When he did, he smiled at me and invited me into his office. I held my head down. He knelt down in front of me and asked me what I had done. I told him I hadn't done anything and explained what had happened. I said I didn't want to go back to that classroom and I didn't want to go home either. He asked me to sit down. He pulled his chair from behind his desk and pointed to it. He told me to sit in his chair. I climbed into it. He pulled up an old wooden chair from the corner of the room and placed it across from me. Then he sat down on it and looked at me real serious-like. He said he wouldn't want to go back to that classroom either, and then he smiled. He looked right into my eyes. He said we could make a deal — that if I returned to the class-room, he would make sure I was never touched again by the teacher. He said we would be partners in this agreement, but that I would have to do my part and try hard to do my schoolwork. He said he would keep an eye on me, just to see that I was okay."

Jackie said he talked to her a few minutes longer, asking her about what she liked to do outside of school. She told him about baseball and they discussed sports for a few more minutes. Then he took her by the hand and led her back to the classroom. He called the teacher out of the room as he sent Jackie in. When the teacher returned, nothing more was said.

Jackie's described feeling response: "I felt great happiness, important, the center of attention, elevated, rapturous and excited. Then, I felt des-perate to stay with him, and fear of going back to the classroom, fol-lowed by a constant feeling of desperation and anticipation and desire to return to the principal's office."

Jackie's described physical symptom response: "Feeling of lightness, nerv-ous excitement and physical pleasure like euphoria which drained away on the way back to the classroom and turned into extreme anxi-ety, mental preoccupation and distraction, physical fatigue and depres-sion, agitation and stomach distress."

Jackie's described behavior response: "I waited for him to invite me back — to say hello or to notice me. I waited and waited. I placed my-self in the hallway where he would pass. I waited outside by his car. I watched his office door and went to the secretaries office frequently. I thought about this constantly. I planned ways to capture his attention. I figured out ways to keep his attention as long as possible because it always went by so fast. I acted different with classmates and teachers — more important. I let it be known that he was my friend and would protect me. I got really involved in school activities and school sports so he would notice me."

When Jackie shared her experience as focus of group, she did not at first seem aware of the implications of her disclosure in relation to her present-day behavior. But as she was sharing the behavioral aspects of this episode, she described how her attachment to the principal was followed by an attachment to her middle-school baseball coach and then her high school gymnastics coach and so on. In each case, the person was her sole preoccupation and was stalked by her at every opportunity. In the midst of this disclosure, it slowly dawned on her that she had revealed the extent to which she would go to replicate the feelings that were generated that day in principal's office. Since that day, she had developed masterful skill in every area of behavior that became necessary to being the center of such caring, concern, attention, defense and protection within a system that provides some level of security. When she became aware that she had revealed information that might threaten her position and security, her demeanor changed and she became quiet and reflective.

Once her disclosure was fully addressed over the remaining weeks of her treatment, she was able to honestly assess why and how her dependence on the hospital system had developed, and how this dependence related to her childhood abuse. Seven years previously, she had been progressing toward a degree in physical education, when a series of events generated in her a progression of alcohol dependence and a re-emergence of early abuse issues. The worsening situation resulted in a deteriorating condition that led to repeated hospitalizations and repeated addiction treatment. During this decline in functioning, Jackie formed an attachment to, and became increasingly dependent upon, the hospital environment that cared for her and provided her with attention, stabilization and security.

This had not been the case when she was in college and first began having problems. At that time, she was estranged from her family and felt lost in the large campus environment where she had acquired no powerful source of support or protection. She had become involved in a relationship with her present partner, who had family members involved in Satanic cult activity. Her partner was trying to break away from her family and the cult while Jackie was attempting to come to terms with her sexual identity and their new relationship. The cult members began to threaten both of them for rejecting involvement in their group and activities. Jackie said she and her partner were terrorized during this period. She started having nightmares, could not concentrate on her studies, started drinking heavily and began "spinning out of control." She said memories of horrible experiences with her mother and aunt began to fill her daily thoughts and sleepless nights.

Jackie's mother and aunt were reportedly members of some kind of secret Indian cult. Members engaged in ritualistic/sacrificial ceremonies involving their children. The children were allegedly placed in outdoor burial pits and threatened with symbolic fear tactics that included using black crows flying overhead to represent death. Jackie and her brother were forced to participate in these activities as early as age 2-3. According to Jackie, infant sacrifice, sexual abuse and a series of horrific experiences were hidden beneath what appeared on the surface to be "a normal home environment." Jackie perceived her early forced involvement as complicity and believed herself to be "evil." She said it was only through her involvement in sports and extra-curricular activities at school, after the experience with the principal, that she began to feel differently. She explained, "School and home were two separate and very different realities."

Throughout her education, Jackie spent most of her time involved in sports activities at school and after school. She said "things" at home "stopped" when she was around age 9. With special education assistance, she was accepted into a physical education program at college. She initially did well, but had trouble keeping up scholastically. During the third year, when her problems began, she began falling behind, dropping classes and was eventually placed on probation. She dropped out of college during this probationary period. She and her partner then relocated to another state. They resettled, obtained employment, and became active in the Gay community. But Jackie's condition worsened. She became increasingly dangerous, suicidal and explosive. She was drinking daily. An alcohol overdose resulted in her first treatment admission. Her eventual diagnosis resulted in disability benefits. She had been in and out of the hospital since that time.

In the year prior to current treatment, she had a sustained period of abstinence, active participation in AA, and weekly sessions with a therapist; she had worked off and on with the help of Vocational Rehabilitation Services. She expressed desire to return to school, but was not able to recognize that she had been sabotaging her progress toward that goal because it might eventually deprive her of the system upon which she had come to depend. During current treatment, she came to acknowledge her fear that the college environment would not provide her the same security level as the hospital environment. This was a major step forward that enabled her to collaborate with treatment staff on developing a highly structured plan that could move her toward her educational goals.

After she completed treatment and made the transition into continuing care, Jackie's recovery plan involved maintaining an extensive support system and support network that included a continuum of psychiatric care and interventions (anti-depressant medication, weekly therapy and active 12 Step program involvement). She made a commitment to a long-term planned strategy for returning to school. This plan required a gradual transition based on a sustained foundation of support. Jackie progresses at high risk despite her present commitment and this highly structured plan.

Through HRIPTM, Jackie identified patterns of behavior that she had constructed, long before her addiction, to relieve an extreme negative emotional state and to replicate an extreme arousal state. She recognized these behaviors as potentially threatening to her current life and plans, and a contributing factor to her risk of addiction relapse. The identified behaviors include: obsessive mental preoccupation, strategic planning, observation, manipulation, maneuvering and excessive efforts to gain access to needed and desired sources of attention; rebellion, destructive action, rule-breaking and defiance; acting, dramatizing and deception; self-sabotaging, self-abusive behaviors enacted to achieve objectives and to self-punish; creative use of already-present problematic and symptomatic conditions to achieve objectives; stalking, intimidation, self-harm, and life-risk to achieve objectives; and verbal and physical aggression that is harmful to self and others.

Given Jackie's limited ability to cope with stressors that trigger these behaviors, she has accepted that her addiction and behavioral recovery requires a commitment to continued weekly therapy for an extended period of time, ongoing psychiatric care and AA attendance. The high-risk nature of her case is better understood as a result of her efforts to reveal significant information that fully reflects her condition. Her condition revealed to this degree, presents substantial criteria to advocate for a highly structured continuum of care that includes ongoing medical and therapeutic interventions.

Notes

1. Nashawaty, C. (November 19, 1999). "A Head of Its Time." *Entertainment Weekly*, #513.
2. Dostoyevsky, F. (1846). *The Double*.
3. Stevenson, R.L. "Memoirs of Himself," in Memories and Portraits, in Stevenson, R.L., *The Works*, Vol. 20, p. 281.
4. Wolf, L. (1995). The Essential Dr. Jekyll and Mr. Hyde. Including the complete novel by Robert Louis Stevenson. USA: Penguin Books.
5. Stevenson, R.L. (1990). *The Strange Case of Dr. Jekyll and Mr. Hyde*. Lincoln: University of Nebraska Press.
6. Wolf, L., *op. cit.*
7. Fuentes, C. (1995). Introduction to: *The Diary of Frida Kahlo: An Intimate Self-Portrait*. New York: Harry N. Abrams, Incorporated. A Times Mirror Company. Frida Kahlo: "La gran ocultadora" ("the great concealer"; plate 125). The mask-like features of her visage in many of the self-portraits are a manifestation of this very self-control (p.26). She was considered a Surrealist and used psychic automatism or automatic drawing to bypass the rational mind and unlock the unconscious. Part of Kahlo's preoccupation with details of her infirmities springs from her interest, in her youth, in physiology and biology. Of all her biological and botanical metaphors, Kahlo made the most effective use of roots and veins, tendrils and nerves, all routes transmitting nourishment or pain (p.29).
8. Herrera, H. (1991). *Frida Kahlo: The Paintings*. New York: Harper Collins Publishers, Inc.
9. Lowe, S. M. (1995). "Essay." The *Diary of Frida Kahlo: An Intimate Self-Portrait*. New York: Harry N. Abrams, Inc.
10. Kahlo. F. (1995). *The Diary of Frida Kahlo: An Intimate Self-Portrait*. New York: Harry N. Abrams, Inc.
11. Tibol, R. (1993). "An Open Life." Mexico: University of New Mexico Press. The Original Frida Kahlo Home Page.
12. Fuentes, C., *op. cit.*
13. Herrera, H., *op. cit.*
14. Fuentes, C., *op. cit.*

He called himself a man, a real bad man at that. But when he forgot
himself with a friend and laughed, or when he was looking on at life
rather than being looked at, his eyes gave him away for the boy he
was. When men looked on he made his eyes stern and forbidding;
take him unaware and they were clear and untroubled. He was at
that age which is at once the ending of boyhood with its ideals and
the beginning of man's estate with its responsibilities. He was but
going through the debatable land, passing through the mists where
all things are formative and wherein one finds himself.[1]

The Outlaw
— Jackson Gregory, 1914

The most problematic conduct documented in the HRIPTM research is linked to a dynamic that stems from childhood experiences
that produce behaviors created to relieve or replicate highly intense-to-
extreme levels of emotional and physiological distress and/or arousal.
Children who have multiple experiences of this nature have the potential to develop extreme behavioral conditions more rapidly. When
problematic patterns repeat, evolve and multiply rapidly during the
course of early development, the compounding nature of these patterns
can reach their full destructive potential long before adulthood. In such
cases, the behavior can be dangerous, explosive and tragic. When this
occurs, shocking and incredible behavior is often deemed a "mystery"
and the child is sometimes described as "inherently evil." But at what
point should behavior be called something other than what it is, and a
severe condition be considered "evil?" And, how does behavior reach
this point without being recognized as a potentially dangerous condition?

After a two-year study of school shootings, an FBI report said
educators should be alert to students exhibiting certain specific risk
factors, such as obsession with violence. The most consistent factor in
these cases was evidence of years of relentless teasing (the students

who fired the bullets were picked on, bullied, teased, harassed). The report, written by the FBI's National Center for the Analysis of Violent Crime in Quantico, Virginia, lists dozens of risk factors gleaned from a study of 18 school shooting cases (which are not identified in the report). The factors were grouped into four categories: personality traits, family situations, and school and social interaction. The report raises the following questions for educators to ask about a troubled child:

1. What is the culture of the school and how is it affecting the child?
2. Does he or she have difficulty expressing anger?
3. Does he or she show an inordinate fascination with violent movies, books and music?
4. Has the student talked or written about committing violent acts?

Other traits included:

5. Poor coping skills
6. Access to weapons
7. Signs of depression
8. Drug and alcohol abuse
9. Alienation
10. Narcissism
11. Inappropriate humor
12. No limits to, or monitoring of, television and Internet use.

In four of the 18 cases studied, school officials and police had detected and pre-empted planned school violence, but the report stresses over and over that it is not a profiling tool. The authors caution school officials not to use the results to predict student behavior, or use those predictions to violate privacy rights. Bruce Hunter, a lobbyist who represents school superintendents for the American Association of School Administrators, said school leaders do keep an eye on children who act strangely, many who exhibit some of the behaviors listed in the FBI report. Often troubled children are referred to the alternative classrooms and schools that have doubled in number in the last few years, he said. But officially profiling students is not the answer, Hunter said. "I doubt that would hold a lot of promise for us. Kids are forming their personalities."

But some child advocates say law enforcement involvement has clouded the response to fears fueled by rare but deadly multiple shootings. School suspensions and juvenile crime codes have increased in the wake of Columbine, said Schiraldi of the Justice Policy Institute. "I'm fearful once we start putting these things out, every principal in America is going to come up with (the names of) 10 kids," Schiraldi said. "Putting out a profile booklet, slapping a couple of cameras up, a metal detector or two, are bromides — while the ulcer festers beneath. I think when we're trying to figure out what makes kids tick, we ought to talk to parents, teachers, child psychologists, students themselves, not people called 'special agent,'" he said.[2]

Communication with children is essential when trying to identify a problem condition. Identification should not be limited to observed behavior. The HRIPTM research demonstrated that the feeling/physical symptom components that are associated with the most extreme states can be as diverse as the diverse behavior that arises from them. Individual behavior construction and pattern development is the way in which behavior evolves and manifests itself into a complex disorder. The physical symptoms associated with the behavior can also develop into serious physiological conditions. Research that focuses on ways to identify individual symptoms associated with the identified problematic behavior can help provide a foundation for interventions that recognize the symptomatic indicators that underlie and perpetuate problematic behavioral actions.

The beginning seeds of behavior that can astound, shock and confound, and that are rooted in individual experiences of an extreme nature, are hard to identify in some children. While problem identification should not be limited to observation, objective observation is critical to identifying problems at the earliest stages of pattern development. Behavior repetition is the key to identification. If a suffering child experiences something that creates an internal condition that is better than anything he or she has felt before, or relieves an internal condition that is continually fearful or painful, the child will feel compelled to repeat this action with little regard for consequences. Behaviors repeat when they become essential to the child for reasons he or she may not even understand. They evolve with repetition as the child develops, much as the young pianist becomes more skilled and proficient with practice. The repertoire expands with increased proficiency. If the child realizes or comes to realize that the behavior is wrong, guilt and shame then begin to reduce self-regard. Preoccupation with the action (compulsion) is born of need and/or desire to continue. Obsession develops when the action continues to be repeated despite attempts to stop the behavior.

The child then enters a period of submission to the behavior. This conversion occurs when the behavior, whether consciously or unconsciously, is accepted as necessary and therefore will be repeated despite obstacles, consequences, punishment, self-harm, harm to others, life risk, and condemnation. At some point, from the seed action to obsessive repetition, the behavior is likely to be identifiable before the condition becomes severe.

The *Crime Report*[3] on Jeffrey Dahmer rejects the notion that childhood abuse, bad parenting, head trauma, fetal alcoholism and drug addiction are responsible for Jeffrey's behavior. Jeffrey also insisted in several interviews that he alone was to blame for his behavior. But this type of unrealistic broad dismissal and self-blaming disclosure is common when the individual and others are convinced that there is no plausible explanation for reprehensible behavior other than the "evil nature of the child." By the time the child with this type of pattern becomes an adolescent or adult, an adopted self-view, much like that held by others, facilitates self-condemnation and fuels the obsession.

Head injury, hereditary and corrosive environmental factors are recognized influences to problematic behavioral conditions. But there are also an unlimited variety of factors that are peculiarly individual to each child. For example, a shift in what makes a child feel secure can be keenly felt when there are changes within the home environment, such as absences or presences that have altered in some disturbing way, even if the child's perception of what is occurring may not be accurate. For example:

> Davy, an only male child, was the central focus of affluent and very loving parents. His mother and father mistakenly assumed that Davy was unaware of their marital problems. He received consistent positive attention from both parents and had many other advantages. One day, he came home early from school and overheard his parents discussing divorce. He recalled that he was "struck dumb with terror" and hid in the hallway alcove listening until they left the next room. That night, he listened at their bedroom door and overheard what seemed like normal conversation. Relieved, he was then able to go to

bed and sleep. But the fear returned in the morning. He was so afraid that his parents might divorce that he listened every night at their door before he could go to sleep. He began to prepare himself for a "divorce" that never happened. He developed an obsessive pattern of secretly watching, listening and spying to alleviate his recurrent anxiety states. During adolescence, he found that alcohol initially relieved his anxiety symptoms. However, he repeatedly sabotaged his relationships with girlfriends with his persistent suspicions and worry about potential "break-up." By young adulthood, he married a woman he deeply loved. He was also abusing alcohol and entered treatment because his wife threatened divorce. He promised her he would remain sober and was committed to recovery. She agreed to support him completely, but only if he recognized that the cause of their divorce was not just alcohol, but his constant spying on her, which she could no longer tolerate.[4]

When children become aware of, or witness, frightening changes inside or outside the family environment, events that may have a tremendous impact on one child may have little impact on another. Catastrophic weather, ominous warnings on television, graphically depicted broadcasts of violence, accidents, horror, and death will be perceived differently by every individual, and sometimes a combination of circumstances and variances come together in one experience that even the best parent couldn't predict or prevent.

A Hollywood cinematographer once described what it takes to make a brilliantly photographed film. Every element of the production is important: the story, the setting, the score, the actors, the direction, besides the natural or created surroundings that are to be filmed. And then, sometimes by pure chance, something else occurs in the atmosphere or the circumstances, or in the face of an actor, or in the lighting, that brings it to another level. Something unplanned and different from anything previously captured — something magical. Unfortunately (and more often), he said, the opposite occurs. The funny thing is, it's hard to see the difference until it's too late. Even with all the experts examining the daily rushes, expectations get in the way of differentiating a great film from something the audience will reject completely. An entire production cast and crew can be doing all the right things and the magic doesn't happen, or everything can be going wrong and something unforeseen happens that changes the whole direction of things.

In this regard, the idea that a child's individual perception can be easily understood or a child's experiences prevented is not only impractical, it is virtually impossible. But there are ways to recognize if a child is developing a condition that is increasingly problematic to the child and others. In some of the most horrifying recent cases involving child and adolescent crime, evidence has accumulated to suggest a link between animal mutilation and certain homicidal patterns. While this may be a true common factor, the wide range of less observable behavioral indicators may be overlooked by a too narrow focus on the obvious. The challenge is to know what to look for, where to look, and at what age to begin. Emotional/physiological symptoms are possibly the most promising area for identifying problematic conditions, particularly in cases where the child does the behavior in secret or as a internalized mental process.

For example, one patient recalled a memory from his fourth year in which he overheard his mother and her twin sister discussing the premature death of their mother. His mother and aunt were 10 years old when their mother died. The vivid center of his memory involved a portion of the conversation in which his mother expressed fear that she might die at an early age, like her mother. He described becoming overcome with terror and panic at the thought, even the possibility, of losing his mother. From that day on, he said tried to stay as close to her as possible. He followed her from kitchen to garden and spent sleepless hours every night worrying that she might die in her sleep. As a result, he was deprived of sleep, was restless when he did sleep, and plagued with imagined scenarios in which he would find his mother dead.

When he was sent to kindergarten the following year, he said he could not concentrate and spent the day watching the wall clock, counting each minute. When his fear became so intense that he could not endure it, he feigned sickness so he would be sent home. Sometimes, he said he actually became sick from the panic that increased as the hours slowly passed. He described how he tried to focus on captivating objects that helped him avoid looking at the clock. He tried to listen to his teacher but could do this only for short periods. He started counting images on the focused objects, like how many letters were on a milk carton or a box of crayons, to keep himself from counting the minutes. He said in later life he became obsessed with calculations that he repeated over and over whenever he had to make a decision about a change in his life or any decision of importance.

The self-harming and self-defeating patterns that grew out of these identified actions stemmed from the sicknesses that made it possible for him to once again be able to function. By becoming sick, he could go home and be reassured that his mother was still alive. Sickness, whether real or feigned, became the means of alleviating panic symptoms at their most extreme level. Avoidance of school and absence became a pattern. His attachment to his mother increased while his relationship with his father deteriorated.

He later discovered that alcohol and drugs relieved his fear-related symptoms. When addiction became a problem, he entered treatment. He remained sober within the secure treatment environment, but symptoms returned and episodic panic immobilized him to such a degree that he feared leaving treatment. He said he felt better when he became involved with a female patient peer. Upon discharge, he returned to his parents' home until he could find employment, regain his independence, and move in with the woman he met in treatment. He relapsed shortly after the move and the entire dynamic became a pattern that repeated for the next 25 years.

With each failed attempt, his self-loathing increased. Anger related to his dependence on his mother was transferred to his relationships (which always began in treatment). He began to physically abuse these women in sudden outbursts of rage that usually preceded or followed relapse. Alcohol dependence and violent aggression towards women led to repeated hospitalizations and arrests.

This patient had been in treatment 20 times and was awaiting a court hearing for a DWI and violation of probation. He was 43 years of age and had maintained no permanent employment during his adult life. He has since completed a lengthy period of treatment in one of the finest facilities in the country, followed by entry into a structured halfway house where he continues to live and is now employed. His treatment was made possible by his very wealthy father, who continues to believe in his potential for recovery, but who also continues to have difficulty understanding his only son.

Although this case does not fall into what might be considered an "evil" category, behavior that does fall under that rubric evolves from its seed formation just as powerfully, and can be just as hard to spot when, initially, it is predominately enacted as an internal mental process.

Evil is a word that is spoken when behavior crosses an imaginary line drawn to separate the explainable from the unexplainable. Once a child or adult is placed in this category, the explanation ends there and compassion disappears. Genetic influence is included if it is assumed that it is possible to inherit a propensity toward evil — that is, if evil was previously identified in the person's ancestry. In his book, *Dark Nature*, biologist Lyall Watson presents his view on this subject:

> Our behavior is most often the result of a complex interaction between nature and nurture, between inheritance and experience. We are astonishingly plastic in such matters, drifting in the direction determined by natural selection, becoming predictable where resources and access to them are involved. Theft, burglary, assault, homicide and even war can often be described in sociobiological terms and given evolutionary significance. I have tried in most of my inquiry to show that such things often have clear biological roots and can contribute, in the final analysis, to reproductive success. These perhaps can be defined as 'weak evil' in the sense that they are, even if only weakly, adaptive. But we also have a tendency to behave, from time to time, in very unpredictable ways that are clearly maladaptive. Arson, pedophilia, and the pathic peculiarities of serial murder are beyond logical or biological comprehension. They defy every reasonable attempt to make sense of them, though we are bound, as scientists, to try to understand uncomfortable facts such as the overwhelming tendency of serial killers to be white men. Attempts to do so are bedeviled, of course, by the equally awkward fact that those who do such things are frequently as bemused by their behavior as the rest of us. . . . I have no intention or inclination to dwell on the sadistic horrors of much serial killing. These have been well documented in Jack Apsche's chilling probe into the mind of 'Bishop' Gary Heidnick who abducted, raped and tortured, impregnated, killed, carved, cooked and ate his victims in Philadelphia a decade ago.[12] A psychiatrist's report on him in 1987 noted that: 'with continued psychotherapy, Mr. Heidnick's prognosis is good.' But at that very moment, he had three naked, abused, malnourished women chained to the plumbing in his basement, and the remains of another in his freezer. There are painstaking analyses of the charismatic Ted Bundy by Ann Rule (p. 329); of lonely Dennis Nilsen by Brian Masters (p. 266); and of the insatiable Jeffrey Dahmer by Anne Schwartz (p. 340). But however you look at it, murderous misogyny and homosexual necrophilia are unattractive and unproductive. There is little in any of

these studies to help us understand what such excesses are really about. Although Nilsen's reply to a question about the motive for his fifteen killings may come as close as we are likely to get. He said: 'Well, enjoying it is as good a reason as any' (p. 266). Many of these killers appear to have no inner being."[5]

Watson's analysis of behavior is fascinating and riveting because it is based on years of study that includes extensive observation of nature. He describes evil as an entity that is real in relation to an intangible line that is crossed into a realm of behavior that is difficult to understand. But in the cases presented, if one to were to take the diabolical and inhuman label off the offending behavior, and objectively pinpoint, as close as possible, its origin and development, the word tragic might better describe a dynamic that can overwhelm a person so powerfully.

In his book, Watson also refers to the child murderer, Eric Smith. Smith presents an excellent case for argument and one that deserves careful scrutiny. Watson's inference that the concept of evil is being reconsidered by a growing number of people is accurate. It is much easier to explain this type of behavior in terms of evil when a cloud of mystery surrounds the case. The mystery is often created and perpetuated by family members, friends, media reports and others associated with the case who describe the murderer from their own perspective. Speculation prevails, particularly when the offender (even when making a detailed confession) cannot fully explain a motive.

An example of this is demonstrated in Watson's review of the Eric Smith case, and Special Reports by *CBS*[6] and *ABC*[7] that encapsulate some of the questions and speculations that arose following the murder of Derrick Robie. On August 2, 1993, in the small town of Savona in New York State, 13-year-old Eric Smith led 4-year-old Derrick Robie into a patch of woods, choked him into unconsciousness, battered him to death with rocks, sexually abused him with a stick and doused the child's body with red Kool-Aid from his own lunch pack. Eric is freckled-faced and red-haired with glasses draped over slightly folded ears. He confessed to the killing six days after it occurred, describing in detail what he had done. He appeared to be enjoying the attention of his interview with the local District Attorney. When asked why he had killed the boy, he replied: "I don't know. I just saw this kid, this blond kid — and I wanted to hurt him."

The two boys had known each other and had played together, on occasion; enough, perhaps to make Eric (who had often been teased about his looks and speech problems) jealous of the out-going, bright, attractive younger child. Nothing unusual here, just the normal and inevitable growing pains of being adolescent and insecure. Enough to hate, but not enough to kill. Eric's family is extensive, with four generations all living nearby — lots of hugs and kisses, no social isolation. Eric visited frequently with his thirteen aunts and uncles and twenty-eight cousins, with whom he was invariably gentle — "like a babysitter." An older boy with whom he went fishing said Eric "was so soft that he couldn't even bait his own hook." It was his great-grandfather who went with him to the police, and his grandfather who sat outside with his mother, while Eric confessed. Both later described him as "very loving" and found his actions totally bewildering. "My God," said the grandfather, "I should have been able to see somehow. There should have been something there to see!"

CBS television covered every stage of the year-long prosecution of Eric Smith. They called their special report on the murder: *Why Did Eric Kill?* And came to no useful conclusion. He was brought up in an apparently happy home in a quiet little middle-class town. A "good boy," who was "happy" — this was the word the police used to describe his attitude — to take part in the investigation. The following is an excerpt from the CBS report:

> The murder of Derrick Robie devastated his family and their community, and left everyone with one question — why? Eric's mother, Tammy Smith, shares the sense of disbelief and horror. "A child just doesn't all of a sudden kill someone," she says. "Something went terribly wrong, and I don't know why, and I might not ever know why."
>
> It is a question which Eric Smith himself struggles to answer; he still sees himself as "just a normal kid, just like anybody else." His parents remain frustrated by his seeming inability to comprehend the enormity of his crime. "Do you think Eric understands the impact of what he did . . .?," Ms. Vieira asks Tammy Smith. "Do you think he gets it yet?" "I don't think he does," Tammy Smith replies. "It's like it's, what happened, is in one place, and he's in another."
>
> What happened on an August day in 1993 changed two families' lives forever: Eric Smith admits that on that day he lured Derrick Robie into a patch of woods on the way to a recreation center. He stran-

gled the child, battered him with rocks, and sodomized him with a stick. Ms. Vieira says one of the things she hoped the report would do is help people understand how this crime destroyed both families. "All of us can try to imagine the despair of Derrick Robie's parents," she says. "Do we have space in our hearts for the parents of the killer, even if the killer is a child himself? Ted and Tammy Smith don't seem to want sympathy; they, like the rest of us, are trying to figure out how their son was capable of such an atrocity."

ABC News Thursday Night explored the legal system that prosecuted Eric Smith as an adult, and talked to lawyers, psychiatrists, and trial witnesses involved in the case. The program also brought viewers up-to-date on how Eric, then age 18, was faring in a maximum-security juvenile facility and his parents' assertion that he had yet to get the personal psychological attention he so desperately needed. The report continued:

> While mystery certainly seems to surround this case, and it is easy to see how Eric's behavior was described as "evil," a more plausible explanation can be found in the accumulated interviews that were collected for this ABC report. Reviewing the case they had covered in 1993, the report began with a recount of how shocking the murder was at the time. Eric's identity was known to the public almost immediately after his confession. He showed little emotion after his arrest and became a national symbol of evil and child crime. At the same time, the parents of Derrick Robie appeared on all the talk shows and they received much public sympathy. After his conviction, Eric gave an interview to ABC. He was then age 14. His voice had changed. He described himself as a normal, red-headed, regular kid. He said he hated school and math because it had too many numbers. He said he likes funny jokes and wanted to move out west and become a country singer. He appeared to shut off when asked about that day.

During this review, a more in-depth picture of the family emerged. The parents, Ted and Tammy Smith, were interviewed. Ted, a factory worker and Tammy, a housewife, described problems with Eric from the time of his birth. Eric was their second child and only son. He had an older sister Stacey and younger sister Holly, who were also interviewed for this report. Tammy said she blamed herself because she had taken medication for epilepsy during her pregnancy. Eric was born with physical and neurological birth defects. He was small for his age, with low-set ears that bent toward the front of his face. He didn't walk or talk until age two. He threw repeated tantrums and when doing so held his breath until he turned blue. Tammy said the doctors told her Eric would be okay. He was a slow learner and had to repeat the fourth grade. One day, she recalled, he scratched himself out of his school picture.

His sister Holly was younger, but close to Eric in age; she described her brother as a nice kid and her best friend. She witnessed what Eric experienced at school and described how he was "picked-on constantly and called dumb." She cried while talking about it. When Eric was interviewed about this, he said he tried to make friends by being the class clown. He said this made him happier because when he did this, he couldn't hear the negative — and if he picked on himself it didn't hurt so much. He said he was hurt by the teasing, "It bugged me." He described the school bus as a "nightmare." The other kids made a gauntlet for him to get through to his seat. His sister said he came home in tears and wouldn't fight back. Eric wet his bed until age eleven. Other reported behaviors were repeated episodes of fire-starting and killing small animals. He was caught trying to strangle a neighbor's cat.

When his defense psychiatrist, Steven Hermitt asked Eric about what led to his savage behavior, Eric described himself during childhood as sad and depressed, and deadly angry. He recounted two vivid memories of experiences that had a significant impact on his growing rage. At age 9, he said, a kid at school had told him that Ted was not his biological father: that his mother had been married previously and he and his older sister were from that union. The boy then told him that his real father didn't want him, but did want the older sister. The other incident occurred a few months before the murder. Eric complimented his older sister on her hair. She told him to shut up; he lunged at her. He said he was full of tension, and went to his father for help. He said his anger was building and that he was getting angrier and angrier. Ted verified Eric's recollection of the episode and recalled telling Eric to "go hit a punching bag." He explained that Eric did what he had suggested, but instead beat on a tree until his hands were bleeding. Ted said he is haunted by his son's bloody hands and how he had failed him.

There were also other problems in the home that surfaced after the murder. Ted had a violent temper and was accused of fondling his step-daughter. Tammy passively defended Ted by explaining that Ted only touched Stacey a few times. The community turned against the family after the murder and the family received hate mail. During the trial, Eric kept quiet, but in his confession given to the DA at the time of his arrest (in which he described the murder in brutal detail), he also recounted an event that took place right before the murder.

Eric rode his bicycle into a local park where a group of men where sitting at a picnic table having lunch. His bicycle bumped the table, as he passed. One of the men began taunting Eric, jeering, "I bet I can beat your head in." The man even threatened to go to his car and get a gun. Eric rode away from the men overwhelmed by rage. While riding away from the picnic area, he came upon Derrick Robie.

During the earlier interview with Eric, at age 14, he described his life as "junk." "My older sister treated me like trash and people were always spitting on me." He described his rage as his "mad switch." He said, "It is like going from A to B with a line going through it." It was in this extreme state of B, that Eric murdered Derrick Robie.

Eric's case is an example of a suffering child who began exhibiting behavioral signs very early. His behavior patterns evolved because they were effectively maintaining his ability to function in a world that was becoming increasingly unbearable. The murder did not "just happen." It was an immediate advancement in a pattern of behavior that had been evolving for years into a dangerous, severe and volatile condition.

Recent evolutionary studies in nature are witnessing similar dynamics as environmental stressors make it increasingly difficult for certain species to survive. Behavior not previously recorded in animal populations is making it possible to study evolution as it is occurring because it is happening at a rapid rate in areas that are most affected by severe conditions.[8] Scientists view this change in animal behavior as alarming and a warning sign of environmental disaster.

Early behavioral signs in children should be viewed with the same degree of alarm. The signs are there but are too often unidentified, overlooked, underestimated, unaddressed or ineffectively addressed and disregarded. It is interesting to note that animal rights activists are already crying out for this type of identification in relation to the alarming rate of animal abuse. The following, taken from the recent *Addendum to The Humane Society of the United States News* article, Summer, 1989 by Dr.

Randall Lockwood and Guy R. Hodge, begins with a prophetic quote by anthropologist Margaret Mead: "One of the most dangerous things that can happen to a child is to kill or torture an animal and get away with it."

- Jeffrey L. Dahmer: Serial Killer, Sexual Deviant. Dahmer confessed to killing, dismembering and, in some cases, cannibalizing, 17 men and boys. As a child, Dahmer impaled frogs, decapitated dogs, and staked cats to trees in his backyard. Dahmer was sentenced to death, but before the sentence was carried out, he was killed by another inmate in 1994.
- Ted Bundy: Serial Killer, Rapist. Bundy killed numerous females who looked like a woman for whom he had a passion. In the 1970s he brought fear to college campuses in many states after killing three women in the Chi Omega sorority house at Florida State University. He was ultimately convicted of two killings, but is suspected of murdering over 40 females, primarily in the northwest. During his childhood, he witnessed his father's brutality toward animals and he himself tortured animals. Bundy was executed in Florida.
- Richard Allen Davis: Accused killer and rapist of 12-year-old Polly Klaas. Davis has been charged with kidnapping Polly Klaas from her own home, raping and strangling her. As a 14-year-old, he set cats on fire and used dogs as targets while practicing knife-throwing. In 1993, he was charged with the shooting death of Marlene Voris 20 years before. "When he was little, it was animals. When he got bigger, it was people." said Zak Backet, a neighbor.
- Michael Wayne Echols (18), Jesse Lloyd Misskelley Jr. (17), Charles Jason Baldwin (16): Killed three 8-year-old boys. The three teenagers were arrested in 1993 for the brutal murder of three 8-year-old boys in West Memphis. The three young boys were lured into the woods, beaten into unconsciousness, one was sexually mutilated, another raped, and all three killed. For some time prior to the killing, the three teenagers were involved in satanic-type rituals. During an initiation ceremony they killed dogs, skinned them, and ate their flesh. Echols was also carrying the head of a cat with him.
- Eric Smith: Adolescent killer of 4-year-old boy: When Smith was 13 years old, he bludgeoned 4-year-old Derrick Robie to death and was charged with murder. Four years prior to killing Derrick, Smith killed the neighbor's cat with a garden hose. There is no specific reason why he killed the little boy or the cat.

- David Berkowitz: Serial killer: David Berkowitz killed a number of his neighbors' pets, as a youth. When he grew up, he became New York City's "Son of Sam" murderer. He shot thirteen young men and women; six died and at least two suffered permanent disabilities. He poisoned his mother's parakeet, out of jealousy.

The problem with any simplification or categorization of behavior as a profiling marker to specific later behavioral conditions is that it limits the view in relation to identifying problems. The FBI warns against reliance on profiling as a method of prevention in its report on school shootings. The HRIPTM research documented the unlimited diversity of behavior leading to problematic conditions. The common factors lie in a child's individual emotional/physiological condition. How the individual child is progressing in his or her emotional and physical health and behavioral development is the key to early identification and intervention of problematic behavior that leads to disorder. When these conditions reach a well-advanced or chronic stage, they are much more difficult to identify, understand and address. Whether addiction is present or not, problematic patterns that begin in early childhood have the potential to destroy health, happiness and life.

In Hare's book, *Without Conscience*[9], he argues that we live in a "camouflage society," a society in which some psychopathic traits — egocentricity, lack of concern for others, superficiality, style or substance, being "cool," manipulative, and so forth — increasingly are tolerated and even valued. Hare challenges the *Diagnostic and Statistical Manual of Mental Health Disorders (DSM-IV)*[10] criteria for antisocial personality, arguing: "The distinction between psychopathology and *antisocial personality disorder* (ASPD) is of considerable significance to the mental health and criminal justice systems. Unfortunately, it is a distinction that is often blurred, not only in the minds of many clinicians but in the latest edition of the *DSM-IV*. . . . it is easy to see how both psychopaths and those with antisocial personality disorder could blend in readily with groups holding antisocial or criminal values. It is more difficult to envisage how those with ASPD could hide out among more prosocial segments of society. Yet psychopaths have little difficulty infiltrating the domains of business, politics, law enforcement, government, academia and other structures. It is the egocentric, cold-blooded and remorseless psychopaths who blend into all aspects of society and have such devastating impacts on people around them who send chills down the spines of law enforcement officers."

In a letter to Asa Gray,[12] Charles Darwin once wrote: "What a trifling difference must often determine which shall survive, and which shall perish!" But there are also many trifling differences that change, alter and redirect a child's life in such a way that, without help, the life that survives does ultimately perish. And it is at the beginning of these lives that action must be taken.

Case Summary: Gary

Gary, a 43-year-old white, married male, was voluntarily admitted for severe pain from chronic reflex sympathetic dystrophy and for loss of control of the opiates he was taking (until his anesthesiologist would be able to do a nerve block). The previously scheduled nerve block had been postponed because his physician had become ill. During this postponement period, Gary was given opiates for pain but admitted to overtaking them, while feeling depressed, hopeless and very fearful of a "seizure" or of relapsing into drinking. He was given Methadone, for pain, in the hopes that he would not become euphoric with this drug; but he reported "feeling stoned" and unable to function. Methadone was stopped and the nerve block was scheduled, with discharge medication supervised by the hospital physician. This was followed by admission into addiction treatment.

During his initial participation in treatment, Gary followed all treatment directives. He began attending Narcotics Anonymous and obtained a sponsor. He responded to the program format from the onset. He said he had been in treatment many times, but wanted to "really try hard to make it this time." In addition to NA, he and his wife began attending a nearby church. The pastor took an interest in Gary and gave him individual attention and pastoral counseling. These efforts helped Gary to stabilize and focus on treatment goals and objectives.

Gary was referred for psychological testing in order to help determine if bipolar disorder or post-traumatic stress disorder (PTSD) were present. He was interviewed by the consulting psychologist and took the Personality Assessment Inventory (PAI). He reported a wide array of symptoms on the PAI (which is not surprising, in view of his multiple hospitalizations for a wide variety of problems). His score on the Traumatic Stress subscale of the PAI was unusually high and suggested the presence of PTSD. He reported "horrible experiences" (severe physical, emotional, and sexual abuse in his childhood) that he continues to relive to this day. His score on the Mania scale was only slightly elevated and, by itself, would not indicate bipolar disorder. When questioned during the interview, however, he reported chronic and severe mood swings, sleep problems, racing thoughts, rapid speech, and periods of hyper-energetic behavior. He also reported a good response to his current medication. It was determined that PTSD was a likely diagnosis while the evidence for bipolar disorder was somewhat equivocal but strong enough to justify a trial on mood-stabilizing medication.

Gary was of average height, weight and appearance. He had short brown hair and brown eyes. He dressed neatly and was polite in manner. He always appeared to be eagerly waiting for something to happen. There was heightened expectation in his eyes, rather than hyper-vigilant apprehension. This was his most disarming feature. He appeared to expect something positive, despite self-depreciating dialogue that invariably focused on the negative.

Gary verbalized everything he felt. This often irritated treatment peers. He had difficulty being quiet and sitting still even for a moment unless occupied in an assigned project or role. When working on an assignment, he responded to encouragement and praise with increased effort and willingness. He did well in group process, but had problems with dialogue boundaries. This also caused problems in his 12 Step group and contributed to his diminished attendance after an initial positive beginning. His relationship with his pastor continued because he had the pastor's undivided attention.

Gary had suffered extreme abuse as a child. He was plagued by painful childhood memories and was prepared to share a multitude of horror stories with anyone who would listen. His memories were continually present and could be vividly recalled in detail. The HRIPTM program is structured to address underlying symptoms before individually focusing on episodic experience; therefore, Gary was encouraged to address current issues in process and meditation group, while learning to be objective in identifying feelings, physical symptoms and behavior that contribute to his addiction and chronic relapse.

An organized method for individual disclosure is often initially difficult for patients who are eager to share experiences without taking the time to learn a structured process for doing so first. However, once Gary began to follow the organized group process, his dialogue became more constructive and less disruptive.

Gary is an example of a child who experienced ongoing trauma from the time he was born. Even in cases such as his, where a multitude of traumatic experiences are present in daily thoughts, predominant and pivotal events can be identified within this maze of trauma. Those prioritized experiences, identified as most pivotal, are often the most driving and disruptive force in the present-day behaviors that sabotage progress and recovery.

The lifespan charting assignments helped Gary begin a process of objective review of his life in order to pinpoint areas that he came to prioritize. His willingness to begin writing, despite difficulty with spelling and grammar, was an indication of a natural inclination in this area. During the first week of treatment, Gary began to reveal consistent feeling and physical symptom responses to a variety of presented situations. Imagining himself at various age periods in his childhood, he repeatedly identified confusion, fear, humiliation, shame, despair, deprivation, hopelessness, loneliness and hatred as far back as he could remember. Associated physical symptoms were described as mental pain, mental confusion, pressure in head, tears, audio-visual distortion, intense anxiety and nervousness, increased energy, hyperactivity and sleeplessness.

During the second week in treatment, Gary revealed consistent behavioral responses to a variety of situations. He repeatedly described behavioral actions that included running away from situations that produced identified distress symptoms, destructive and self-abusive behavior, verbal screaming, physical and violent aggression, suicidal ideation, threat to self-harm, hiding, lying and stealing.

Alcohol and drugs were introduced early in Gary's childhood at a time that coincided with his extremely problematic behavioral pattern development. However, the behaviors that repeated and developed into his most destructive patterns precipitated substance abuse that began around age 6-7. This important factor helps to explain Gary's behavioral actions prior to substance relapse, and how these actions contribute to, but are not a result of, relapse. It also identifies the potential for dangerous high risk behavior that can arise from conditions other than substance use and also present a high risk for relapse to substance abuse.

Gary's efforts to address his feelings, associated physical symptoms and behaviors began to have a positive effect on his ability to recognize how easily he could be triggered into self-destructive and destructive actions. By the third week of treatment, he had produced volumes of written material mapping out and prioritizing his lifespan experiences. By recognizing factors related to his limited ability to cope with daily stressors, he began to recognize that his level of risk was high and that his need for a solidly structured support system was undeniable. Sadly, he was not able to identify one positive period in his early life. He could not identify a time when positive coping skills were developed. He clearly identified periods when many destructive behaviors were constructed in his effort to survive the nightmare of his childhood.

Gary's written work demonstrated creative talent. With limited reading and writing skills and education, he produced material that was interesting and quite remarkable. While writing about his experiences, he also began writing short stories. Some were personal vignettes, often written in rough poetic verse. Others were short horror stories not unlike those written by Stephen King. The more he was encouraged, the more he wrote, until he had produced many pages of revealing homework.

Before long, he was able to identify an experience that he said stood out from the rest. He chose this experience for his focus of group disclosure, which was scheduled for presentation during his fifth week of treatment. Gary said that the following experience happened when he was 6 years old, and was a regularly occurring and vividly present recollection. His disclosure began with a brief background of his family and home environment.

Gary was the second youngest child and only son. He had three older sisters. He lived with his mother and stepfather. He had believed his stepfather was his real father, until he reached the age of 6. Conditions were terrible in his home environment. Addiction, neglect, abuse and violence prevailed. As an infant, he was removed twice from the home by local Social Services for severe neglect. His written descriptions of his early life were a horrifying account of childhood physical and sexual abuse to an extreme degree. By the time he entered first grade, he had developed a pattern of self-protection. He described this behavior as "putting himself in a big Bubble." The following experience, taken from his written preparation for group disclosure, describes an episode that gave him a first glimpse of something other than brutality. The following is a facsimile of the written account he prepared.

"I remember going to first grade in school. Did not want to go because I did not have clothes or shoes. I remember going with pants that were too small and my shoes did not have shoestrings. I remember just sitting there and I would put myself in a big Bubble so no one would see what I didn't have. I remember the school principal calling me to his office — can remember what his office looked like. I remember he sat me down and started asking me why don't you have shoestrings. By now I knew my bubble was broken and I felt awful and embarrassed to death. He took some twine to wrap boxes with and made shoestrings. I remember he dipped the ends into glue so they would not come apart, and put them on my shoes. He was a kind man."

Gary's described feeling response: "My bubble was broken. I felt awful and embarrassed to death. I felt ashamed and bad."

Gary's described physical symptom response: "Racing thoughts, inside screaming noises, blurred vision and confusion, intense pressure in head, accelerated energy in body and tears."

Gary's described behavior response: "I ran away, all the police and neighbors, just everybody in town was looking for me. I was so embarrassed when they found me, and I set fire to the grass outside and ran away again. Finally, after being caught over and over, I stopped running away and started drinking a lot and sniffing glue, gas, just everything, was always out of my mind — felt normal to me. Just over shoe strings look what happened to me and how I felt."

Gary has been alcohol and drug dependent since pre-adolescence. His formal education stopped at eighth grade. Despite this, he learned the trade of auto mechanics and automobile restoration. He worked hard when focused on a job. He was innovative and creative.

Gary had few sustained positive periods in his life, but they occurred as a result of his own initiative. His behavior, addiction and mental and physical illnesses sabotaged these efforts repeatedly throughout his life. The fact that he continued to try at all demonstrated courage and persistence. The kindness he received from the principal was the only early experience in his life that could be linked to his capacity for kindness. Although he initially responded to the principal's kindness by running away, he began to enact kindnesses to others from that time on. This behavior was most prevalent when he was able to maintain some level of stability. For example, whenever he earned extra money, he spent all of it on presents for his wife. One day, when he mistakenly thought he had won the lottery, he excitedly announced his plans to buy a building for the treatment program. He then had to be told by his counselor that the letter he received was just a gimmick; but he was completely sincere in his intention.

His wife was a stabilizing factor, although she too had been diagnosed with mental health problems more than once — they had each been hospitalized for psychiatric and addiction problems several times during the course of their 8-year marriage. They had occasionally separated due to Gary's violent episodes. Most of these explosive episodes were alcohol/drug related, or involved arguments with his family of origin. His relatives, unfortunately, lived in the vicinity. Several arrests resulted in a criminal record that included charges of assault with intent to harm, and arson.

On one occasion, Gary exhibited what officers described as "demonic" behavior. He was committed for psychiatric evaluation that resulted in a transfer into substance abuse treatment. Once he was hospitalized and stabilized, Gary completed his treatment and reestablished his relationship with his wife. After he was discharged, he relapsed and the same pattern ensued. But with each treatment, he gained knowledge of recovery principles and spiritual concepts. He had entered treatment this last time of his own accord, which was a major step forward. His willingness to attend church and form a relationship with the pastor was also a significant change. He said he had previously been too filled with hatred and anger to have faith in anything except his wife.

A typical scenario with Gary and his wife occurred the last time he was placed on the locked ward for involuntary detox. It was his birthday, and although it was she who had called the police and helped to have him committed, she showed up at the hospital the next day with a birthday cake, wanting to surprise him. He was restrained at the time. Both could be very child-like, and this is how they were with one another.

Another example occurred when, prior to Gary's treatment completion and transition into continuing care, he had to appear in court for pending charges for violence against a police officer. After the court hearing, in which he was granted a continuance, he returned to the hospital, opened his coat and displayed a stash of three bottles of medication. He announced that he had been hoarding them, and had devised an escape plan in case he was sentenced. He planned to take all the medication, overdose, and then be transferred to the hospital where (if he lived) he would resume treatment. He was quite pleased that he had worked out such a "recovery-oriented" solution to incarceration! His plan also demonstrated his still-present running and escape pattern that had begun with the school principal and the shoestring episode. It clearly demonstrated his high level of risk.

Gary was diagnosed with inoperable cancer soon after this event. Although he continued to maintain sobriety and his pain-management medication was supervised by his physician, he stopped attending 12 Step meetings. He continued church attendance and counseling with his pastor. He expressed regret and remorse for his wrongdoings. In his prayers, he repeatedly questioned the meaning of his life and why it had been so filled with pain and suffering. When emotionally and physically distressed to an extreme degree, he continued to threaten to kill himself. When relatively stable, he continued to be likable, child-like, humorous and kind.

Gary's was the progress of a complex patient who begins treatment from the depths of a labyrinth. The climb to the top, in many such cases, seems an impossible goal to attain. Some make it to a certain level, and others start nearer the top; but each one's climb is marked by stumbles, setbacks and periods of regression. Regression is heartbreaking when one witnesses the struggle that is necessary for some to achieve even the slightest level of stability and recovery. In Gary's case, toward the end of his life, his struggle was recognized as a remarkable *achievement*.

Gary died at the age of 43. His pastor presided. Everyone agreed that he was finally at peace, and without pain. But there was one person there who could think of nothing but what life must have been like for a man who remembered just one act of kindness during his entire childhood.

Notes

1. Gregory, J. (1914). *The Outlaw*, p. 1. New York: A.L. Burt Company/Dodd, Mead and Company.
2. FBI National Center for the Analysis of Violent Crime. "Report on School Violence." Quantico, Virginia. Internet access website.
3. Dahmer Internet website: "Crime Report."
4. Excerpt from the case history of a patient.
5. Watson, L. (1995). *Dark Nature: A Natural History of Evil*. New York, New York: Harper Collins. Drawing on the latest insights of evolutionary ethology, anthropology, and psychology, biologist and naturalist Lyall Watson explores the problems our species. Watson utilizes a vast array of sources to examine the motivations and driving forces behind evil behavior and the delicate balance between "civilized" society and anarchy.

   The following titles are cited in Watson's book.

   Dalgaard, O.S. & Kringlen, E., "A Norwegian Twin Study." *British Journal of Criminal Psychology*, 16:213, 1976.

   Apsche, J.A. (1993). *Probing the Mind of the Serial Killer*. Philadelphia: International.

   Rule, A. (1993). *The Stranger Beside Me*. New York: Signet.

   Masters, B. (1985). *Killing for Company*. London: Jonathan Cape.

   Schwartz, A.E. (1993). *The Man Who Could Not Kill Enough*. New York: Birch Lane.
6. CBS Report. (1994). "Why Did Eric Kill?" Internet access.
7. ABC News Thursday Night (1998) Update Report on Eric Smith.
8. Weiner, J. (1994). *The Beak of the Finch: A Story of Evolution in Our Time*. New York: Alfred A. Knopf.
9. Hare, R.D. (1993). *Without Conscience: The Disturbing World of the Psychopaths Among Us*. New York: Pocket Books.
10. Hare, R.D. (February, 1996). "Psychopathology and Antisocial Personality Disorder: A Case of Diagnostic Confusion." *Psychiatric Times*.
11. American Psychiatric Association. (1996). *Diagnostic and Statistical Manual of Mental Disorders* (DSM-IV) (4th ed. rev.). Washington: Author.
12. Weiner, J. (1994) *The Beak of the Finch*, op. cit..

What I Wanted to Be.

Well it all Began on april 3rd 1955
I came into this World not Wanted
and from day one i knew it. from as
far Back as i can rember, It was not
a good fealing to have. at age one
the man's name that I go by Wallinger
tryed to posin me in my crib By
putting a lot of sleeping pills into
my mouth and all over the crib.
I found out by my older sister. I almost
didn't make it. then i found out By
my uncle that he tryed to get me
taken from my mother and I think
my real father Chester Cash. Because
of the pain I was suffer ing under
the hands of them. By Now I was
about two and he told me that their
was shit diapers all around me in a
room, that I was a mess and had
a diper rash so Bad. that he called
Police, But they did nothing this was
In north carlonia then we moved to
new Jersey, that's when my life of
hell started Because I can rember it.
every night.

Pages 278—280: Excerpts from Gary's journal.

I always wanted To Be some one other than my self and also day dreaned all the time about it, One of the reason's for it was I go by two names I went To school as gary Steven Cash then when it came time to get my driver licens my birth certifiat said Gary steven Wallinger then i new why every Body called me a bastard, their's always been heart acke in my life even with to names or three if i count Bastard as a name, Boy its hard to Belive in any thing But I do belive in you conime and want to thank you for trying to fix me

so what i want to Be when i grow up is me I never knew me and i am Just starting to find my self. and I am scared to death to find out what Happens if their is another name for me or if i can be saved

Gary Wallinger
Gary Cash
or Bastard

Gary W,

I rember going to first grade in school did not want to go because I did not have cloths or shoes, I rember going with pants that were to small and my shoes did not have shoe strings. I rember Just sitting their and I would put my self in a big Bubble so nowon would see what I didn't have, I rember the school prinobull calling me to his office can rember what his office even looked like, I rember he sat me down with and started asking me why dont you have shoe strings, Buy know i new my bubble was Broken, and I felt afull and emBarith to death, he took some twine to rap Boxes with and made shoe strings, i rember he dipped the ends, into glue so they would not come apart, and put them on my shoes, he was a kind man, But I fealt so Bad about what happened I ran away, all the police, melbos Just every Body in town looking for me, I was so ENBARSed

2

they found me, and i set fire to the grass out side and ran away agine, So I stopped running away. and started drinking alot and snuffing glue gas Just every thing, Was always out of my mind, felt normal to me,

I ust over shoe strings look what. happened to me and how I felt,

CHAPTER XIV
THE FINALE: THE PROBLEM IN PERSPECTIVE

A child, more than all other gifts
That earth can offer to declining man,
Brings hope with it, and forward-looking thoughts.
　　　　　　　　　　　— Wordsworth

George Eliot's novel *Silas Marner*,[1] written in 1861, begins with the introduction, "A story of old-fashioned village life." When Hillary Clinton wrote *It Takes a Village*,[2] she may or may not have been influenced by Eliot, but her ideas on child rearing and child care responsibilities of parents, schools, government and the larger community speak once again to the need for child care at every level of our society. While this may not solve the problem of problematic behavior identification, it may have a great impact on the level of security felt by children. Early indicators can easily be missed when children are out of view, alienated from others, and are left alone to construct their own devices for dealing with real or imagined fears.

George Eliot, born in 1819 as Mary Ann (Marian) Evans, was one of the greatest and most influential of English novelists. She combined her formidable intellectual ability with imaginative sympathy and acute powers of observation to address social issues. She was a woman torn by contradictions — between the desire to conserve the past and yet to change the limitations imposed by class and gender. She wrote *Silas Marner* at a time in her life when these contradictions converged during a period of mental depression.

Eliot rose above from her feelings of alienation and depression by writing about her recollection of village life. At the center of her novel was the weaver who emerged in her memory during moments of deep despair. Eliot described her childhood recollection of the weaver as a man with a stoop and an expression of face that led her to think that he was alien from his fellows. She understood from the depths of her depression the loneliness and alienation of separation from community. Hating the conditions of life in London, she remembered her childhood not only for its green fields and her mother's dairy but for the whole agricultural way of life which, she saw, enhanced the aesthetic aspects of nature as well as shaped the lives of the people whose human achievement in creating community she deeply respected. She felt the loss of these things the more for having pined for them for ten years in London among the claustrophobic streets, the choking smoke and the anonymous crowd — facts liberally documented in her letters and Journal. An intellectual circle she had, but this was no substitute for the neighborliness of "old-fashioned village life." With this sense of her own loss went her realization of what it must mean for the utterly disinherited masses, no longer folk, deprived of a community by the forces of modern progress.

In her story, the weaver Silas finds salvation through a return to community and resurrection through his care for a motherless child, Eppie. Eppie's influence on Silas would have been inadequate without the village there to take both into its neighborly care. In the spirit of Wordsworth's poetry is the description of how Eppie forges a bond between Silas and all animate and inanimate life. "There was a love between the child and the world from men and women with parental looks and tones to the red ladybirds and the round pebbles." Eliot interweaves the healing power of unity with the intuitive spirit of Wordsworth and Einstein and all who see life and nature as inter-related in its effort to thrive.

George Eliot grew up at a time when the pastoral life she knew was being destroyed by the rapid rise of industrialism. Her striking intelligence brought her to the attention of publisher John Chapman, who enlisted her to work on the intellectual *Westminster Review* in London. Her relationship to the married George Henry Lewes gave her the support needed to begin her career as a novelist. Long a favorite among Eliot's novels, *Silas Marner* is often regarded as a mere moral fairytale. It contains, along with its genial humor, many complex ironies and a great deal of pointed social criticism while examining the dire effects of the industrial revolution.

In a later edition, Leavis writes: "Our first knowledge of this book is a note in George Eliot's *Journal* (28 November 1860): 'I am now engaged in writing a story — the idea of which came to me after our arrival in this house [a depressing furnished London house] and which has thrust itself between me and the other book [*Romolo*] I was meditating. It is *Silas Marner, the Weaver of Raveloe*.' That same day, her Journal opens: 'Since I last wrote in this Journal, I have suffered much from physical weakness, accompanied with mental depression. The loss of country has seemed very bitter to me, and my want of health and strength has prevented me from working much — still worse, has made me despair of ever working well again.'

Six weeks later, in writing to tell her publisher of her new book, she again stresses the involuntary nature of this new undertaking: "a story which came *across* my other plans by a sudden inspiration." She adds: "It is a story of old fashioned village life, which has unfolded itself from the merest millet-seed of thought." On 10 March 1861, she notes: "Finished *Silas Marner*." Previously, replying to Major Blackwood's comment that, so far as he had read he, found it "sombre," she said that she was not surprised and doubted if it would interest anybody "since Wordsworth is dead," but assured him that it was not sad on the whole, "since it sets in strong light the remedial influences of pure, natural human relations." Thus the Weaver's story belonged to the village life of the past and exemplified a theory congenial to Wordsworth (and Coleridge); and the impulse to write it sprang from a deep depression of health and spirits due to living in conditions which were the very negation of "old-fashioned village life," a depression that, as we see, was morbid, since it involved irrational despair of ever succeeding again as a novelist, in spite of the great success of her novels *Adam Bede* and *The Mill on the Floss*. The letter to Blackwood ends:

> It came to me first of all quite suddenly, as a sort of legendary tale, suggested by my recollections of having once, in early childhood, seen a linen weaver with a bag on his back; but as my mind dwelt on the subject, I became inclined to a more realistic treatment.

Eliot's memory emerged as the "merest millet-seed of thought" and was transformed into a novel and theory emphasizing a need for security and community. She lived in an era of dramatic change and understood its impact on society. In today's rapidly changing global era, many children are feeling increasingly insecure and alienated. Elementary school children are being treated for anxiety and depression as never before. Problematic patterns of behavior that take root in early childhood and develop into disorder conditions have a monumental impact on our society.

According to The Carnegie Task Force on *Meeting the Needs of Young Children*,[3] "Across the United States, we are beginning to hear the rumblings of a quiet crisis." Their Goals Panel reported that nearly half of our infants and toddlers start life at a disadvantage and do not have the supports necessary to thrive. They cite the first three years as a crucial "starting point" — a period particularly sensitive to the protective mechanisms of parental and family support.

Parents and experts have long known that how individuals function from the preschool years all the way through adolescence and even adulthood hinges on the experiences children have in their first three years. Babies raised by caring, attentive adults in safe, predictable environments are better learners than those raised with less attention in less secure settings. Recent scientific findings corroborate these observations. With the help of powerful new research tools including sophisticated brain scans, scientists have studied the developing brain in greater detail than ever before. The Carnegie research points to five key findings that should inform our nation's efforts to provide our youngest children with a healthy start: First, the brain development that takes place during the prenatal period and in the first year of life is more rapid and extensive than previously realized. Second, brain development is much more vulnerable to environmental influence that ever before suspected. Third, the influence of early environment on the brain is long lasting. Fourth, the environment affects not only the number of brain cells and number of connections among them, but also the way these connections are "wired." And fifth, we have new scientific evidence for the negative impact of early stress on brain function.

The risks are clearer than ever before: an adverse environment can compromise a young child's brain function and overall development, placing him or her at great risk of developing a variety of cognitive, behavioral, and physical difficulties. In some cases these effects may be irreversible. But the opportunities are equally dramatic: a good start in life can do more to promote learning and prevent damage than we ever imagined. A range of other "protective factors" — such as good nutrition and sensitive parenting — helps the child to achieve good outcomes and avoid bad ones.

Research focused on assessment and testing strategies for identifying underlying symptoms associated with repetitive behavior at the earliest stage of pattern development is crucial. Total reliance on behavioral observation and diagnosis based on observation and a too narrow range of experiential indicators will result in overlooking many potentially destructive evolving patterns.

Richard Hughes, in *A High Wind In Jamaica*,[4] tells the story of a child who killed, and of seeing her later standing among other little girls at her new school in England:

> Looking at that gentle, happy throng of clear innocent faces and soft graceful limbs, listening to the careless, artless babble of chatter rising, perhaps God could have picked out from among them which was Emily: but I am sure I could not.

Recently, the Substance Abuse and Mental Health Services Administrations (SAMHSA) Center for Substance Abuse Treatment (CSAT) released a new treatment guide compiled by a consensus panel of non-federal experts entitled, *Substance Abuse Treatment for Persons with Child Abuse and Neglect Issues*. It is estimated that two-thirds of adults in substance abuse treatment programs were abused or neglected as children. The guide emphasizes the need for alcohol and drug treatment providers to properly screen and assess their patients for childhood sexual, physical or other abuse, in light of recent statistics which indicate that reported cases of abused and neglected children have more than doubled over the past decade — from 1.4 million in 1986 to more than 3 million in 1997. According to CSAT Director H. Wesley Clark, in the absence of recognizing signs of prior abuse and neglect, treatment providers may wrongly attribute symptoms of childhood trauma-related disorders to consequences of current abuse. This mistake, he said, can result in a missed opportunity to break a terrible cycle.[5]

The recommendation in many of these reports, including the *FBI*

Report on School Violence, is the stated need for improved communication with children on an individual level. But there is a need for communication at the earliest stages of development that includes testing, screening and assessment that identifies emotional and physiological distress symptoms. While assessment procedures focused on abuse and neglect issues are vitally important, the broader range of childhood experience should not be excluded. Questions and observations that are solely directed to pinpoint abuse may miss symptoms and problematic conditions that arise from experiences that are not abuse related, even if abuse is a factor in a high percentage of cases. Assessment therefore need not be limited to specific types of experience, but any experience that emerges as a result of investigations that address problematic feeling and physical symptoms.

We are verging on a decade of medical and scientific breakthroughs that will transform the way we understand and diagnose medical and mental health problems. The perspective presented here is based on listening to patients and convicted offenders with chronic behavioral, mental health and substance abuse disorders. In each case, there was once a child who had a chance for a different life, but the problems were not identified and the child was not heard.

> There is an arm around my shoulders, a brown robe, click of black
> rosary beads, a Franciscan priest.
> My child, my child, my child. . . .
> My child, sit here with me. Tell me what troubles you. Only if you
> want to. I am Father Gregory.
> I'm sixteen today, Father.
> Oh, lovely, lovely, and why should that be a trouble to you?
> I drank my first pint last night.
> Yes?
> I hit my mother.
> God help us, my child. But he will forgive you. Is there anything else.
> I can't tell you, Father. . . . I can't, Father. I did terrible things. . . .
> I can't tell, Father. I can't. . . .
> But you could tell St. Francis, couldn't you?
> He doesn't help me anymore.
> But you love him, don't you?
> I do. My name is Francis.
> Then tell him. We'll sit here and you'll tell him the things that trouble

286

you. If I sit and listen, it will only be a pair of ears for St. Francis and Our Lord. Won't that help?

I talk to St. Francis and tell him about Margaret, Oliver, Eugene, my father singing Roddy McCorely and bringing home no money, my father sending no money from England, Theresa and the green sofa, my terrible sins on Carrigogunnell, why couldn't they hang Hermann Goering for what he did to the little children with shoes scattered around concentration camps, the Christian brother who closed the door in my face, the time they wouldn't let me be an alter boy, my small brother Michael walking up the lane with the broken shoe clacking, my bad eyes that I'm ashamed of, the Jesuit brother who closed the door in my face, the tears in Mam's eyes when I slapped her.

Angela's Ashes[6]

Notes

1. Leavis, Q. D. (1967). Introduction to: Eliot, G. (1861). *Silas Marner: The Weaver of Raveloe.* (Q. D. Leavis, Ed.), (First published 1861). Middlesex, England: Penguin Books. Q. D. Leavis was a fellow of Girton College, Cambridge, from 1929 to 1932, and taught in Cambridge for many years. Her publications include *Fiction and the Reading Public,* two volumes of *Collected Essays, Lectures in America* and *Dickens the Novelist,* the two latter books written jointly with her husband, the distinguished literary critic Dr. F. R. Leavis. Leavis died in 1981.

2. Clinton, H.R. (1996). *It Takes a Village.* New York: Simon & Schuster.

3. Carnegie Corporation of New York: "Report on Meeting The Needs of Young Children. (1994)." Internet access website.

4. Hughes, R. (1929). *High Wind in Jamaica.* London: Collins Publishing.

5. Hayes, L.L. (April, 2000). "Child Abuse Linked to Drug, Alcohol Abuse." *Counseling Today.* American Counseling Association.

6. McCourt, F. (1966). *Angela's Ashes,* pp. 342-343. New York, New York: Scribner.